Contents

LIBERATING SHAHRAZAD

LIBERATING SHAHRAZAD
FEMINISM, POSTCOLONIALISM, AND ISLAM

SUZANNE GAUCH

 University of Minnesota Press
Minneapolis
London

An earlier version of chapter 3 was published as "Telling the Tale of a Body Devoured by Narrative," *differences: A Journal of Feminist Cultural Studies* 11, no. 1 (Spring 1999): 179–202; reprinted with permission of Indiana University Press, the publisher of the journal.

Published by the University of Minnesota Press
111 Third Avenue South, Suite 290
Minneapolis, MN 55401-2520
http://www.upress.umn.edu

Library of Congress Cataloging-in-Publication Data
Gauch, Suzanne, 1965-
    Liberating Shahrazad : feminism, postcolonialism, and Islam / Suzanne Gauch.
       p. cm.
    Includes bibliographical references and index.
    ISBN-13: 978-0-8166-4882-5 (hc : alk. paper)
    ISBN-10: 0-8166-4882-4 (hc : alk. paper)
    ISBN-13: 978-0-8166-4883-2 (pbk. : alk. paper)
    ISBN-10: 0-8166-4883-2 (pbk. : alk. paper)
    1. Arabic literature—History and criticism. 2. Women in literature.
3. Scheherazade (Legendary character). 4. Muslim women—Social conditions.
I. Title.
PJ7519.W66G384 2006
892.7'09—dc22
                                          2006015345

Printed in the United States of America on acid-free paper

The University of Minnesota is an equal-opportunity educator and employer.

12 11 10 09 08 07   10 9 8 7 6 5 4 3 2 1

I am Shahrazad.
The poem and my voice are the song of the wronged.

Rise up, captives! I am Shahrazad.

—*Fairuz, "Shahrazad"*
(composed by the Rahbani Brothers)

Preface ∞ Why Shahrazad?

Like [Scheherazade] I have to face the daily threat of political violence unarmed. Only words can save me.

If the West has the power to control time by manipulating images, I thought, then who are we if we do not control our images? Who am I—and who makes my image?
> —*Fatima Mernissi,* Scheherazade Goes West: Different Cultures, Different Harems

Shahrazad then speaks. But woman's voice is more than a physiological faculty. It is the narrative instrument that permits her to be a literary medium, to vie with the male in the process of textual creation. To control the narrative process, however, is no small task.
> —*Fedwa Malti-Douglas,* Woman's Body, Woman's Word: Gender and Discourse in Arabo-Islamic Writing

Scheherazade/Shahrazad

Almost everyone is familiar with at least one of her oft retold stories. Even those unacquainted with Scheherazade, as she is known to most Western readers, recognize the tales of Aladdin, Sinbad the Sailor, or Ali Baba and the Forty Thieves, thanks to their Hollywood or Disney incarnations. Yet Scheherazade's voice is often absent, or nearly so, from these tales that Western translators of *The Thousand and One Nights*, or *The Arabian Nights*, have long attributed to her.[1] Instead of presenting the stories they tell as the product of Scheherazade's brilliance, daring initiative, and political acumen, filmed versions of *Nights* stories depict women as lavishly, yet revealingly, attired harem beauties, slaves to the pleasure of their master. However, Scheherazade, or Shahrazad as Arabic speakers commonly call her, was more than the sum of those enticing, sexually charged images; she was that courageous woman who confronted a king so enraged by the infidelity of his first wife that he took to marrying a virgin every evening and putting her to death the following morning. Offering herself as the king's next victim, Shahrazad postpones her execution by telling him a lengthy and intricate story each night, leaving it unfinished as dawn breaks. Over the course of many nights, her stories divert the king from his obsession with women's infidelity, both entertaining him and altering the manner in which he looks on human behavior. Shahrazad, then, saves not only her own life but also the lives of countless other women, employing her narrative skills to alter those representations of women—as deceitful beauties dominated by physical desire—that the king had so cruelly acted on.

While the number of actual stories varies from version to version of the *Nights*, most Western compilations conclude with an elaborate scene in which King Shahrayar renounces his vengeance and capitulates to Scheherazade. Yet the moment he does so, she leaves off telling stories, a veil of silence descending on her as she presumably devotes herself to her duties as queen and mother. No longer a spokeswoman for the multifaceted intelligence and limitless abilities of women, she becomes a model of the womanly virtues of the translator's era. Yet the fourteenth-century Arabic manuscript of the *Nights* from which the first European translator, the Orientalist Antoine Galland, worked was incomplete, breaking off midstory after some 270 or so nights.[2] Thus, early in the eighteenth century, Galland was the first European to seek out tales and anecdotes from various "Oriental" sources in an effort to create a work that lived up to its title by arriving at the thousand and first night with some finality. As for the conclusion, Galland may well have derived his inspiration from a short notice on story collections in a tenth-century catalog of books, the *Kitāb al-Fihrīst* of Ibn al-Nadim:

> The first book to be written with this content was the book *Hazar Afsan* which means "A Thousand Stories." The basis for this [name] was that one of their kings used to marry a woman, spend a night with her and kill her the next day. Then he married a concubine of royal blood who had intelligence and wit. She was called Shahrazad and when she came to him she would begin a story, but leave off at the end of the night, which induced the king to ask for it the night following. This happened to her for a thousand nights, during which time he [the king] had intercourse with her until because of him she was granted a son, whom she showed to him, informing him of the trick played upon him. Then, appreciating her intelligence, he was well disposed toward her and kept her alive.[3]

In Galland's version, however, there is no child, only the king's recognition of Scheherazade's prodigious memory, worthiness, and great wisdom. Subsequent translators accused Galland of excessive prudery and modified the scene so that Scheherazade concluded her final story by producing a son, and later two more, on whose behalf she implored the king's mercy. Scheherazade's silence on this final night consequently says more about her translators' battles to confirm their authoritative knowledge of the Orient than it does about her "true" character. Of indeterminate origin, property of no known author, Scheherazade seems open to a host of appropriations, even such as may be in contradiction to her own aims.

Over the years, Scheherazade has evolved from chaste beauty to wily seductress, from prisoner to liberator and back again, her character shaped by European rivalries with the Ottoman Empire, colonial incursions into Islamic regions, anticolonial struggles, decolonization, globalization, and international terrorism.[4] Despite many efforts, no one has been able to trace either her origins or those of her stories back to a single place and time. Even the two oldest notices on the frame story featuring Scheherazade, both from the tenth century and very brief, diverge regarding the relationship of the characters to one another, and neither corresponds exactly to the description of their affiliation as set out in the introduction of the earliest extant manuscripts.[5] Scheherazade's history alone, therefore, everywhere belies the Orientalist contention that the Islamic world was a static and unchanging place. Now, in the postindependence era, new writers and artists, many of them from the Arab and Islamic worlds, reject the authority of those European translators and scholars who sought to embody Scheherazade and her tales definitively in a determinate, finite, and final work. For these artists, Scheherazade's indeterminacy constitutes not a flaw to be overcome but an inspiration. In contrast to images of Scheherazade as undifferentiated Oriental or Muslim woman, their work foregrounds Shahrazad—as I will henceforth refer to her—as a speaking agent whose stories have never ended and whose resolve has only increased in the face of both rising fundamentalisms and proliferating Western media images of Arab and Muslim women as silent, oppressed, exploited, and uneducated victims.

As a result of her journeys between East and West, Shahrazad has become a powerful trope for contemporary Arab and Muslim women writers, particularly those who address international audiences. Moroccan feminist scholar Fatima Mernissi eloquently summarizes the dual challenge that Shahrazad's project exemplifies for women writers and filmmakers from the Islamic world: to combat symbolic and political violence at home and to struggle against co-option by imperialist or anti-Islamic critics abroad.[6] Speaking to the complex legacy of Shahrazad,

Mernissi asserts that when the storyteller stakes her life on the power of her stories, she affirms her intelligence, sangfroid, courage, and political astuteness. She contrasts this representation of Shahrazad as a strong yet subtle character with the image that Western readers glean of her, that of an essentially submissive, exotic woman who survives King Shahrayar's "Oriental" excesses of cruelty and power because of her extraordinary beauty and talent as a seductress. Fedwa Malti-Douglas persuasively argues that the source of these conflicting receptions of Shahrazad lies in the simultaneous emphasis that the *Nights* places on her voice and body, for Shahrazad is "a sexual being, who manipulates discourse (and men) through her body."[7] To be sure, in order for contemporary Arab and Muslim writers and filmmakers to counterbalance the emphasis European-language translations and adaptations of the *Nights* have placed on Shahrazad's appearance, they must keep telling stories at all costs, asserting their roles as manipulators of discourse rather than as mere characters in a series of global dramas.

Shahrazad's more recent past consequently poses myriad obstacles, as well as offering an empowering opportunity, for Arab and Muslim writers. If scholars of Arabic literature have taken pains over the years to point out that the *Nights* editions are by no means typical of medieval literary production in Arabic and that, on the contrary, they have never figured in the canon of this literature, women artists find themselves additionally obliged to compete with an endless stream of Western images of an exotic Shahrazad and the mysterious, oppressed women she represents.[8] The very covers of Western editions of works by women writers from the Arabo-Islamic world often boast reproductions of noted Orientalist odalisques and harems or photographs of veiled or barely glimpsed Muslim women, even when the written works within offer the most pointed cross-cultural critiques. Because their images have been so overdetermined, any Arab or Muslim woman writer's traversal of the imaginary frontier between Orient and Occident always reverberates bidirectionally. Where unequal distributions of wealth and power create seemingly insurmountable divisions out of religious, cultural, and social differences, a writer who appears to identify too closely with the West as she struggles to assert her agency abroad risks losing her credibility at home.

Postcolonial feminists such as Chandra Mohanty and Gayatri Spivak have, in very different ways, pointed out for some years now that the exploitation of gender as a justification for Western intervention in and control of non-Western cultures threatens to bind the hands of "native" women struggling against the various forms of gender-based oppression. In her breakthrough article in the field, Chandra Mohanty warns that "one such significant effect of the dominant 'representations' of Western feminism is its conflation with imperialism in the eyes of particular Third World women."[9] Spivak, however, discovers an equally pernicious imperialism in the withdrawal of Western or other intellectuals from political involvement in the global South on the premise that the subaltern should be allowed to speak for herself. Her concern to demonstrate that those situated on the margins of the structures that guarantee the reproduction of ideology possess no natural or true voice with which to disrupt the prevailing order leads her to the (in)famous declaration that "the subaltern cannot speak."[10] Shahrazad is neither subaltern nor Western feminist, however. Nor are these artists who invoke her by name or through their narrative techniques; mindful of the strange journeys of the medieval heroine, they have learned to speak the different languages of transnational feminism in order to forestall the co-option of their own words and images. Like their model, they elaborate complex relations to those they represent as well as to their audience, their stories, like Shahrazad's, calling for boundary-crossing, multidirectional, ever-evolving analysis.

While Shahrazad, character and speaking agent, and the history of her reception in both the Occident and the Orient highlight the problematic of representation so central to postcolonial studies, the vantage point occupied by the artists I analyze in this study facilitates their engagement with the kind of multiperspectival study for which postcolonial critics often call. All in one way or another connected with the Maghreb, these artists speak from a space that presently incarnates the very much contested and quite porous line between Occident and Orient. (In Arabic, the word *Maghreb* denotes "west" and is conventionally used to refer to Northwest Africa, particularly Morocco; here I will use the term in its broadest sense to indicate the western reaches of the Arab world: Tunisia, Algeria, Morocco.) From that place, they deploy words and images that undertake an intricate set of negotiations on the border between Muslim Orient and "secular" Occident, exploring sites of resistance to both overt and more subtle forms of imperialism and fundamentalism. Examining as well the tenuous boundary between written and filmed text and lived reality, they strive to intervene against the oppression of women in the Maghreb while examining what is at stake in the continued centrality of gender in postindependence relations among North Africa, the broader Islamic world, and the West. Moroccan Fatima Mernissi, Franco-Moroccan Tahar Ben Jelloun, Algerian Assia Djebar, Franco-Algerian Leïla Sebbar, and Tunisian Moufida Tlatli compose their internationally renowned works in Arabic, English, and French. They entertain and educate by addressing a subject that has fascinated Western audiences since precolonial times and has become a central topic of debate in postindependence nations: women in Islamic societies. Working from the premise that the *Nights* tales have never ended, that Shahrazad's repertoire of stories must continue to endure, mutate, and grow as Arab and Muslim women control the representation of their worlds, Tlatli, Mernissi, Ben Jelloun, Djebar, and Sebbar test as well the boundaries of the "merely" textual.

No End in Sight

No matter how many tales European translators included within the *Nights,* their inevitable relegation of Shahrazad to the silent shadows served the purpose of reinscribing stereotypes of the Islamic world as inherently misogynist and retrograde. After all, this ending appears to affirm that change from within the Orient itself is impossible, that even after Shahrazad has mobilized all of her learning, skill, wisdom, and wit, she convinces the king definitively to renounce his cruelty only by embracing the models of good wife and mother, much as Malti-Douglas contends. By contrast, the Maghrebi artists who are the focus of this study dismiss the conclusion of the *Nights* as premature, implicitly or explicitly integrating Shahrazad's lessons into new, unforeseen narratives. Sidestepping the traps of comprehensiveness and definitiveness in which many editors and translators of the *Nights* became entangled, they instead draw on the story collection as a fluid work elaborated in and by its circulation between Occident and Orient. Highlighting this steady exchange, which has intensified since the start of the colonial period but which Robert Irwin suggests is indeed characteristic of the story collection since its inception, these writers and filmmakers show how neither Shahrazad nor her stories will ever be set once and for all.[11] Juxtaposing the legacy of the *Nights* with the consequences of social, historical, cultural, political, religious, and ethnic narratives (both Western and North African) that position women as models of identity and community, these artists simultaneously dispute the naturalness and deleterious effects of such a positioning. Calling on Shahrazad's unique heritage, they insist on the irreducible heterogeneity intertwining societies, cultures, and nations on both sides of the imaginary divide between Orient and Occident, Islamic world and West.

Following a short introduction that examines how Shahrazad and her stories have been reappropriated and reconfigured by different translators and scholars of the *Nights*, chapter 1 analyzes a work that recontextualizes a familiar tale of singing slaves and princes. Tunisian filmmaker Moufida Tlatli's *The Silences of the Palace* sets the coming-of-age tale of an illegitimate servant girl in a palace of Tunisia's ruling class during the turbulent years just prior to Tunisian independence. I show how Tlatli retains only the bare elements of a popular tale of romance in which a king is smitten with love for a beautiful and talented slave, transforming them into the stuff of a melodrama by portraying a social universe in which the servant girl's looks and accomplishments relegate her to the marginal world of the prostitute rather than miraculously elevate her to the rank of princess. The social segregation, sexual violence, and economic realities that Tlatli highlights put forth a social critique in the guise of a familiar entertainment, I argue, while blending genres in a way that calls for new models of feminist film criticism. *Silences* crafts a particular tension between image and word, and I demonstrate how it calls on tropes of repetition and techniques of doubling in order to reveal how the gaze can only ever partly substitute for the voice of those it takes as its objects. Thus addressing the reality of cross-cultural audiences in an era of uneven global exchange, *Silences* challenges formulations of both authenticity and personal and textual legitimacy within and beyond Tlatli's native Tunisia.

In chapter 2, I examine a work that directly addresses a North American audience by playfully engaging with the particular Hollywood Orientalist imagery that has shaped many fantasies of Muslim women. Moroccan sociologist Fatima Mernissi's memoir *Dreams of Trespass: Tales of a Harem Girlhood*, I show, entices its readers by briefly conjuring a world of seduction, intrigue, and adventure reminiscent of classic Hollywood films and then pointedly contrasting it with the daily frustrations of life in a Moroccan harem. Like *Silences*, Mernissi's memoir portrays the domestic world of women against the backdrop of nationalist struggles, yet in such a way that their personal battles for access to education and the public spaces of Moroccan society take inspiration from and contribute to the realization of Moroccan independence. I propose that Mernissi invokes the conventions of autobiographical writing while self-consciously constructing a fictional universe in order to test the limitations of non-Arab readers' perceptions of an Islamic world long cast as Europe's other. At the same time, I reveal how *Dreams* reconfigures Moroccan history with a view to justifying discourses promoting equal rights for women as integral to Moroccan identity. For Mernissi's story is a highly strategic one, casting the years prior to independence as a model of dialogue between the sexes and also among classes. Consequently, Mernissi succeeds in promoting a feminist agenda that cannot be easily silenced by the claims of conservatives in the Islamic world or appropriated by readers elsewhere as ethnographic evidence of Arab women's oppression.

While the first two chapters demonstrate that Tlatli's and Mernissi's works displace stock images and perceptions of Arab and Muslim women, chapter 3 explores a work that throws into question even the seemingly given category of identity that is sex. In an effort to construct a narrative that breaks through the postcolonial writer's obligation to authenticity, Moroccan writer Tahar Ben Jelloun's novel *The Sand Child* weaves a surreal tale that promotes artistry over realism, in turn positing change and imagination as hallmarks of Moroccan identity. By recounting, through a succession of storytellers, the tale of a female child raised as a boy against the backdrop of pre- and postindependence Morocco, Ben Jelloun's novel stresses the act of telling as a way to resist the spectacularity with which all postcolonial narratives, especially those that treat issues of gender and sex, must contend when they circulate outside their presumed site of origin. Despite their infinite character, Shahrazad's stories take as their point of departure an urgent scenario that imparts a specific purpose to each of her words as well as to their utterance. By contrast, I argue that in *The Sand Child* the main character's intentions remain diffuse and uncertain, so that the tales each storyteller struggles to articulate reach an impasse whenever they seek to bestow a future on him or her. For audiences abroad, which often perceive in postcolonial works a kind of authentic self-representation, Ben Jelloun's novel insists over and over that the stories generated by the Moroccan people are everchanging and inexhaustible.

Written during that ambiguous period midway between the war of independence and the senseless civil war of the 1990s, the short story collection and breakthrough novel of the Algerian Assia Djebar depict a writer struggling with her representative role. In chapter 4, I examine how Djebar's *Women of Algiers in Their Apartments* and *Fantasia: An Algerian Cavalcade* theorize the engagement of the postcolonial writer on behalf of her female subjects through the trope of embodiment. Often positioning their narrators as sisters of Shahrazad, Djebar's works portray Western-educated women's negotiation of culture and power in an increasingly monolithic postindependence Algeria that more and more excludes the contributions of women to the narrative of national identity. Djebar's narrators question how they may challenge dominant discourses of power by means of the long-silenced stories of women whose social, educational, and linguistic backgrounds differ from their own but with whom their own futures are intertwined. I demonstrate how the struggle of these narrators, who confront the violence that representation in the former colonial language perpetrates on those on whose behalf they would speak, develop an ethical relation through women's shared experience of disembodiment across the different languages of Algeria. Scrupulously culling fragments of lost or forgotten narratives and setting them into dialogue with accounts of her personal history, the narrator of *Fantasia* urges readers to face the women of her fragmented narratives as necessary interlocutors rather than as objects of study.

Shahrazad's descendants all find themselves obliged to confront the final silence that European translators imposed on the storyteller of the *Nights*. In chapter 5, I argue that Franco-Algerian writer Leïla Sebbar's trilogy—*Sherazade*, *Les carnets de Shérazade* (The Notebooks of Sherazade), and *Le fou de Shérazade* (Mad for Sherazade)—targets the limitations imposed by this final silence in a new way. Sebbar's novels relate the adventures of the teenage, Franco-Algerian, runaway Sherazade in France and the Middle East, drawing on avant-garde French film, Orientalist art, European colonial and revolutionary history, fashion, and global culture. I explore the limitations and potential of this translation of Shahrazad into a heroine who speaks with her looks rather than with words in a world dominated by the visual. I show how Sebbar's characters *take on*, in every sense of the term, Orientalist, exoticist, colonial, and postcolonial reifications of difference. At the same time, the descendants of Shahrazad that populate Sebbar's novels expose and trouble more recent social fantasies of easy multiculturalism. In a world where hopes of revolutionary change have fallen by the wayside, displaced by the allure of a global capitalism under which (superficial) difference is sought out and commodified, the narratives of Sherazade proliferate without ever reaching any neat conclusion. Continually eluding those who would coerce or persuade her to authenticate their narratives, Sherazade again and again thwarts finalizing scenarios. Through her increasingly slippery protagonist, Sebbar suggests that the goals of Shahrazad's stories have not yet been met either north or south of the Mediterranean.

Noting the proliferation of stories in that elastic, ever-shifting work, Moroccan critic Abdelfattah Kilito claims, "In general, one only knows a few of the stories in the collection and promises oneself to read others. One has never finished reading the *Nights*."[12] Those who revive Shahrazad in ever new guises continue to add an endless stream of stories to her already vast repertoire, defying us to continue reading, watching, and listening while revealing to us that we have never ceased to do so. The following study proposes that at a time when many are writing off postcolonial studies as a retreat from material forms of resistance, the vital legacy of Shahrazad draws attention to a model of change as old as her undatable stories. Operating by means of an endless stream of elaborations on the themes of gender and power, her stories pave the way for and perpetuate change not immediately perceptible as revolutionary, mired as we are in notions of revolution as violent rupture. One of the longest works in progress ever, Shahrazad's story unrelentingly tests the historical, linguistic, and psychic limitations that inevitably bear on any artistic work and on any project of social, political, and economic change. Shahrazad is no political radical; the changes at which her storytelling ultimately aims are not violent. Rather, her stories bit by bit overcome what were once seemingly insurmountable boundaries and limitations to change. They begin by aiming at the transformation of her audience's most intimate experience of themselves; is that not the desired outcome of any revolutionary project? As for the title of this work, *liberating* should not be interpreted as an action to be performed on Shahrazad. No, *liberating* must be read as Shahrazad's distinguishing attribute.

Note on the Transcription of Arabic Words

THE MULTIPLE CONVENTIONS for transcribing Arabic proper names and words into English can give rise to confusion. This is particularly true when dealing with words from Algeria, Morocco, and Tunisia, because the North African vernacular pronunciation differs greatly from that of "standard" Arabic. While the transcription system of the *International Journal of Middle Eastern Studies* is widely used to render Arabic sounds in English, a French standardized spelling predominates in French works about the former colonies of North Africa and often influences how North Africans choose to render Arabic in Latin characters. Thus, *Maghreb* is far more common than *Maghrib*, for example. I have generally respected each author's or translator's choice of spellings, while occasionally placing a transcription more familiar to English readers in brackets. There are instances, however, where adhering to French spellings would appear contrived because of familiarity of the words in question. I therefore always, for example, employ *Qur'an* rather than the French *Coran* (or the now dated English *Koran*). The transliteration of the name Scheherazade/Shahrazad, presumed to be Persian in origin, is another matter, and it is discussed in the chapters that follow. If a certain inconsistency prevails, it is part of the story.

Introduction ∞ A Thousand and One Shahrazads

It is human to search for the completion and end of every affair and to think that one can know the end from knowing the beginning. It is also human to fail to recognize that some things have no known beginning and may not have a knowable end. The desire to know the beginning is thus satisfied by inventing it, and the desire to know the end is satisfied by fabricating it. Such, in any case, have been the human failings from which the *Nights* have suffered most.
—*Muhsin Mahdi*, The Thousand and One Nights

SHAHRAZAD — BEAUTIFUL, EXOTIC SEDUCTRESS, or supremely learned, courageous, political strategist, or both—emerges at the confluence of many histories of domination and resistance. While the legacy of a Shahrazad who is little more than stunning seductress vexes many Arab and Muslim women scholars, writers, and filmmakers, disproving this portrayal is far more challenging than simply holding it up against her original in *The Thousand and One Nights*. For anyone who attempts to do so confronts a bewildering array of variant editions of the *Nights*, each claiming definitive authority on different grounds: completeness, date of "discovery," consistency of style or lack thereof, inclusion or exclusion of particular stories, and popularity.[1] In the absence of one original authorized by either the signature of an author, or traceable, transparent origins in the Arab Middle Ages, or universal resonances in subsequent editions, any author of fiction or film who seeks to recast Shahrazad's image must proceed otherwise than by traditional methods of textual and historical justification. That author is obliged, instead, to follow the model of the *Nights* themselves, each time defining Shahrazad anew in the telling, justifying the characterization of the heroine by prolonging Shahrazad's stories in a manner that pays tribute to her.

1

The indeterminate origins and instability not just of the stories in her repertoire but of Shahrazad herself have made it very easy for translators, compilers, and copyists to place words in her mouth over the years.[2] Yet this instability and uncertainty signal a fundamental irreducibility that no final silencing of Shahrazad has been able to overcome. They demand a particular attentiveness at the same time that they grant those who seek to follow in her footsteps a particular flexibility in reshaping her character and stories. Given the Persian overtones of Shahrazad's name, her tale surely had its origin somewhere in the Islamic world of the Middle Ages; yet the stories she tells, whether in the European or the earliest Arabic manuscripts, represent a compendium of cross-cultural, transnational influences. If European translators of the *Nights* each sought to have the final word by producing a definitively "complete" version, none has been able to impose his version as the enduringly authoritative one.[3] At the outset of her influential study of poetics in the *Nights*, Ferial Ghazoul underscores both this volatility and intangibility of the work and its authors: "There is neither an original text nor an individual author. *The Arabian Nights* is an artistic production of the collective mind; its specificity lies in its very emergence as a text. The typical text is often conceived as a limited and defined object—as a singular event. In contrast, *The Arabian Nights* is plural and mercurial, and herein lies its challenge."[4] Because the tale lacks an author, the only master—or rather mistress—presiding over these changes and challenges is Shahrazad herself. A character who has taken on many lives of her own, she cedes control of her destiny only temporarily.

Although *The Thousand and One Nights* has entertained European readers and attracted the attention of scholars since its first appearance in French in 1704, Muhsin Mahdi proposes the first sustained study to consider in depth how Europeans formed part of that collective mind to which Ghazoul attributes authorship of the *Nights*. From the vantage point of the late twentieth century, Mahdi frames his full-length study of the *Nights* in terms of the questions of representation and power raised by Said's study of Orientalism and three subsequent decades of postcolonial studies. Ultimately, he concludes, the European reception of the *Nights* inflected not just the way the work was subsequently read but also the very shape it assumed and how it was (re)produced from the eighteenth century on. Studying and finally editing the unfinished fourteenth-century Syrian manuscript that was in Antoine Galland's possession when he began the first translation of the *Nights* (it breaks off in the middle of the tale of Qamar al-Zaman), Mahdi demonstrates how Galland fabricated the work we know today as the *Nights* by adding to this stylistically uniform Syrian work texts from diverse sources, inserting night breaks, and bringing Shahrazad's tale to a conclusion.[5] Determined to present readers with a work that literally realized its title, Galland and his successors, Mahdi argues, reworked the collection in this manner until it contained to their estimation one thousand and one nights of stories that together exemplified the Orient:

> The number and size of the stories included under the title of the *Nights* kept growing, and the *Urtext* was identified in the minds of nineteenth-century students with the most complete text, that is, the text that contained the largest number of stories regardless of their provenance. This enormous corpus became the fertile field for anthropological, historical, linguistic, and cultural studies, without anybody having the vaguest idea as to how and why the same title was called upon to embrace them. The only notion that justified this process in the public's mind was the idea of the Orient as the *Urtext* of the *Nights.*[6]

More than a literary work, the *Nights* stood in for the Arab Orient itself, the elusiveness of a complete version paralleling the failure of the geographical region and its people to conform to the work's representations. Yet Mahdi goes further, demonstrating how the Arabic recensions of the *Nights* that appeared in the nineteenth century are all in one way or another outgrowths of retranslations of Galland's French version. Cheap Arabic copies of these *Nights* presumably returned these recensions to the Arab world, where they undoubtedly circulated and mingled with different variants, were absorbed into popular Arab culture, and were readapted by storytellers for their own purposes.[7] As we shall see, readers and storytellers in Arab countries had their own ideas regarding Shahrazad's character.

Meanwhile, as the era of decolonization approached, the nature of the attraction that the *Nights* held for European readers changed. In the mid-twentieth century, Jorge Luis Borges pinpointed the source of translators' longstanding fascination with the *Nights,* not in its function as a mirror of the Arab world, but in its ability to be endlessly reformulated so as to reflect the literary and worldly preoccupations of particular nations and ages. Alleging that the flowery descriptions of the "literal and complete" French translation of the *Nights* by J. C.

Mardrus betray the original text yet render it perfectly for fin-de-siècle France, Borges compares it with his own rendering of the original:

> I had the indolent pleasure of comparing the three German versions by Weil, Henning and Littman, and the two English versions by Lane and Sir Richard Burton. In them I confirmed that the original of Mardrus's ten lines was this: "The four drains ran into a fountain, which was of marble in various colors."[8]

The process whereby Borges arrives at this "original" claims for him an authority equal to that of past translators of the *Nights* only in order to expose that authority as entirely contingent on the translator's ability to tell a persuasive (scholarly) story that draws on and transforms the expectations of his particular audience. In replacing the notion that translations of the *Nights* transmit knowledge of an original other with the conviction that the *Nights* reflect the image of their translators and in speaking to the expectations of his own audience only to transform those expectations, Borges pronounces himself a student of Shahrazad rather than her master. When, in a famous line near the conclusion of his essay, Borges claims that the king heard his story from the lips of Shahrazad on night 602, does he not refer to his own experience?[9]

What of Shahrazad's fate in the course of these many transformations of the *Nights?* In retrospect, she and her story appear limitless in more ways than one, the subjects of endless permutations restrained only by the disposition of the reader and the interpretative fashions of the times. As soon as she arrived in Europe via Galland's 1704 translation, she became a beauty whose image merged with that of the odalisques and other women of the harem, who increasingly became the subjects of Orientalist paintings. However, in 1927, some two centuries and numerous translations later, Parisian writer and activist Marie Lahy-Hollebecque declared Shahrazad a feminist. Citing Shahrazad's role as originator of the *Nights*, Lahy-Hollebecque called for contemporary Europe to hearken to her example: "If one recalls that this occurs in an Islamic land, and in an era where all forms of slavery subsisted the world over, one rests astounded by the audacity of views, the absence of prejudices, that permitted an Arab narrator to assign to a woman a role that our Middle Ages never contemplated and that our twentieth century envisions only with great reluctance."[10] Yet in the years since Lahy-Hollebecque's study, critics have arrived at dissenting conclusions with respect to Shahrazad's feminism or lack thereof. At the end of the twentieth century, Fatima Mernissi insists on Shahrazad's courage and intellect but expresses amazement that, "for many Westerners, Scheherazade was considered a lovely but simple-minded entertainer, someone who narrates an innocuous tale and dresses fabulously."[11] Ghazoul asserts that Shahrazad represents the agency of women, transforming them "from sexual objects into erotic subjects."[12] Breaking with both these readings, Fedwa Malti-Douglas affirms that the conclusion of Shahrazad's tale problematizes readings of her as feminist icon by reinstating her corporeal identity to the detriment of her role as narrator.[13]

Each scholar's reading of Shahrazad's fundamental character is entirely corroborated by one or more translations or manuscript editions of the *Nights*. Lahy-Hollebecque and Malti-Douglas each base their analyses on a particular European translation or a late Arabic edition. In Lahy-Hollebecque's case it is the Mardrus translation, often faulted for its too obvious fin-de-siècle aesthetics; Malti-Douglas, by contrast, references an Arabic edition, the nineteenth-century Cairo I, or Bulaq, as well as Sir Richard Burton's epic version. Ghazoul, who stresses the multiple and oral sources of the *Nights*, refrains from attributing authority to any one edition, although for the sake of simplicity she does select the popular Bulaq edition as her primary reference, relying on the English translation she deems most suitable in each instance instead of retranslating the passages in question herself. Only Mernissi refuses to single out any one edition, taking as definitive the versions of *Nights* stories that her female relatives allegedly recounted during her childhood and alternately citing various popular European translations when they support her points.[14] While hers is less a study of Shahrazad or the *Nights* than a strategic invocation that advances a contemporary Islamic feminism, it is also perhaps the most "true" to the "original." Mernissi and the contemporary Maghrebi writers and filmmakers who rewrite the fiction of Shahrazad wrest her image back from the male translators of the *Nights*, discovering a real power in the multiple storytellers, characters, and narratives that she continues to inspire.

The very attempts by translators and adaptors to usurp Shahrazad's voice by carefully delimiting her role in the *Nights* have thus only succeeded in endowing her character with an eternal quality that makes of her a powerful literary ancestor for those who call for a new status for Arab and Muslim women within and beyond the Arab world. Ghazoul's comparative study of *Nights* editions prompts her to credit the work's structure with eternalizing Shahrazad's speech: "The most fundamental victory in *The Arabian Nights* is transformation of past and future into perpetual present. The tense of Shahrazad is the present indicative."[15] Captive of no known author, powerful in her ability to elude finalizing representations by continuously creating in the present, Shahrazad continues to cross cultures in various guises as a valuable trope for Arab and Muslim women writers and filmmakers. Were it not for the closure Galland and his European successors so insistently imposed on the *Nights*, we perhaps would have remained more attentive to the enduring urgency of Shahrazad's words. For the *Nights* stories really are infinite; many rulers have come and gone and still many remain, and now is no time for Shahrazad to fall silent.

Shahrazad's Algerian Guises

Between Shahrazad's arrival in Europe and the emergence of internationally popular North African, or Maghrebi, writers and filmmakers in the second half of the twentieth century, a number of Algerian women, in various ways, took up Shahrazad's role as a voice for presumably silent women. Largely as a result of the extent and duration of the French presence in Algeria (from 1830 to 1962), the colony, which was the oldest, largest, and most extensively settled of the three North African colonies, proved fertile ground for "native women's voices," voices that at one time or another confirmed the necessity or success of French colonization, its shortcomings, its oppressiveness, and its demise. As the era of colonization progressed and gave way to struggles for independence, the terms of these women's role and the tone of their voices also evolved. Fantastic romances set in "traditional Oriental" societies gave way to tales revealing the harshness of women's lives in rural societies fiercely resisting the incursions of colonialism and then to accounts of women braving colonial atrocities in an emerging nation. In response, European characterizations of Maghrebi women shifted from beautiful seductresses, to docile or dedicated representatives of cultural authenticity, and finally to courageous freedom fighters. The three writers discussed below confront, in ever-evolving ways, the representational legacies of the colonizer along with their correlates in Algeria: Elissa Rhaïs authored once wildly popular novels about transgressive and ill-fated North African lives and loves; Fadhma Aïth Mansour Amrouche, a Christianized Kabyle woman, reaffirmed the vital autonomy of Amazight, or Berber, society and culture in her autobiography; and Djamila Boupacha was an Algerian freedom fighter who mobilized French public opinion against the war in Algeria with accounts of her torture by French soldiers.

Elissa Rhaïs perhaps best illustrates the process whereby North African women who asserted agency as speakers were quickly reduced to characters in a colonial drama. Storyteller and author, the long-dead minor literary celebrity resurfaced in 1982 as the subject of an eventually televised controversy regarding her true identity, a controversy that exposed how an aura of mystery and exoticism promoted by Orientalism continues to hover over postindependence Algeria. Author of twelve French-language novels, novellas, and collections of short stories in an eleven-year span from 1919 to 1930, Rhaïs is notable primarily for being the first indigenous woman author to emerge from Algeria. Her work, as Jean Déjeux describes it in a meticulously documented article, was set in an exotic Arab and Jewish North Africa and encompassed "novels and tales of passion-fueled intrigues and dark vengeances, but also tales reminiscent of the marvelous ambience of *The Thousand and One Nights*."[16] Déjeux further relates how Rhaïs's editors fabricated a persona for her that tapped into the French public's concern with the efficacy of the French colonial school system, presenting her as "a Muslim Arab, an Oriental, who attended French school until age twelve, then adopted the veil of Muslim women and left the harem in order to write French stories."[17] He also convincingly suggests that in literary circles many knew that Rhaïs was in fact an Algerian Jew who had adopted the persona and clothing of a Muslim woman in order to further her literary career. A pseudonym, the (non-Muslim) name Elissa Rhaïs was designed to conjure the mysteries of the Orient, the world of Shahrazad. In reality, Elissa Rhaïs was Rosine Amar, née Boumendil, some forty years old, the divorced wife of an Algerian rabbi, and the mother of three children. Remarried to a wealthy Jewish Algerian merchant, she separated from him in order to pursue a career as a writer in Paris.[18]

To this plausible account of Rhaïs's life was added a third that rivaled any of Shahrazad's tales, not to mention the plots of Rhaïs's own novels. It emerged in 1982 when Paul Tabet, the son of Rhaïs's nephew, published the biography *Elissa Rhaïs*, in which he alleged that Leïla Boumendil, born of a Muslim father and Jewish mother, married at the age of seventeen to a wealthy merchant who cruelly locked the rebellious girl in a harem for fifteen years, was illiterate.[19] The real author of the novels signed Elissa Rhaïs was therefore Tabet's father, Raoul Dahan, an impoverished and much younger relation of Leïla's who, hired as her secretary, became her lover and scribe. Drawn to and yet horrified by the much older, ignorant woman who had committed the stories of a cowife to memory in order to survive terrible years in the harem, Raoul became her virtual captive. In tormented tribute, he fashioned her stories into novels and offered them to the public as her own.[20] Storyteller and spectacle, star and usurper, victim and despot, emancipated woman and slave of colonial stereotypes, Elissa Rhaïs thus conjures anew fantasies of the decadent, despotic Orient, albeit one strangely regendered. While Déjeux concedes the probable veracity of some of Tabet's allegations, he questions the narrative into which Tabet fashions them, commenting that Tabet's tale only reinscribes the servitude he attributes to his late father, "prisoner of the Occidental imaginary."[21] To be sure, Tabet's narrative simply inverts the sex of Shahrazad and the king, reviving an Orient of shadowy intrigues, uncertain identities, and perverse sexualities.[22] For Emily Apter, the debate inaugurated by Tabet's revelations also highlights the fundamental indeterminacy of Rhaïs's conventional, "realistic" prose: "For all we know, the novels could have been written by a French colonial officer—the mere fact that such doubts prove difficult to dispel on the basis of the writing alone points to the fundamental unreliability of time-honored notions of historical narration, authentic voice and national literature."[23] Speaking perhaps too much to European readers' expectations, Rhaïs seems now forever trapped in an antiquated Orient of endless dissimulation, revived now and then with nostalgia or as a curiosity. Yet the doubts retrospectively cast on her person also trouble this space, making painfully evident how the force of its imaginary existence has irretrievably overwritten countless other stories.

Women authors critical of the colonial project thus set out to strip themselves of veils of exoticism and to examine how colonialism's denial of existing and emerging ethnic, religious, cultural, and national identities sought to deny them a constitutive voice. Completed in 1946, Fadhma Aïth Mansour Amrouche's autobiography *Histoire de ma vie (My Life Story: The Autobiography of a Berber Woman)* testifies to the burden of an uncertain identity resulting from her problematic positioning vis-à-vis both indigenous and colonial society during a period of considerable historical upheaval.[24] Born in Kabylia in 1882 or 1883, Amrouche was a contemporary of Rhaïs/Boumendil, yet her difficult life shares none of the earlier author's glamour and mystery. The illegitimate daughter of a defiant Kabyle woman disowned by her family for reject- ing clan traditions (she refused to return to her family after the death of her first husband), Amrouche was educated and grew up primarily in French-run orphanage schools. She eventually converted to Chris- tianity, and she criticizes the oppressiveness of the Kabyle mores that obliged her mother to send her away out of fear for her safety. At the same time, however, she underscores the meanness and cruelties of many of her French "benefactors," professes her admiration for her courageous mother, and never ceases to long for her native Kabylia. Indeed, despite her continuous exiles and status as an outsider in the eyes of many Kabyle, who saw in her alternately a child of transgression, an infidel, and, during the war of independence, a potential traitor, Amrouche never ceased to proclaim her Kabyle identity. Her children, the poet Jean Amrouche and the singer and novelist Marguerite Taos Amrouche, preserved and performed the songs, poems, and tales of their mother, through them elevating her to the status of premier promoter of Kabyle language and culture.[25]

Amrouche's autobiography straightforwardly chronicles its author's lifelong tribulations: the losses of family, home, friendships, husband, and children, her poverty, and her final exile in France. At the end of this French-language memoir, however, she defies her audience by de- claring that she has preserved her Kabyle self despite all her losses and uprootings:

> I have just reread this long account and I perceive that I have omitted to say that I always remained "la Kabyle." . . . Today more than ever, I aspire to finally be home, in my village, among my people, among those who speak the same language, who have the same mentality, the same superstitious and candid soul, starved for liberty, for independence, the soul of Jugurtha![26]

Calling out to ancient history, Amrouche confirms colonialism's fail- ure. Taking the legendary figure of the ancient Amazight (Berber) king Jugurtha, whom her son Jean declared a symbol of the absolute liberty of the Amazight people, Amrouche proclaims her fundamental differ- ence from the colonizer, while celebrating qualities of her people that are negative in colonial eyes. A component of the French colonial pol- icy consisted of holding up the "Berbers" as more noble, civilized, and European than their Arab counterparts as a result of their interactions with ancient Rome. Having seduced her presumably French readership with this tale of her colonial, Christian education, Amrouche now concludes her autobiography by telling her readers that she is not the sum of what she has written up to that point. Still, this French colonial policy of divide and rule had postindependence repercussions when those determining the parameters of Algeria's new identity officially insisted on its Arab and Islamic character, effectively excluding the Amazight peoples from recognition as full citizens.[27]

In his 1967 introduction to Amrouche's memoir, the internationally renowned Algerian writer Kateb Yacine cautions readers not to fall prey to this colonially constructed rift. Holding up Fadhma Amrouche as the first Algerian woman to assume control of her own drama, Kateb pleads with postindependence Algerians to receive her as their own, to listen to her voice, to bear witness with their own stories: "Algerians, women and men, bear witness for yourselves! Accept no longer to be positioned as objects; take up the pen for yourselves before someone seizes the drama that belongs to you, in order to turn it against you!"[28] Amrouche's story, however, is swept aside by the drama of a postindependence nation striving to overcome the colonial past by fixing once and for all the history, voice, and culture of its people. Many others will need to reiterate her lesson, each one adding a new twist to the tale.

Just as Amrouche's memoir troubled the bases and markers of identity, those women who triumphantly supported the new Algeria also found their stories circumscribed by their representative obligations. The outspokenness of a young nationalist freedom fighter, Djamila Boupacha, came to symbolize the colonized's will to independence, the decadence and horrors of colonization, and the promise of a new Algeria. Yet her story, related by others, also begins to make visible the postindependence limits placed on women's (self-)expression. *Djamila Boupacha*, the book-length account of Boupacha's illegal arrest, torture, and rape by French soldiers and of her quest for justice in a corrupt colonial legal system, mobilized public opinion in France and abroad against the unjust war in Algeria.[29] Narrated and presented by the Franco-Tunisian lawyer Gisèle Halimi, who transformed Boupacha's case into a groundbreaking legal struggle against the colonial system, and the French philosopher Simone de Beauvoir, the book that bears Djamila Boupacha's name testifies to an international feminist movement that recognized the Algerian people's struggle for self-determination. Arrested and repeatedly tortured until she confessed to a crime she did not commit, Djamila Boupacha refused to accept her conviction in silence. Throughout the work, Boupacha's simultaneous pride in her role as a freedom fighter struggling for an independent, just Algeria and her belief in the French principles of liberty, equality, and fraternity render all the more horrific the crimes of the colonial authorities. Not the first, the last, or even the most horrific example of torture and rape, not even the first instance to be publicized abroad, Boupacha's case nonetheless captured public attention worldwide as no other had.[30]

What became of Djamila Boupacha, powerful symbol of an independent Algeria committed to respect and equal rights for all? Halimi's narrative leaves us hanging after emphasizing the determination of the Committee of the Friends of Djamila Boupacha to continue fighting recalcitrant and complicit legal and military systems in order to bring to justice Boupacha's torturers.[31] While it is easy to trace the influence of Boupacha's case inside and outside Algeria through the many representations—verbal, visual, and musical—that she generated, Boupacha herself seems to have vanished from the world stage with few traces after Algerian independence. At the time that her case was publicized, Boupacha possessed precisely those attributes that would ultimately elicit the empathy of both Western feminist activists and a broad public: not only was she determined, outspoken, and unapologetically committed to Algeria's independence, but also she and her family appealed to the French values her supporters embodied.[32] Of equal importance was Boupacha's visibility; immediately following the title page of the book that bears her name is a close-up photograph in which she looks confidently out at the reader, the inspiration for the sketch by Picasso that precedes the title page. Unveiled and French-educated, Boupacha seemed to prefigure Algerian women's liberation from a Muslim tradition long viewed by Westerners as oppressive. Yet her defiance of the colonial legal system, and by extension of her torturers, stemmed from her request that she be seen by a doctor primarily in order to establish the status of her virginity. For Halimi, Boupacha's concern for her virginity reflects the religious puritanism and taboos of her patriarchal society, and she all but dismisses the centrality of the young woman's body as motive for the authorities' crime. Boupacha's insistence on her virginity reveals the multiple obligations to which she must answer, and Halimi's dismissal of her concern exposes the interpretive impasses that Maghrebi writers confront. It shows how women were obliged, on behalf of the emerging nation, to legitimate their activism variably to different audiences, vastly complicating their quest to forge narrative agency.[33]

Like Shahrazad, all three of these Algerian women promise to confirm in one way or another the prevailing European impressions of North African women of their particular time, only to undercut those impressions in the narratives they relate, as well as through their very act of speaking. By addressing multiple audiences on both sides of the Mediterranean, all three also challenge "from within" women's obligation to represent the integrity of religions, cultures, and ethnicities. Yet they are also constantly reinscribed on both sides of the Mediterranean as mere pawns of colonial, national, and international narratives. In Morocco, independence was followed by the ratification of the Code of Personal Status, which affirmed men as the head of the household and conferred the status of minors on women. Tunisian women, by contrast, were granted legal equality with men in the post-independence Personal Status Code, yet within the private domain they continued to confront pressures to subscribe to normative feminine behavior. Algerian women long struggled for the recognition of equality between the sexes but saw the defeat of their efforts in 1984, when Algeria instituted a conservative Family Code.[34] In all three countries but most tragically in Algeria, the decades since independence have seen a sharp rise in religious extremisms that challenge nationalist governments.[35] Meanwhile, in Western media Maghrebi, Arab, and Muslim women continue to figure as largely helpless victims of new incarnations of the Oriental despots of the past.

Yet the words of these three authors resonate in the work of their successors, Algerian, Moroccan, Tunisian artists inspired by their example. As the narratives of these later women writers multiply available perspectives on the past, present, and future, they continually reject the kind of pessimism that would claim them as victims. Instead, these writers resist narrative closure, whether it originates at home or abroad, in the form of definitive characterizations of North African women's circumstances and aspirations. Like Shahrazad, they endlessly defer the final word, promising always that the next tale will supersede the previous one in as yet unheard of ways. In the interval that is the telling, however, amazing transformations are already underway.

1 ∞ Silent Reflections

Perhaps this culture of the indirect has advantages
over a culture valuing simple and direct expression.
Here everything is a little bit devious, a bit unformulated—the unsaid, and so on. This is why the camera
is so amazing. It's in complete harmony with this
rather repressed language. A camera is somewhat
sly and hidden. It's there and it can capture small
details about something one is trying to say, so in a
sense it can be an instrument for poetry.
—*Moufida Tlatli, "Moving Bodies," interview by
Laura Mulvey*

THAT FIRST NIGHT, with death hanging over her head and no viable means of resistance, Shahrazad enticed King Shahrayar into an alternate realm. Refocusing the king's attentions away from her and his immediate desires and onto the actors of the myriad dramas that she conjured for him, Shahrazad succeeded in diffusing the murderous rage that had gripped him ever since he had seen his wife in a passionate embrace with a slave.[1] In Shahrazad's stories, powerful figures reconsider their categorical judgments of apparent wrongdoers after listening to elaborate tales of the unexpected and marvelous.[2] Drawn into this world, King Shahrayar surely catches sight of his own reflection in the characters brought to life for him by Shahrazad's voice. As he postpones his vengeance, we cannnot but assume that he takes the lessons of these judges as his own.

In her recent introductory remarks to an abridged edition of Sir Richard F. Burton's *Nights,* British author A. S. Byatt remarks that audiences around the world identify with this tale because of its "deeply satisfying image of the relations between life, death, and storytelling."[3] Like Shahrazad, Byatt implies, we all attempt to transcend the finite "biological time" of our lives with stories. Yet the exoticizing and eroti-cizing of Shahrazad by European translators often limit the degree to which audiences outside the Islamic world are able to identify with the storyteller. For more even than the appendage of a final night, in which Shahrazad returns to center stage, the insistent interpolation of night-breaks into *The Thousand and One Nights* announces a refusal on the part of European retellers of the tales to permit Shahrazad to cede place to her stories. European and North American films, plays, ballets, paintings, and illustrations, not to mention pornography, intensify this preoccupation with the appearance of the storyteller, assigning her a starring role in dramas of desire that largely ignore her purpose and resolve.[4] In the frame story of the *Nights*, however, a defining facet of Shahrazad's character is her skill in deflecting the king's gaze from her person. Like any accomplished storyteller, she fathoms the interpretative universe that King Shahrayar shares with her, calculating the correct proportions of the fantastic and the mundane required to maintain the engagement of her royal audience. By contrast, translators, playwrights, choreographers, and artists from the eighteenth century onward have often approached the tales as the faithful mirror of an exotic, mysterious, enticing Orient and its peoples.[5] The *Nights* stories therefore long prompted European audiences to look outward rather than inward, to relegate the lessons of Shahrazad's tales to other times, places, and peoples.

For Arab women artists such as Moufida Tlatli, Fatima Mernissi, Assia Djebar, and Leïla Sebbar, Shahrazad's agency constitutes the real lesson. Locked within the confines of the palace, this storyteller profoundly transforms the manner in which its ruler perceives not just her but also himself, his subjects, and his authority. Night after night, Shahrazad makes herself heard by using language in such a way that the king remains unaware of the power he cedes to his seemingly innocent entertainment. This is the message that many Arab writers and filmmakers adapt from the *Nights* in the 1970s, 1980s, and 1990s, those decades when the hopes that accompanied national independence faded as governments turned increasingly autocratic, the left lost ground as the Soviet Union collapsed, and Islamism emerged as a formidable political and social force.[6] Some, including many women artists from the Maghreb, explore the models of gender in the *Nights* in order to emphasize how the relationship between Muslim women's visibility and their agency everywhere inflects both internal and external postindependence politics. Understanding that their commercial success, indeed the viability of their message, depends on the goodwill of powerful groups whose interests may not coincide—on the publishers, film distributors, readers, viewers, and, in some cases, censors who guarantee access to the work in its country of origin and internationally—these writers and filmmakers often draw on the seemingly apolitical aspects of the *Nights*, their love stories, fantastic occurrences, comedic details, interpolated poems, and narrative structure.[7] Following Shahrazad's example, they keep their audience always in sight, challenging the status quo while playing to readers' and viewers' expectations.

Seemingly complicit with the premise that visibility constitutes the first condition of authority and authorship, a premise upheld by audiences in the global North, Tunisian filmmaker Moufida Tlatli nevertheless begins to redirect this lesson in her 1994 film *The Silences of the Palace (Ṣamt al Quṣūr)*.[8] Offering a glimpse of hitherto unseen women, the servants who are virtual slaves of a ruling elite tottering on the brink of irrelevance as Tunisian independence looms, Tlatli's film broaches such difficult themes as slavery, rape, abortion, and death. The harsh realities of these women's oppression are chronicled through flashback scenes that feature soft lighting, seamless editing, abundant close-up and full shots of the actors, and a color palette reminiscent of Delacroix's Orientalist paintings. As such, the film taps into both Orientalist and filmic traditions of narrative pleasure, which everywhere it yet seeks to disturb. Tlatli produces a narrative of fractured repetitions, employing shot-reverse shots and mirrors, not to produce an illusion of seamless unity, but to double asymmetrically the images of the protagonist and to withhold narrative closure. From the opening sequence, point-of-view shots establish Alia, the protagonist, as an active looker rather than as an object of others' gazes. At the same time, she is doubled, appearing first as a young woman and then as a girl, with the result that her gaze simultaneously advances the narrative and folds back on itself. Employing an ostensibly classic narrative film structure and drawing heavily on the tropes of melodrama, *Silences* nonetheless problematizes the illusion of lifelike presence that film fosters, accumulating reflections on the possibility of self-authorship outside dominant frameworks of identity.

Tlatli's first feature film after a twenty-year career as a film editor, *The Silences of the Palace* quickly became the most internationally acclaimed and distributed North African film, making *Time* magazine's list of top ten films of 1994.[9] Until recently, it remained in wide VHS and DVD distribution in Europe and North America. A coming-of-age tale set on the eve of Tunisian independence, *Silences* reassesses the postindependence social, political, and economic climate for women and lower-class groups in Tunisia. Film and media theorist Ella Shohat includes *Silences* in a larger group of "post-Third-Worldist" works, remarking that in it, "[t]he gender-conscious open-ended narrative destabilizes a euphoric closure of the 'Nation.'"[10] The popular success of Tlatli's film stems not from an overtly political critique of postindependence Tunisia, however, but from a formal strategy tailored to entertain even while the film deliberately focuses on the psychological drama of those who cling desperately to old mindsets in times of dramatic change. In spite of its long shots, slow pace, and evocation of historical moments and settings unfamiliar to younger and non-Tunisian audiences, *Silences* quickly draws audiences into an intimate world rife with the familiar themes of melodrama: façades of respectability maintained through disavowal and repression, a burden of domestic order borne silently by women for the benefit of men.

Aside from Laura Mulvey's brief treatment of the issue in her interview with Tlatli for *Sight and Sound*, few have examined the particular formal strategies of *Silences*.[11] In her historical study of cultural identity in Arab film, Viola Shafik dubs *Silences* a sophisticated, formal study, yet her analysis of the film remains spare; she devotes barely two paragraphs of her book to it.[12] Meanwhile, the few scholars to offer critical readings of Tlatli's film to date have largely focused on the personal dilemma of the central character, Alia, as a snapshot of colonial or postcolonial female subjectivity or as a critique of narratives of nationhood.[13] None of these readings finally examines how Tlatli's film might draw on narrative and feminist traditions distinct from Euro-American ones. Unlike a classic Hollywood film or even an experimental European film, then, *Silences* seems to escape the kind of rigorous feminist reading that identifies a work as paradigmatic, as more than a mere exemplar of a historical condition or theoretical current. Certainly, the female-centered filmic perspective of *Silences* and its open-ended conclusion lend the film to readings based in now-classic feminist film theory. Yet the film's skillful amalgam of history and fiction—easily elided for audiences unfamiliar with the details of Tunisia's colonial past and postcolonial present—and its nod to the narrative art of Shahrazad call for theorization on its own terms. For even before the full social, historical, geographical, and cultural context of the film comes into view, its opening sequences introduce a complex set of issues that exact multiperspectival readings, from which a lesson emerges about feminist authorship, a lesson not restricted to Arab or Muslim women.

Looking

In the opening shot of *Silences*, an extreme close-up of the protagonist, Alia, fills the screen. Over the sounds of an instrumental melody, her eyes move slowly from left to right, as if taking in the source of the steady hum of conversation, laughter, and clatter that is just audible above the music. After a long moment, she intones the opening lines of "Amal Ḥayaati" (Hope of My Life), a song that any Arab viewer would immediately recognize as part of the repertoire of larger-than-life Egyptian singer Umm Kulthūm.[14] A slight rise in the level of conversation greets Alia's rendition of the song, and an eyeline match now reveals a room of socializing women apparently oblivious to her presence. When the camera returns to Alia, who is standing on a makeshift stage, it reveals her stiff posture, her cramped hands held at her sides. Several minutes elapse as she sings of hope, generating no response from her audience (the lyrics of the song are left untranslated for non-Arabic speakers).[15] Finally, her voice falters. Dipping her head abruptly, then raising her hand to it with a grimace, Alia looks once more at the indifferent women before decisively abandoning the stage. Positioned in this scene as an ineffectual imitator of Umm Kulthūm, "the voice of Egypt," whose performances nourished a mix of cultural and national pride that promoted pan-Arabism and united Egyptians, Alia appears both invisible and unheard, except to the film's audience.[16]

Any interpretation of the film spectator's gaze as privileged, however, must soon take into account the differential positions occupied by various audience members vis-à-vis the narrative content of *Silences*, positions based not just on gender but also on national, ethnic, cultural, and social identities. For those spectators who are outsiders to the largely sex-segregated wedding celebrations that serve as the backdrop to the opening scene, the camera may seem to offer a forbidden look into an exclusively female space. Insofar as Tlatli's editing in this opening scene draws us into the very "voyeuristic-scopophilic look" that Laura Mulvey dissects in her now famous essay on the gaze, these film spectators, whether male or female, find themselves "masculinized" by the scene's apparent actualization of colonial fantasies of unveiling Muslim women.[17] When Alia exits the villa, two men in the background eye her appraisingly while addressing inaudible remarks to each other. In this brief moment and in the dialogue with her reproachful boyfriend that immediately follows, Alia is reintroduced as an erotic object for the male characters of the film in a way that disrupts the reverie of the film's spectators. Indeed, by including Arab men within the frame, if only apparently to reinforce stereotypical notions of their sexism, the two sequences disrupt the voyeuristic pleasure of any spectator who holds him- or herself above such conduct, establishing a kind of complicity with Alia that is absent, for example, in Orientalist paintings of harem scenes.[18]

When *Silences* returns to a past that foregrounds Alia and her mother, the film's male characters also grow more complex, their different class and cultural affinities and their relationship to colonial authorities emerging more clearly. Alia's presumed father, the bey, or "prince," Sidi Ali, is portrayed as secular and European, as well as classically educated and sympathetic to modern nationalist ideals. A member of the ruling elite who reported to Ottoman rulers before 1881 and to their French colonizers after that date, yet a rebel who skips palace functions to discuss democratic rule with proponents of the opposition, he fills the role of potential, enlightened savior as well as that of oppressor.[19] Like his brother, he takes only one wife and frequently dresses in Western-style clothing. Furthermore, they do not impose "traditional" dress on the women of the palace, servants and aristocrats alike. None of the women veil, most wear Western-style dresses, and religion is nowhere an issue. In this manner, *Silences* chips away at the colonial pretext that an obvious embrace of the colonizer's values would rescue Arab and Muslim women from all manner of sexist oppression. Indeed, the film's visual text and narrative content alike reveal the common blind spots of spectators from both sides of the former colonizer/colonized divide.

At the same time, *Silences* cautions that those outside Alia's world cannot presume to furnish the recognition she requires. For those positioned as insiders to Tunisian and Arab society, the film's initial scene adds another degree of discomfort to the dynamics of the gaze that it establishes. Alia's performance in this opening scene adapts a filmic strategy, the device of the showgirl, which Mulvey identifies as a classic-film technique that reinforces woman's "to-be-looked-at-ness," explaining of this device that it "allows the two looks [of the spectator and of the male characters] to be unified technically without any apparent break in the diegesis."[20] In Tlatli's mise-en-scène, however, Alia performs for a primarily female audience (a handful of men are present in the background, along with the bridegroom), one that additionally refuses to dignify her with so much as a look. For an audience immediately attuned to the sociocultural codes at work in this scenario—the stigma that accrues to the female performer in Arab culture—and able to understand the Arabic words to, and thus the irony of, Alia's song, identification with the camera's gaze is fraught with unease. Rather than a titillating violation of private space, this gaze assumes the quality of an embarrassed obligation when the film foregrounds a disavowed subject who belongs "to the very marginal area outside the ordered opposition between public and private." In Hollywood cinema, Mulvey specifies that the "underworld of prostitution" occupies this marginal space, which complements "the repression of the sexual within the private citizen's home." While Alia is not, so to speak, a prostitute, her profession as singer and her unmarried status effectively designate her as one in Tunisian society.[21] And as the film makes clear, she is a subject whose effacement is necessary to uphold the appearance of social order, both before and after independence.

Tlatli eases viewers into this confrontation. In her interview with Mulvey, she hints at the multiplicity of readings to which *Silences* lends itself when she reflects that cinema from the Islamic world should be regarded as possessing a cultural function similar to that of its poetry:

> [P]oets frequently had to make use of symbols and metaphors to express something that could not otherwise have been spoken. Poetry allows this: it gives a fantastic freedom. You only have to have a small amount of imagination to extract another reading from the words. Perhaps the cinema is the same. It too has to make use of metaphors and symbols, in keeping with this lack of directness that so characterizes Islamic society.[22]

These remarks do more than align cinema with a foundational Arabic cultural practice; they also allude to the material reality confronting artists and intellectuals in 1990s Tunisia. Despite Tunisia's reputation as the most progressive Arab country for women's rights and its model economic growth in the 1990s, it remains notorious for its centralized rule, repression of government critics, and censorship of the media.[23] By thus playing with classic cinematic camera and editing techniques and combining them with Arabo-Islamic poetic and narrative traditions, Tlatli, much like Shahrazad, produces a narrative that contains multiple stories within each frame, the entertaining giving way to all manner of serious messages.

In Alia's apartment after her performance, the issue of her social marginality dominates her conversation with her boyfriend even as she remains the central focus of the camera. Lying on the bed fully clothed, her boyfriend Lotfi gently rubbing her temples, Alia declares, "I'm scared of the eyes of the neighbors. They stare at me all the time. Every eye accuses me as if they could read something in my face." Her words accentuate the unspoken tension that saturates looks among the characters of the film and stands in contrast to her act of looking in the film's opening scene. Here, Alia's inability to return the neighbors' gazes reveals that she remains trapped by a web of internalized as well as societal taboos. Unable to defy her neighbors' censorious looks, Alia cannot engage a dialectical process whereby she might wrest recognition from those who deny her. Lotfi dismisses Alia's fears as all in her head, before adding, "Tomorrow this burden will be lifted." The dialogue that ensues reveals that the following day Alia is to have an abortion, not her first, and that, despite his protestations of love and certainty that the child is his, Lotfi steadfastly refuses to marry her. Suddenly, without turning to look at him, Alia blurts out that she wishes to keep her child. He responds with muted exasperation: "You're crazy. . . . A child needs a name, a family, a marriage." In later flashbacks to the palace in which Alia spent her childhood as the fatherless daughter of a servant, the social and legal implications of her present situation grow clearer. In retrospect, Lotfi's refusal to marry Alia seems less a function of cruelty than one of cowardice, one that echoes the cowardice of her presumed father. Nevertheless, the sequences that follow continue to foster viewers' complicity with Alia.

In the "to-be-looked-at-ness" of Alia and the other women servants, then, *Silences* places on display a vital social issue that complicates Western feminist film theory. If spectators positioned on the inside of Tunisian society in the mid-1990s employ only "a small amount of imagination," they can read Tlatli's film as a critique not just of the national government's failure to uphold its revolutionary promises but of their own collusion with the status quo. At Tunisia's independence in 1956, the new, secular republic, headed by Hassib Borguiba, divested the beys of their power and ratified the Personal Status Code, which abolished polygamy, instituted judicial divorce, raised the minimum marriage age to seventeen, and granted women a host of other social, legal, and political rights.[24] Nonetheless, the "class" of servants into which Alia was born eventually vanished after independence more as a result of the emergence of new economic models and social classes than as a result of legal action. While the experience of Alia's mother, Khedija, makes clear that poor families from the country continued to sell their girl children to wealthy households in the early twentieth century despite an official ban on slavery, by the time Alia returns to the palace in approximately 1966, the servants' quarters are almost deserted.[25] Indeed, the death of Sidi Ali, the man presumed to be Alia's father, signals the demise of such preindependence models of social hierarchies. For in spite of his professed modernism, he cannot, or will not, recognize that his union with Khedija is structured by a dynamics of power that has nothing to do with romantic love.

As Alia journeys back in time, the parallels between her and her mother's life trajectories call attention to the fact that the denial of subjectivity on which the old servitude depended is more difficult to eradicate than that servitude itself. Like her mother, Alia clings to existence on the edge of nonbeing, visible to the spectator and to the disapproving neighbors but unnamed and therefore invisible in the eyes of the law and the state. It is up to audiences to recognize that in 1994, nearly thirty years after the fictional events in the film's frame, Alia's story continues, for it is only in 1998 that an amendment to the Tunisian Personal Status Code finally guarantees children a first and last name and the right to sue for paternity if born out of wedlock. *Silences* therefore seems to interpellate the gazes of Tunisian and Arab spectators toward a distinct, politically immediate end. However, even the ratification of this later law only touches the surface of the problems that Tlatli lays out in *Silences*. In her brilliant study of kin relations and postcolonial state formation, Mounira Charrad stresses that Tunisia's Personal Status Code was not so much concerned with the rights of women as it was with promoting "the conjugal unit and its progeny, to the detriment of the extended agnatic group."[26] In other words, it merely reformulated patriarchal structures in order to strengthen the authority of the central government. Like the Personal Status Code, the amendment of 1998 in no way undermines the patriarchal foundations of the modern Tunisian state, guaranteeing access to, rather than challenging, the structures of patrilineage. At the outset of the film, Alia's concessions to Lotfi's reasoning indicate that she continues to believe that only the name of the father can authorize a life, whether her child's or her own, as the flashback scenes demonstrate. By the end of *Silences*, the father's name has lost its value for her. She has decided to keep her child in the hopes that it will be a girl on whom she may bestow the name Khedija, after her mother. In the film's closing scene, she sits alone in the palace garden after nightfall, challenging audiences to envision social transformations as fantastic as any Shahrazad imagined.

Naming

Shahrazad, the daughter of the king's vizier, never had to face the social invisibility that Alia confronts. Knowing herself worthy of the king's attentions, Shahrazad does not hesitate before speaking but rations her words in order to extend her audience. Alia, by contrast, lacks any subject position within the social hierarchy of the palace; her silence is thus presupposed. Yet silence is also a survival tactic by which the servants refuse to identify with the daily humiliations to which they are subjected. Not yet versed in this silence, Alia thus observes the world around her—surreptitiously more often than openly and defiantly—witnessing the degradations that the servant women bear and noting her mother's suffering on her behalf. In the absence of anyone with whom to share her discoveries, her voyeurism alternately proves deficient and overwhelming as a source of self-knowledge. Without any instruction from the other servants as to how she might control the narrative of her life, Alia finds herself again and again at the mercy of others, of a father who refuses to recognize her, of a boyfriend who fears jeopardizing his respectability by marrying her. Although it shows that which has been silenced, the visual narrative of *Silences* thus remains troublingly incomplete. As Alia travels back to the palace to pay her respects to the recently deceased Sidi Ali, a voice-over foreshadows the tone of the narrative to come: "My former pains resurface, as well as the past I thought I'd buried with my mother." Yet the interior monologue ends once Alia arrives at the palace, and she remains a character in, rather than the narrator of, the story that follows, with the film's spectators positioned as voyeurs rather than addressees. Alia expects until nearly the film's very end the authorizing word of her father's name. She takes control of her life story only when she at last realizes that this gauge of authorship no longer holds final meaning for her.

In the introduction to her foundational article on voice and cinema, Mary Ann Doane reminds us that in silent film, "[t]he absent voice re-emerges in gestures and the contortions of the face—it is spread over the body of the actor."[27] *Silences* is by no means a silent film, for no sequence in the film, with the exception of the young Alia's nightmare, is truly soundless; synchronized sound and a musical soundtrack compensate for the lack of dialogue. Moreover, the characters minimize their gestures and strictly control their facial expressions, the only clue to their emotions the often guarded expression in their eyes. In this, the servant women make visible the limitations of their strategy of silence, how it transforms from a tactic of resistance into a form of oppression when it serves the interests of their employers and the state. Khedija's and Alia's abortions, for example, convey the degree to which the servant women efface all traces of their own presence, the extent to which they have internalized their official nonexistence through self-silencing. While the deepening political crisis (the nationalists' ever bolder challenges to the beys' authority) increasingly insinuates itself into the palace via radio and the tales of male servants who run errands in the city, those few women who begin to seize on nationalist narratives of resistance to voice their despair or discontent are chastised by Khalti Hadda, their matriarch. For her, the servants owe their absolute loyalty to the beys, who rule the palace and who, in her eyes, guarantee the continued existence of the servant family, rather than the other way around. Although the servants sing while working or celebrating and jest with one another regarding their charms and prospects as a self-nurturing community, they rarely broach the topics of social relations, personal circumstances, and politics. Because no one ever articulates for her how the interests of the servants are at odds with those of the ruling family, the young Alia fixates on full membership in that family as the only possible entry into subjectivity.

On a formal level, the paucity of dialogue in *Silences* prevents the full emergence of the illusion that "reality speaks and is not spoken, that film is not a constructed discourse."[28] In the absence of narrative or dialogue spoken by women, every scene of the film appears only partly realized. Despite Tlatli's use of rather conventional sound and camera techniques that usually support the illusion of self-evident meaning, the figures of the servant women who are the film's central focus never quite attain the status of unified, self-present individuals. Viewers may gloss over a nagging lack of presence by willfully reading *Silences* as a mirror of Tunisian realities, a temptation that is perhaps facilitated by the dedication at the film's opening: "to my mother." Still, while *Silences* has hardly been celebrated as a technically innovative or paradigm-shifting film, it lacks those qualities that make certain African

films easily relegated to the category of ethnographic works: low production values (read, modest budgets and restricted access to equipment
and editing facilities) and an uncertain sense of cinematic language
(read, rejection of dominant narrative conventions). Aside from its long
takes and slow pacing, then, *Silences* falls into an intermediary category:
not quite a film that documents the foreign and not so entirely familiar
as to elide the gap between spectator and fictional reality. To reduce
Silences to a reflection of reality, to lose sight of its fictionality, is to
dismiss Tlatli's skill as a storyteller and to ignore the scope of her lessons
on the contingency of self-determination.

For Tlatli's treatment of subjectivity is complex, belying the notion
that women outside the global North struggle solely to combat elemen-
tal forms of oppression that bar them from self-expression. Moreover,
Silences does not sustain the kind of fully realized, self-knowing subject
already debunked by European and North American feminist theorists.
Through the theme of the unspoken-unspeakable name of the father,
Tlatli foregrounds the kind of fundamental, pre-Oedipal loss that Kaja
Silverman argues film both engages and glosses over by presenting
spectators with that which is necessarily absent.[29] As she surveys work
on classic cinema's mediation of absence through the figure of woman
constructed as a loss or lack to be disavowed, Silverman attends to the
effects of this disavowal in the production of male subjectivity:

> However, at no point . . . has it been noted that the lack which must somehow
> be disavowed not only structures male subjectivity as much as female
> subjectivity, but poses a far greater danger to the stability of the former
> than to that of the latter. Since the female subject is constructed through
> an identification with dispossession, her exposure to further castrations
> jeopardizes nothing. The male subject, on the contrary, is constructed
> through an identification with the phallus. That identification may be
> threatened by the disappearance of the object, but it is capsized by any
> reminder of the male subject's discursive limitations. It is impossible for a
> subject who knows himself to be excluded from authoritative vision, speech,
> and hearing to sustain a pleasurable relation to the phallus.[30]

While Silverman's analysis targets theoretical discourses of male spec-
tatorship, *Silences*, which is all about looking, incorporates such a figure
of the male spectator into the diegesis, or film narrative, in the characters of Sidi Ali and his brother, Si Bechir. Tlatli's film therefore exposes more than the disenfranchisement of a particular social group of
women by prevailing narratives of communal and national belonging.
Rather, that critical silence that Alia stubbornly strives to overcome

gradually reveals her father's limitations, his lack exposing the fragile constructedness of the male subjectivity on which the essential structures of colony and modern nation alike repose.

From the first flashback sequence, in which Sidi Ali paces nervously in a sitting room of the palace as Khedija gives birth, *Silences* introduces him as Alia's father. The aged Khalti Hadda's reminiscence that Sidi Ali's joy at this impending birth was due to his wife Jneina's barrenness seems to touch off this first flashback, a memory of which Alia cannot possibly have any recollection. Sidi Ali immediately seems a familiar character, a man who turns to another woman because his wife cannot bear him children. However, the film contrasts Sidi Ali's delight with his brother Bechir's more perfunctory celebration of the birth of his daughter Sarra, born just minutes before Alia, Sidi Ali's delight in a female child, as well as his sensitivity to Jneina's subsequent unease, setting him apart from men like his brother. As the flashbacks advance, *Silences* reaffirms Sidi Ali's paternal relationship to Alia primarily through his displayed preference for Khedija and the fatherly gazes, sometimes troubled, that he directs at Alia. In spite of his obvious affection for Khedija and Alia, however—an affection so evident that, time and again, it elicits the scorn of Jneina and the disapproval of his brother's wife—Sidi Ali never formally acknowledges Alia as his daughter, a gesture that traditionally would have granted Khedija social status and freed her from servitude. In this household of outwardly monogamous aristocrats, to do so might undermine Sidi Ali's position as a self-styled modernizer. His silence not only maintains Khedija and his presumed daughter in a state of nonpersonhood, however; it also effectively shores up his masculinity while further diminishing his barren wife's already limited agency.[31]

Tlatli conveys Sidi Ali's reluctance to assume paternity of Alia by a conspicuous paucity of shot-reverse shot sequences between the two characters. Rather than return or engage her presumed father's gaze, Alia relentlessly spies on him and on her mother as she waits on the beys, seeking some visual confirmation of what it seems to her everyone must know. One of the few shot-reverse shot sequences between Alia and Sidi Ali happens after she has fled to an old storage room with Sarra's oud, or lute. She plucks some strings and sings a few lines; as she looks up, the camera cuts to Sidi Ali standing outside the window. He applauds as she meets his gaze, and Alia smiles as if her talent and parentage have together been confirmed. Not long afterward, a sequence shows Alia catching sight of Sidi Ali stealthily entering her mother's room. Tiptoeing up to the closed shutters, she spies through them and sees Sidi Ali tenderly embrace Khedija. Overcome with emotion at this long-hoped-for sight, Alia runs to the garden and races in circles until she falls over in a faint. There, Si Bechir comes upon her, still uncon-scious, as he walks in the gardens reading aloud from a book of French poems; for a long moment, it seems as if he will violate her, but he finally smoothes down her dress and carries her away. This is but the pro-logue to a crucial scene, however. Bechir is tucking Alia into bed in the room she shares with her mother when Khedija hesitantly enters. Turn-ing from Alia with a compliment to her beauty, Bechir stalks Khedija as her face reflects mounting horror. She struggles silently as he grabs her from behind and rapes her. In midrape, the camera cuts to a high-angle shot of Alia, eyes open in frozen terror, bearing witness to the scene. When she closes her eyes, her nightmare—the only truly silent sequence in the film—takes over the screen; in it, Alia runs at night to the palace gates, grasping the bars too late and silently screaming as they close in front of her.

Alia's nightmare represents more than just her personal trauma, despite the tendency of the conventional melodramatic tropes of the sequence to overwhelm its more far-reaching significations. Through its total silence, the nightmare sequence underscores Alia's failure to speak out, to intervene in the scene that definitively shatters her nar-rative of self. In the narrative of the film as well, it marks a crisis. Alia evokes the nightmare's persistent recurrence but claims to have no memory of it, leaving it and the key scene that provokes it uncommented on and unresolved. In order finally to force open the gates and leave the palace behind once and for all, Alia would need, in effect, to confront a number of questions far thornier than her habitual query regarding her father's name: How many previous rapes and abortions have there been? Is Khedija's subsequent pregnancy the result of her tryst with Sidi Ali or of Bechir's rape? Is it perhaps Sidi Ali, and not Jneina, who is to blame for the couple's lack of children, thus making it impossible that he is her father? Does Khedija's growing disgust with herself stem only from her fear of seeing Alia follow in her footsteps, or is it also from a horror of potential incest? Finally, does Sidi Ali neglect to recognize Alia as his child because he prefers the absolutely unverifiable assumption that he is her father to potential challenges to his subjectivity in a culture built on patrilineal kinship structures? These questions disturb the progressive narrative that *Silences* has, until this point, seemingly built. No longer does Alia's personal dilemma stem only from the selfish refusal of her presumed father, otherwise a self-styled rebel, to defy social convention by recognizing her. Rather, the burden to break the silence—a burden she initially rejects through her long, mute illness immediately following her mother's rape—now falls heavily on her. She must forestall the utterance of the name she does not want to hear by becoming complicit in the servants' silence, unless she can assume the seemingly impossible task of envisioning an entirely new narrative of self.

From the rape scene on, it seems that Alia knows there can be no definitive response to her oft-reiterated query regarding the name of her father. This very irremediable uncertainty, in tandem with her new awareness of just how much her mother's silence protects her oppressors, instills in her a new wariness regarding the beys, but also leaves her wavering between disdain for her mother's submissive silence and admiration for her strength. Her conflicting sentiments explode in a pivotal scene after her recovery. Alia confronts her mother as the pregnant Khedija, desperate to abort in secret, informs her daughter that she is to spend some time on the beys' farm after Sarra's engagement party. Again demanding the name of her father, Alia blurts out to Khedija that she knows of her mother's nights spent with the beys. When Khedija attempts to push her daughter from the room, crying out that she doesn't want to see her, Alia looks at the full-length mirror that adorns their room and impulsively shatters it with her fist, shouting that she has no desire to see her mother either. At this moment, Alia catches a glimpse of the endless refraction of their common story, without origin and without resolution. The effect is intensified as Khedija finally discloses her ignorance of her own past and her resultant inability even to contemplate leaving the palace. Alia's sense of self has been thrown into crisis, so that she is forever compelled to return not to the point of "certain" knowledge but to the point of its obfuscation; the film narrative has lost its linear momentum. Only midway through *Silences*, spectators must understand that the film can have no resolution, that this story can make no progress; it can only ever repeat itself.

Looking Back, Renaming

Much of the power of Tlatli's film emanates from the way in which it repeats an all too familiar tale, that of women trapped on the economic, social, and political margins, through a familiar genre, that of melodrama. In many ways, *Silences* foregrounds the very frustration and absence of resolution that Thomas Elsaesser deems characteristic of the family melodrama:

> The family melodrama . . . more often records the failure of the protagonist to act in a way that could shape the events and influence the emotional environment, let alone change the stifling milieu. The world is closed, and the characters are acted upon. Melodrama confers on them a negative identity through suffering, and the progressive self-immolation and disillusionment generally end in resignation: they emerge as lesser human beings for having become wise and acquiescent to the ways of the world.[32]

Yet while *Silences* shares elements of the family melodrama, it portrays a social universe in which the definition of family cannot be taken for granted, in which the extended clan still vies with a more recent nuclear model. Taking the perspective not just of women but also of the lowest of the low, the film intensifies even further the climate of repression characteristic of melodrama. In the claustrophobic world of the palace, looks reveal the silencing of the fundamental supporting roles of those servants whose very existence belies the "modernity" of the beys as well as the "liberation" promised by the nuclear family. Still, as political upheaval causes the palace walls to tremble, women are pitted against women rather than against the patriarchal sociopolitical structures that so oppress them. The aristocratic Jneina's persecution of Khedija, for example, prevents Jneina from ever recognizing how both of them shore up the social façade that grants Sidi Ali such power over their lives. Khedija, for her part, rationalizes that silence protects Alia from the realities of her life, not understanding how it actually exacerbates her daughter's dependence on the prevailing social and symbolic order, how it condemns Alia to return forever to the scene of her undoing.

However, *Silences* also draws on the narrative model of repetition proposed in the *Nights* in order to evoke a potential for change. In the *Nights*, each repetition of and variation on a fantastic tale—a tale that suspends or transgresses the limits of the possible—realizes and confirms the power of hitherto unheard of worlds of experience that lie beyond the limits of the immediately perceptible. While theories of repetition often emphasize that each repeat performance reinforces the status quo while yet introducing occasions for slippage and change, storytellers in the *Nights* repeat variations on fantastic, excessive, and impossible tales with the declared intention of challenging their audience's everyday experiences. In her narratological study of repetition in the *Nights*, Sandra Naddaff argues, for example, that only through "the final dissolution of the repetitive structure" at the end of a story like "The Porter and the Three Ladies" is (narrative) control reestablished.[33] At the same time, repetition "creates time," in Naddaff's words, by breaking the forward, teleological movement of narrative.[34] Stories in the *Nights* conclude when the caliph, king, or judge recognizes the exemplarity of the speaker's excessive story and decrees that it be consigned to writing. *Silences* ends when Alia breaks free of her need to repeat a question whose answer would but further entrap her in the past and when she finally realizes the vital exemplarity of her and her mother's life stories, permitting her to escape the melodramatic mode of resignation. Long lived in silence because deemed beyond the margins of appropriate speech, their experiences provide her with the necessary elements for a new life narrative while requiring yet another cycle of repetition so as to ensure their eventual inscription.

Alia recognizes her own life as a repetition of her mother's at the same time that she relives the formerly repressed events that led her to her present predicament. For the first time, she hears a new meaning in her mother's silences. Yet the film's juxtaposition of flashbacks with the frame story also underscores the changes that have taken place since Alia left the palace, the critical differences between her life and her mother's that have made this new way of hearing possible for her. For in a number of ways, Alia's situation improves on Khedija's, even as it mirrors her mother's fundamental disenfranchisement. As a financially successful wedding singer whose companion is a schoolteacher, Alia possesses a certain intellectual and material independence to which her mother had no access; she has survived, materially at least, in the outside world that her mother so feared.[35] Moreover, when she returns to the palace at the outset of the film, the sparsely furnished, dimly lit, and virtually deserted lower floors contrast sharply not only with the opulent palace of her memories but also with her own modern, brightly lit apartment. Her beauty, youth, and talent seem to have helped her to succeed in the very much changed world of postindependence Tunisia, while the women who remained behind in the palace, aristocrats and servants alike, seem trapped in a static, crumbling world.

Nonetheless, when the elegantly dressed adult Alia returns to the palace, she barely meets the mourning women's eyes and quickly whispers to her childhood companion Sarra that she must visit Khalti Hadda.

Significantly, it is in the presence of this now ailing and blind woman, matriarch of the servants and mother figure to Khedija, that Alia's flashbacks begin, and it is to her that Alia will confess the fears she has hidden in the ten years since she left the palace. Oblivious to the signs of Alia's material success, Khalti Hadda relates to her how, following her flight, the old woman effaced all traces of Alia's existence in an effort to spare Sidi Ali any further anguish: "So he would calm down, we never uttered your name." As if in response to this renewed subordination of her existence to the needs of the prince, Alia conjures up her past, which is at the same time the story of her mother's life. As her tale highlights decisive silences, it indicates that Alia's obsession with her father's name is simply a screen for a more critical lack. After revisiting the formative experiences of her life, Alia seems finally to see her mother as the real author of her life. At the film's conclusion she abandons her objective of integration into Tunisian society, shunning normalization in order to explore the possibility of a different narrative of personhood.

Before that final scene occurs, however, Alia revisits her earlier failed attempt to assert her subjectivity. In it, she challenges the omnipotence of the beys only to look to the nationalists, as represented by her boyfriend, Lotfi, to provide the recognition the former have denied her. In the final flashback, which mirrors the opening scene of the film, the young Alia performs before a crowd of female guests at Sarra's engagement party. Taking the stage at her cousin's request, Alia interprets "Ghanni li Shwayya Shwayya," a song exalting the power of love that Umm Kulthūm first sang in a film where she played the role of a singing slave girl.[36] Throughout Alia's performance, a play of shot-reverse shots encompasses a pensive Sidi Ali at the window of the men's quarters, a proud Lotfi (the tutor to the beys' children) at the entrance to the room, a visibly uncomfortable Khedija near the door to the kitchen stairs, and the disdainfully tolerant and long-suffering wives of the beys. As she concludes the verse, "the darkness of the night becomes light in the eyes of lovers," Alia abruptly breaks off the song. In the long moment of silence that ensues, all eyes rest on her. A sequence of close-ups and shot-reverse shots foregrounds Alia's reproachful expression; Khedija, who now sways briefly, winces, and carefully turns; and Lotfi, composed yet discomfited. When the scene briefly shifts to Khedija staggering in pain on the steps to the kitchen, Alia's voice suddenly rings out again, singing the words of the forbidden nationalist anthem. Tlatli builds tension by cutting between scenes of Khedija in the throes of a self-induced abortion in the rooms below and close-ups of Alia, Lotfi, and the aristocrats upstairs. When the guests file from the room after an initial moment of shock, Alia continues to sing without accompaniment. She reaches the line "but under the ashes glows an ember for every loving heart" when Khedija screams in the agony of her death. Abandoning her song, Alia rushes to her mother's room, pursued by Lotfi. Her earlier conversation with Khalti Hadda has already revealed that she left the palace with Lotfi that night, never to return, even for her mother's funeral.

While there are no storytellers among the slave women, all are singers. They sing to celebrate and sometimes to accompany their work. Their songs recount often earthy tales of flirtation, seduction, and falls from grace, underlining the isolation and oppression of these women, who have neither suitors nor illusions of freely chosen loves. By contrast, the songs of Umm Kulthūm that enter the palace via the radio draw on the literary tradition of secular Arabic love poetry and explore themes of all-consuming, enduring, and unrequited loves. Herself of humble origins and yet eminently respectable, Umm Kulthūm appeals to slaves and masters alike with her songs. Alia and Sarra, who share their love of music and together listen to the Egyptian singer's famous radio broadcasts despite the disapproval of the adults, hint at the possibility of a new sort of communal identity. Yet Sarra's sheltered life as a princess permits her to cling to the ideals of romantic love that permeate Umm Kulthūm's songs, while for Alia such dreams are shattered by brutal sexual encounters that the songs ignore. Uninstructed in the art of storytelling in order to entertain, edify, persuade, and transform, Alia instead channels her emotions into celebrated lyrics, grasping for idealized models of selfhood in the aftermath of her mother's rape. Her talents as a singer only increase her value as a prized object in the eyes of the princes, however; unschooled and fatherless, Alia has no access to the respectability of Umm Kulthūm and instead, in fulfillment of a destiny that the palace hierarchy has always traced out for her, only accrues the social stigma that habitually attaches to female performers. In the film's final flashback, the song's celebration of a romantic love that transcends all social barriers makes a mockery of both Khedija's suffering and Alia's future.

Urgently casting about for a means to express if not the much more typical tale of the sexual exploitation of slaves by their masters, then at least some rejection of the conventions that permit her mother's life to slip silently away, Alia turns to the anthem of the nationalists. Forbidden by the princes, its lyrics exalt those who sacrifice their lives for Tunisian independence:

> Green Tunisia seems in a daze.
> Its sadness bursts forth in flashes that shake the sky and extinguish the stars.
> Cherish the suffering of those who have fallen so that enlightenment may spread.
> On their foreheads, after the torment, a light appears.
> On yours are written shame and defeat.
> [Twenty times] you have handed Tunisia over to its enemy.
> Plunged for a long time in darkness, the despair of the doves obscures the domes [shrines of the martyrs].
> But under the ashes an ember glows for every loving heart.[37]

These strangely appropriate lyrics find their target, for the quality of Alia's voice and her beauty do nothing to mute their critique of the ruling class. The appalled aristocrats silently turn away. At the same time, the song's lofty metaphors fail to account for or alter the silent victimization of Khedija. Ten years after independence, the political situation has changed, and the beys have lost their political power, but Alia's life, like her mother's, seems on the verge of being lost to silence. Meanwhile, the anthem has lost its potency in a postindependence Tunisia, where the identity of the enemy has grown less clear. Alia has returned to singing of romantic loves in which she no longer believes, her attention merely shifted to another absent name that would legitimate her life story—that of a husband.

At the end of the film, Alia remarks to Khalti Hadda that her mother always refused to divulge the name of her father. In her response, the elderly woman unwittingly exposes the very weakness of those she has devoted her life to protecting: "Is a father simply a name? A father is sweat, pain and joy, an entire life of daily caring. Listen, my daughter, there are things in life one is better off not knowing. What your mother underwent could drive you crazy also." Although Khalti Hadda still piously repeats the lesson of silence that the palace servants were taught, Alia seems suddenly to recognize that it is her mother who has filled the critical role that Khalti Hadda describes. The blind woman means to pay homage to Khedija's exemplary silence, to her commitment to her duty, yet her words instead induce Alia finally to confront the assumptions on which the entire social edifice reposes. Although she once perceived herself as unrealized and her existence as unspeakable, Alia now seems to discover that no father or husband can authorize her life narrative for her. Sidi Ali may have praised her singing, and Lotfi may have taught her to read and write, but neither man "authored" Alia as her life with her mother did. Nor does either man really want to hear the story that Alia has to tell, the story that her mother toiled to shape in the hope that she might one day attain, if not a happy conclusion, at least peace. Alia now recognizes, it seems, that it falls to her to legitimate in turn her mother's life, to reawaken its purpose and intention by insisting on this narrative that she has too long permitted society to ignore.

At the film's conclusion, Alia, alone in the palace garden after nightfall, resolves to keep her unborn child. Her resolution sets the conditions for a repetition of the story viewers have just witnessed, yet the self-consciousness of that repetition marks a change, a will to challenge the dominant social order and its notions of female subjectivity. Difficult, it is not a seductive story; only through insistent and painful repetition might it take on the power to edify and transform. In the voice-over that concludes the film, Alia muses to her dead mother, "This child . . . I feel that it has taken root in me. I feel it bringing me back to life, bringing me back to you. I hope it will be a girl. I will call her Khedija." In his study of plagiarism and forgery in the classical Arabic tradition, Abdelfatah Kilito notes that only a text whose origins and originator are known can become authoritative, a condition that excludes a work like the *Nights* from the literary canon on the grounds of illegitimacy.[38] In this epilogue to the film and prologue to her story, Alia emphasizes her mother as primary, rejecting the genealogical conventions of personal and textual authentification that authorize only those whose paternity is established. Repeating this act that norms of social propriety would silence and hide, Alia affirms the authority and influence of her mother, an authority and influence that become her own. Her decision to bear a child out of wedlock without any hope of conclusiveness is meant to endow with authoritativeness her own voice as well as that of her child, voices that may tell hitherto unheard tales.

Beginning, Again

Two interior monologues inaugurate and conclude the flashback sequences of the film. Each represents voice and body simultaneously, offering up, in Doane's words, "what is inaccessible to the image, what exceeds the visible: the inner life of the character."[39] While the first voice-over is a conventional precursor to a diegesis that "speaks for itself," the second concludes the film, leaving it very much open-ended. For it breaks the illusion that all that preceded was in Alia's voice. In this opening that is the conclusion, the inner life of Alia still remains under the shadow of withheld social recognition and a violence all the more insidious because it is disavowed. Alia's final words thus suggest a determination to transform the future, but they also heighten the urgency and fragility of her project. The story still hangs on the voice of a single woman speaking—to an audience obscured by the night—in order to vanquish death.

2 ∞ Speaking in Between

BEFORE SHE BECOMES STORYTELLER to King Shahrayar, Shahrazad briefly figures as an audience member. For when she requests of her father that he give her as a bride to the king, the aging vizier answers her with two tales meant to dissuade. In the first, a donkey foolishly boasts to an overworked ox of the advantages that his stubbornness earns him, and in the second a merchant learns from animals how to beat his demanding wife into silence.[1] The first a plea not to sacrifice oneself for others and the second a warning, Shahrazad nonetheless stands her ground. She dismisses the transparent messages of both tales with an open threat that exposes her father's weakness: "Such tales don't deter me from my request. If you wish, I can tell you many such tales. In the end, if you don't take me to King Shahrayar, I shall go to him by myself behind your back and tell him that you have refused to give me to one like him and that you have begrudged your master one like me."[2] This plain language vanishes once Shahrazad has the ear of the king, however. Like any storyteller who desires to retain her audience, Shahrazad tailors her words, conjuring for the king dazzling, intricate tales that speak to and defy his expectations.

As European translators and scholars vied with one another to set a definitive version of the *Nights*, the needs and desires of particular audiences were nearly relegated to the background. Nevertheless, this oral vestige of the tales never vanished entirely but merely found a different expression. Translators and other adaptors of the tales all, in one way or another, slipped into Shahrazad's role as they reshaped the characters and stories of the collection in order to appeal to their target audiences, whether scholarly or popular. Accordingly, passages deemed pornographic disappeared or multiplied, and learned notes accumulated or diminished; poetry was excised or rendered into rhyming verse, and medieval vocabulary was alternately adapted to colloquial and archaic registers.[3] In the process, Shahrazad was not the only character transformed: King Shahrayar became in the European translations of the colonial era another stock Muslim despot, and the caliphs and viziers of the various stories were transformed into dunces or evil schemers by the makers of Hollywood films.[4] Arab storytellers who wish to reclaim Shahrazad's legacy in today's era of globally disseminated visual media thus confront a situation more delicate than even that in which Shahrazad determined to intervene. For they must keep in mind the competing desires and circumstances of multiple audiences at home as well as abroad. How, then, to interpellate, educate, and transform the members of these disparate audiences?

Tapping into associations of the Arab world with the colorful, simplified, Hollywood versions of Shahrazad's stories, Fatima Mernissi's *Dreams of Trespass: Tales of a Harem Girlhood* proposes a beguiling account of the lives of secluded middle-class Moroccan women during a period that spans roughly from the end of the Second World War to the birth of the nationalist, anticolonial Istiqlal Party in 1949. Its young narrator, Fatima, portrays herself as a wide-eyed witness to the outspokenness of her mother, maternal grandmother, aunts, and female cousins while incidentally establishing her authority as a new kind of storyteller, one who blends firsthand knowledge of oral practices with knowledge culled from a subsequent European-style education. Despite this easy tone, Fatima is no casual native informant. Mernissi selects role models for her characters more from the Islamic world than from the European, emphasizing the climate of uncertainty in which women and men alike fear displacement by those foreigners, Europeans and Americans, whose incursions into Morocco are intensifying. Still, young Fatima's mother, grandmother, aunts, and female cousins argue that only access to formal education, information, and experience—in short, the dismantling of the "traditional" harem—will make of them exemplary

Moroccans. By portraying the small, daily conflicts that result from Moroccans' increased access to goods from and communication with both the rapidly changing Islamic and Western worlds, Mernissi reminds her readers that the Moroccan nation arose from a dialogue between diverse, competing identities. In the process, she hints that the strength of the modern kingdom reposes on a continued ability to reshape old narratives of identity while negotiating new ones.

By the time she published her memoir, Mernissi had achieved worldwide recognition as a sociologist of contemporary Morocco and the larger Islamic world. While her earlier books of scholarship were extremely successful, the engaging *Dreams* reached an even broader audience. Acclaimed in the popular media (a quotation from a review in *Elle* graces the back cover of the U.S. edition), it has been translated, by Mernissi's own count, into at least twenty-two languages.[5] At the same time, the memoir's publication abroad reveals that access to audiences who share one's religion, culture, (colonial) history, or even language continues to be mediated by the global North when artist and audience hail from a country with a soft currency. To circumvent this, Mernissi, writing in English as well as in French and Arabic, has become a savvy global storyteller who modifies her work for different constituencies, adding qualifying notes for more informed readers and slightly altering the narrative itself for different audiences. She also revises and retitles earlier versions of works published in Morocco in Arabic and French, making it very difficult to determine which versions of her work are the originals and which the derivations.[6] In so doing, she evades commercial censorship to insist on her prerogative to enter into dialogue with those her work most immediately concerns, the women of the Maghreb and the larger Islamic world.

By tailoring some of her work for audiences in the United States, Mernissi sends a particularly involved message, strategically intervening in the representation of Muslim women while troubling the alignment of the scholarly and literary production of former colonies with that of the nations that were once their colonizers. Because she also writes in French as well as Arabic, languages that many of her English-language readers do not master, Mernissi plays with the common, if naive, belief that European languages permit Muslim women more direct access to self-expression. Against claims that writing of sex, love, and female subjectivity is impossible in Arabic (a claim repeated in 2005 by the anonymous author of a best-selling novel about a North African

woman's sex life), the young Fatima of *Dreams* refers to the sex education lessons of her formidably authoritative, female Qur'an schoolteacher, to her independent-minded grandmother's pragmatic struggles
to realize an everyday love, to a host of feminist writers from throughout the Islamic world, to the accomplishments of a Lebanese singer
who sacrificed respectability in order to defy the cultural norms of her
time, and, of course, to Shahrazad.[7] Whereas scholars such as Margot
Badran and Miriam Cooke have brought Arab feminism to the attention of English-speaking audiences through studies of Arab women
writers and activists, Mernissi depicts even illiterate women as pathbreaking feminists and feminism itself as a long-standing tradition in
the Islamic world.[8] Much as she did in her major scholarly work *Beyond
the Veil: Male-Female Dynamics in Modern Muslim Society*, she crosses
genre boundaries through her combination of sociological observation
with storytelling, scholarship with entertainment.[9] Looking back to an
earlier period of rapid change in both the Islamic and so-called Western worlds, *Dreams* self-consciously probes all the boundaries that
delimit knowledge in order to speak to global audiences entering into
ever more complex relations.

Certainly, the English-language edition of *Dreams* addresses itself
to North American audiences. From its innocent opening invocation
of colonial-era stereotypes of both Muslims and Christians, to its basic
lessons in colonial history, to its coy photographs, *Dreams* speaks to
readers at a remove from Morocco's past: those for whom the name
Morocco may conjure up a jumble of scenes from the film *Casablanca*
and vague notions of some colonial-era skirmishes between French-
men, Spaniards, and Germans.[10] Speaking to imaginations whose view
of Muslim women may derive on the one hand from the Orientalist
fantasies of Hollywood film and on the other from grim news reports,
Mernissi opens her narrative by provocatively positioning herself as a
childlike character in a vaguely familiar, exotic tale. Earnest, guileless,
and not yet sexualized, the young Fatima sets herself the task of learning to communicate with those who rule her small world. Her address
to the reader strikes a similar chord, for Fatima begins her story as if
attempting to explain herself to outsiders for the first time. While she
depicts her task as terribly daunting and herself as a bit of an unwor-
thy blunderer, she nonetheless displays consummate skill as a storyteller, dropping bits of vital historical and cultural information into
even her most innocent musings. She thereby rescripts her readers'

understanding of the world even as she offers them the kind of stock characters they have come to expect. Of course, these stock characters take the form of the French, Spaniards, Germans, and Americans; Mernissi's Moroccans, men and women alike, are finely drawn.

Although Fatima describes only the Egyptian films that the Mernissi women attend, the pervasive influence of Hollywood cinema in colonial Morocco is made plain from her allusions to her cousin Zin as a Rudolph Valentino look-alike. As if in response to images of the Arab world promoted by such Valentino vehicles as *The Sheik* and *The Son of the Sheik*, the U.S. edition of *Dreams* offers its readers its own images of the Arab world.[11] Prefacing each chapter of this edition is a photograph: the first shows an arched door in a medina; the second a brocade-covered seat below lace curtains in what appears to be a woman's room; the third a djellaba-clad figure standing before an ornate wrought iron gate on the other side of which are gathered women cloaked in shadows; the fourth, two women pictured from the back, about to walk through a courtyard gate into a garden; the fifth, three women, backs to the viewer, hurrying along the side hall of an inner courtyard; and so on.[12] Only in the final photograph does the female model look out at the viewer, the outlines of her face and body barely visible through a lace curtain. In order to catch a more satisfying glimpse of this world and the women who occupy it, then, readers must turn to Fatima's narrative. There, they find dynamic women who ceaselessly do battle with the restrictions that the harem imposes on them as well as with the ideal images to which their male relatives would hold them. Yet these women concern themselves less with how they will physically appear to the outside world than with retelling history in such a way as to assert themselves as the coauthors of their Moroccan identity.

Once upon a Time

Instead of reinterpreting a familiar fiction by contrasting it with the bleakness of material reality, Mernissi transforms the matter of everyday, secluded, mundane, middle-class existence into fabulous stories. An assiduous pupil of her "modernist" female relatives, storytellers all, Fatima learns to assert her agency wherever possible by tirelessly manipulating everyday rituals, accepted truths, and so-called tradition. The Mernissi women recast their chores as adventures (Fatima's grandmother Yasmina and her cowives go dishwashing in the river), mundane procedures as rallying points for independence (Fatima's mother, Douja, resists collective mealtimes and demands instead to eat alone with her husband and children), and institutions of power into manifestations of weakness (cousin Chama creatively fabricates a history of the harem in which the Arabs appear as dupes of Europeans). Although they rarely succeed in transgressing the physical boundaries of the harem, the women purposefully seize on all they have at hand as proof of their desire and aptitude for independence, an independence they place in the service of national independence. When Fatima's mother, for example, dresses her in impractical Western gowns, she models this attitude for her daughter: "'Dress says so much about a woman's designs,' she said. 'If you plan to be modern, express it through what you wear, otherwise they will shove you behind the gates. Caftans may be of unparalleled beauty, but Western dress is about salaried work.'"[13] Ascribing a quite different meaning to the impractical clothing from what might be ascribed by European or North American readers, Fatima's mother gives her daughter a lesson in strategic interpretation, transforming what might seem a symbol of cultural imperialism and normative gender roles into a sign of women's economic empowerment and that empowerment into a vital step toward an independent Morocco.

It is the most disenfranchised women of the Mernissi household, however—those whose lack of fathers, husbands, or sons has left them socially unrecognized (the divorced aunt Habiba and the freed slave Mina)—who seem to teach Fatima the most about the need for and the possibilities of creative self-fashioning. Mina's tale of defying her captors' expectations during her forced journey from sub-Saharan Africa to Morocco serves Fatima as an example of the forms of resistance available even to the most powerless. Aunt Habiba's fantastic tales, by contrast, remind her not to forsake sensuality, joy, and a desire for adventure in her quest for autonomy and recognition. The women's favorite exemplar of these qualities, Fatima relates, is the story of Princess Budur, who "dared to imagine the impossible, the unrealistic" (133). Excerpted from the much longer tale of Qamar al-Zaman, the story of Princess Budur recounts how the princess, abandoned by her husband among strangers, succeeds in passing as a man. So successful is her performance that the king of Ebony City designates the princess his successor and offers her his daughter's hand in marriage. Princess Budur confesses her secret to her new wife, who carefully guards it, enabling the princess to maintain her position as ruler until the return of her hapless, wayward husband. Thus, while Fatima's literate, adolescent cousin Chama regularly inspires the modernists among the women with dramatizations of the lives of Muslim feminists, it is Aunt Habiba who demonstrates that the way to break through the despair that sometimes descends on them when assessing the circumscribed nature of their own lives is all in the telling.

In keeping with the memoir's emphasis on strategic representation, Fatima summarizes the meaning of Princess Budur's story as follows: "The bottom line of her story, after all, was that a woman can fool society by posing as a man. All she has to do is wear her husband's clothes; the difference between the sexes is silly, only a matter of dress" (137). Noting that this was quite an insolent lesson for Shahrazad to offer King Shahrayar, Fatima then introduces the alternate moral that her mother and the others take from the story, that of a need for solidarity among women. Aunt Habiba, unable because of her insecure status to join in the heated debates between modernists and traditionalists that this second moral occasions, discovers yet another message in the story: "'There is nothing wrong with being helpless, ladies!' Aunt Habiba would say, when it was her turn to take over the stage, 'Princess Budur's life is the proof. Not having had the opportunity to test your talents does not mean that you have none'" (138). While thus demonstrating the power of interpretation, Mernissi slips still another lesson into Fatima's relation of the tale. The women's performance of Princess Budur's story crosses several linguistic registers; at times, long passages lifted verbatim from Burton's overwrought translation of the *Nights* issue from the illiterate women's mouths, and at others the bombast of Burton's translation is undercut by Fatima's quick, succinct plot summaries. Mernissi further chooses to censor the tale: in the *Nights*, the story ends with Princess Budur testing her unsuspecting husband by making sexual advances to him while she is still in the character of king. Mernissi's own strategy of fashioning meaning in accordance with audience expectations therefore shows through this mélange of literary styles and morals, appealing to readers' discernment to hear what Fatima/Shahrazad is really saying and to see through to the real meaning of the tale.

Lest readers be tempted to treat her narrative as the unproblematic reflection of an oral, illiterate women's culture, Mernissi continually points out its debt to Arabic literary history, whether through its references to the marginal *Nights*, to a long poetic tradition that endures in popular music, to works of Arab history or treatises on women's condition in Islam, or to autobiographical writing, which has long occupied a distinguished place in this history. The English version of *Dreams* especially plays with this last genre. Perhaps because in the Arab world as elsewhere autobiography was generally the purview of public, usually male, individuals (statesmen, scholars, and religious figures), Mernissi, a public individual in her own right, approaches her memoir differently. She employs the figure of Fatima, a child still anxious to locate her place in the world, to dramatize what Fadia Faqir neatly states in her introduction to the collected autobiographical writings of Arab women, that for many women, "confidence and certitude about the self and its position in history and language are lacking."[14] Yet at the same time, *Dreams* does not accept as paradigmatic those autobiographies of Egyptian feminists that cousin Chama idolizes. For as the Mernissi women complain, "Deep down, though, the problem with feminists' lives was that they did not have enough singing and dancing in them. . . . The feminists' lives seemed to be all about fighting and unhappy marriages, never about happy moments, beautiful nights, or whatever it was that gave them the strength to carry on" (132). Refusing to contribute to those bleak images of Muslim women silenced, disenfranchised, and psychically and physically violated, images that have sold so many books internationally, Mernissi begins to craft new kinds of personae for Arab women through her engagement with pragmatic, yet playful, self-representations.

Examining the poetics of women's self-representation, Sidonie Smith stresses the constraints imposed on the autobiographer by the very interpretative figures she employs to reveal herself: "Those figures are always cast in language and are always motivated by cultural expectations, habits, and systems of interpretation pressing on her at the scene of writing. Cultural scripts of signification, the figures of verisimilitude or lifelikeness reflect privileged stories and character types that the prevailing culture, through its discourse, names as 'real' and therefore 'readable.'"[15] Rather than attempt the impossible task of openly departing from these scripts, Mernissi, writing across cultures and in a language that is not Fatima's native one, demonstrates her mastery of them. Manipulating stereotypes of the Arab world with seeming ease, she almost casually refutes the ethnocentric idea that true apprehension of the self is restricted to Western writers. There is more to her story, though, for *Dreams* also exposes the fragility of a Western individualism and self-consciousness that rely on the opposition between the West and the rest of the world. As the coauthors of a recent study of autobiographical writing in Arabic observe, it is precisely these kinds of presuppositions on which two influential Western scholars, Georg Misch and Franz Rosenthal, relied as they shaped the fields of comparative autobiography and Arabic studies:

> Both sought, not to analyze a history of changing literary conventions for the representation of the human life experience (i.e. autobiographies as literary texts), but rather an essentialized self that they deemed easily and directly discernable through the literary representation. In addition, they believed firmly in the historical development of a culturally defined "Western self," the superiority of which was assumed unquestioningly, as were the existence of a modern western "individualism" and "self-awareness" not found in other societies or other historical periods.[16]

Instead of openly questioning the belief in the transparency of language and existence of self-knowing, self-identical selves on which many early studies of autobiography relied, *Dreams* subjects them to a child's reasoning. When young Fatima studiously attempts to apply these standards to her own small world in order to grasp exactly who she is vis-à-vis the others who are her family members and the figures of authority in her life, she runs into obstacles every time. Uncertainty, a productive rather than a paralyzing uncertainty, prevails until the very end, almost incidentally dismantling every autobiographical convention.

It might seem that Mernissi adopts the perspective that Philippe Lejeune lays out in his influential description of the "autobiographical pact," in which he holds that once the author of the autobiographical work has named his narrator after himself, thereby making a pact to tell the truth such as it seems to the author, the actual accuracy of the narrative matters less: "In autobiography, it is indispensable that the referential pact be *drawn up*, and that it be *kept*; but it is not necessary that the result be on the order of strict resemblance. The referential pact can be, according to the criteria of the reader, badly kept, without the referential value of the text disappearing (on the contrary)."[17] Lejeune's theory has intrigued many for the emphasis it places on the reader of autobiography; in his formulation, autobiography promotes a particular practice of reading as the reader seeks to learn the truth of the author as author rather than as historical actor. Yet, although Mernissi creates in *Dreams* a narrator who learns to be hyperconscious of how she is perceived by others, young Fatima's concern is not at all to put on display her budding artistic talents or to prove herself in any other domain, as it were. On the contrary, Mernissi's purpose is more openly didactic; the lesson of Fatima's tale lies precisely in her lack of self-mastery, in the slippage between self and the dominant languages of power that make it impossible for her to fix once and for all who she is.

Without dismissing the very concrete power imbalances in her childhood world, Fatima/Mernissi immediately begins to draw attention to the strategic constructedness of the tales we tell to identify others and ourselves. The opening lines of *Dreams* establish the work as autobiographical while tacitly acknowledging a respect for the power of representation: "I was born in a harem in 1940 in Fez, a ninth-century Moroccan city some five thousand kilometers west of Mecca, and one thousand kilometers south of Madrid, one of the dangerous capitals of the Christians" (1). With these loaded words, Mernissi engages with images of Muslim women as uneducated slaves of tradition and religion and with representations of the Islamic world as unchanging, backward looking, and superstitious. Yet in the mouth of the child Fatima, those views of the Arab world that we have learned to deem Orientalist are amusingly scrambled, their "realism" undone. Moreover, by pointing out Morocco's distance from the centers of Islam and its rather Western location, Fatima reminds her educated readers of some geographical facts that trouble neat demarcations of the Arab world from the West. Her qualification of Madrid as one of the dangerous capitals of the Christians reinscribes a religious and cultural distance while yet playing on Western readers' notions of what is safe and what is dangerous, in effect mocking such blanket determinations and the simplistic dialectic that underpins them. Sober and assiduous, Fatima does more than present readers with an image of her world; she also models Mernissi's ideal reader, disingenuously proposing lessons in how to read across cultures as she reveals the power of speaking from the margins.

Quickly ushering her readers into the harem, Fatima shatters their perceptions of that space as erotic paradise, as homosocial utopia, or as a prison inhabited by voiceless shadows. Fatima's reiterated desire to understand the origins, forms, and utility of the harem drives the narrative and serves as a pretext for Mernissi to treat one of her favored topics, the realities of the harem as a social institution that impedes the emergence of the modern couple.[18] Studying the rural harem presided over by Fatima's polygamous grandfather and the urban harem shared by her monogamous father and uncles, Fatima concludes that the only commonality between them is that they restrict women's movements. Both harems are further fraught with divisions of class and hierarchies of power, and in each one some women uphold the status quo while others struggle mightily against the restrictions of the prevailing order, Fatima's mother and maternal grandmother, Yasmina, among the latter. Life in the harem, then, models for Fatima the kind of dialogue occurring throughout Morocco in the years just prior to independence; furthermore, aligning herself with the "modernists," she learns never to resign herself to the status quo. Her illiterate, secluded female relatives' fascination with the lives of feminists and female performers from throughout the Islamic world also depicts in microcosm the comparatist, transnational dialogue that Muslim feminists have advocated as a powerful tool for countering repressive interpretations of women's rights under Islamic law.[19] It is this kind of transnational dialogue that *Dreams* engages. Mernissi's audience, however, reaches far beyond the Islamic world, enabling her to bring to bear on the issue of Muslim women's rights broader concerns about power and communication in a globalizing world still fraught with countless inequities.

Deceptively simple on the surface, the tale is nonetheless quite complex. Mernissi writes more than twenty-five years after independence, at a time when harems have largely vanished, many women have abandoned the veil, and others have adopted new forms of it. The voice of an older Fatima even intervenes early on in *Dreams* to evince a desire for palpable boundaries: "But since then, looking for the frontier has become my life's occupation. Anxiety eats at me whenever I cannot situate the geometric line organizing my powerlessness" (3). Reassuring readers that Fatima Mernissi's goal is not to abolish all boundaries and overthrow the established order of Moroccan life, this ironic voice nonetheless stresses not the power that boundaries accord but rather their purpose in withholding power. Embedded in a discussion of the division of preindependence Morocco into Spanish and French zones, the statement suggests that the abolition of borders is constitutive of modern Moroccan identity, while the impulse to enforce them represents a kind of colonization of the mind. Mernissi appeals to a collective memory of frustration over imposed frontiers when Fatima disingenuously notes: "Cousin Samir, who sometimes accompanied Uncle and Father on their trips, said that to create a frontier, all you need is soldiers to force others to believe in it. In the landscape itself, nothing changes. The frontier is in the mind of the powerful" (2–3). In the tales that follow, Fatima relates how Moroccan men sometimes grudgingly learn to accept Moroccan women's apparent transgressions of gender boundaries in order that they may together wrest their country from colonizers who would disempower them all. There is more to the story, though. Mernissi revisits this tale as a positive precedent in a postindependence era in which Moroccan women remain at the mercy of restrictive laws and are again blamed by some for causing the country's hardships with their "transgressions."

In partial response to such critics, *Dreams* exemplifies a give and take not only among women of differing interests but also between women and men. A mundane squabble occasioned by the desire of Fatima's mother to abandon collective meals quickly reveals the fraught relations between men and women under colonial rule. Yet this scenario presents itself as a perfect opportunity for negotiation rather than as the foundation of a potentially tragic outcome:

> Father would say that he could not just break away. If he did, tradition would vanish: "We live in difficult times, the country is occupied by foreign armies, our culture is threatened. All we have left is these traditions." This reasoning would drive Mother nuts: "Do you think that by sticking together in this big, absurd house, we will gain the strength we need to throw the foreign armies out? And what is more important anyway, tradition or people's happiness?" (78)

Frivolous though Douja's dismissal of this ordinary, tangible practice in the name of a vague, even foreign, personal happiness may seem, it resonates with Fatima's father, a character torn between his obligations to the collectivity and his love for his wife. Like Mernissi's other works, *Dreams* holds up recognition of the legitimacy of the heterosexual couple (viewed by many feminists as the root and prop of gender inequality) as a cornerstone of Moroccan women's enfranchisement and of modern Morocco's global competitiveness. Fatima's loving, yet constantly debating, parents represent the ideal couple, Moroccan-style, in this period of critical sociopolitical and economic transformation.

Fedwa Malti-Douglas observes that Shahrazad aims to replace the dynamics of homosocial male society with those of the heterosexual couple.[20] In opposition to Malti-Douglas, who bases her contention in large part on her reading of Shahrazad's silencing in the conclusion of the *Nights*, Mernissi does not view the heterosexual couple as enforcing a patriarchal status quo. Rather, such a couple exemplifies a critical transformation of sociopolitical relations, one that keeps pace with economic realities. In the "Note to the Western Reader" that prefaces *Beyond the Veil*, Mernissi explains: "It appears to me that the Muslim system is not so much opposed to women as to the heterosexual unit. What is feared is the growth of the involvement between a man and a woman into an all-encompassing love satisfying the sexual, emotional and intellectual needs of both partners."[21] The formation of this couple, Mernissi contends, is the natural outcome of the necessary involvement of women in the struggle against foreign domination. Once women had been recruited into the public domain as workers or soldiers, thereby contributing to the founding of independent nations, they could no longer logically be relegated to the harem on the grounds that their public presence would result in *fitna*, or social chaos.[22] Mernissi concludes her "Note to the Western Reader" by inquiring whether a society thus transformed would indeed still be an authentically Muslim one, but in *Dreams*, as in her work on women rulers in Islam, she answers this query with a resounding yes.[23] Based on mutual affinity rather than on a need to cement clan ties and tested through a constant dialogue that the sexual segregation of traditional Moroccan households would inhibit, the couple of Fatima's parents models the kind of relations necessary to establish a modern nation, in which individuals must look beyond a kinship based in blood lines to forge ties with all manner of fellow Moroccans.

Her mother's appeals to personal happiness may serve to naturalize this model of a modern couple that acts as the support of the emerging nation, but Fatima does express some reservations about the dismantlement of other support systems its actualization entails. Mernissi places her doubts conveniently in the mouths of either Fatima's father or others, however:

> The nationalists advocated the end of seclusion and the veil, but they did not say a word about a couple's right to split off from their larger family. In fact, most of the leaders still lived with their parents. The male nationalist movement supported the liberation of women, but had not come to grips with the idea of the elderly living by themselves, nor with couples splitting off into separate households. Neither idea seemed right, or elegant. (76)

Fatima thus points out that without the harem, divorced women such as her aunt Habiba and freed slaves such as Mina would have no place to turn, though she also frequently remarks that as single women, neither do they have any standing within the harem. In a society in which women gain a measure of recognition insofar as they are wives and mothers, only careful strategies of self-effacement guarantee Aunt Habiba's and Mina's acceptance there. The disappearance of this institution, it is implied, would necessarily lead to new possibilities of being for women like them. Yet in many ways, this issue of unattached, unskilled, and illiterate women is left unresolved in *Dreams*, in which it becomes clear that economic circumstances are increasingly making the kind of harem in which Fatima comes of age a thing of the past. Perhaps because *Dreams* is very much an engagement with the prejudices of audiences abroad, the continuing problems of poverty and women's illiteracy are left untouched, problems that today still result for some Moroccan girls in the kind of quasi-slavery portrayed in Tlatli's film *The Silences of the Palace*.[24] Instead, the educated, economically secure Fatima represents the hopes of the future: as a woman who will one day form part of a couple, always in dialogue, that grants new autonomy to both women and men.[25]

Behind this focus on the couple, Mernissi introduces a message as insolent as that which Shahrazad proposed with the story of Princess Budur. She casts into doubt the exact nature of the difference between men and women by insisting that Islamic tradition promotes their equality. This theme of a basic gender equality runs throughout Mernissi's work; already in the 1970s she notes that Islam "affirms the potential equality between the sexes. The existing inequality does not rest on an ideological or biological theory of women's inferiority, but is the outcome of specific social institutions designed to restrain her power: namely, segregation and legal subordination in the family structure."[26] In *Dreams*, the uneducated women of the Mernissi household represent this power of women barely contained despite the restricted lives they lead, and they often insist that present-day gender-based injustices violate the true precepts of Islam. Fatima's narrative reflects this in many places, such as when she relates her mother's insistence that her birth be celebrated as any boy's would: "She had always rejected male superiority as nonsense and totally anti-Muslim—'Allah made us all equal,' she would say" (9). In the climate of rapid sociopolitical change that serves as a backdrop to Fatima's tale, it is the tenuousness of the differences between the sexes that, Mernissi suggests, results in a renewed insistence on boundaries between them. On the surface, her position seems to support Deniz Kandiyoti's contention: "In countries where the most prominent form of cultural nationalism is Islamic, for instance, feminist discourse can legitimately proceed in only one of two directions: either denying that Islamic practices are necessarily oppressive or asserting that oppressive practices are not necessarily Islamic."[27] Still, Mernissi complicates the latter position through a creative retelling of the story, suggesting thereby a broader field of options.

Most pertinently, Fatima's life story stops short of Morocco's independence. Although she alludes to the transformations in women's status that take place in the course of the resistance (her mother's success in leaving the harem in order to march in the streets for independence and her concurrent shedding of the veil), Fatima omits any mention of Morocco's postindependence ratification of family law grounded in Shari'a.[28] By any account a dialing back of the emerging freedoms portrayed in *Dreams*, the Code of Personal Status declared men the head of the household, entitled them to divorce their wives by repudiation (a practice outlawed in all other Islamic countries except Saudi Arabia), to take additional wives (with the consent of the first), and conferred on women the status of minors.[29] Silencing this less than satisfactory response to the struggles of her female relatives, Mernissi instead focuses on a period of negotiations among various interest groups that might have resulted in a more positive outcome. In the process, many of the historical tensions among urban nationalists and independent rural clans, Arabs, Amazighen (Berbers), and other groups and between Islamic law and North African custom are obscured by her very positive characterization of Sultan Mohammed V.

Fatima's Mohammed V appears as a modernist reformer who upholds the interests of the urban-led Istiqlal Party and the emerging middle class and presides over divergent interests. He permits his daughter to tour the country dressed in Western clothing and to make speeches on behalf of independence. Indeed, the popularity of the historical Mohammed V (member of a dynasty that had ruled portions of Morocco since 1649 and never bowed to Ottoman rule, though some of its members had colluded with the French colonizers) grew when he was exiled after attempting to wrest control of internal affairs back from the French.[30] After independence, he returned to Morocco and assumed the title of king, retaining the title of commander of the Believers, to which his descent from the Prophet entitled him; his descendants still rule Morocco.[31] In the process of promoting Moroccan independence, however,

Mohammed V made some not very modern compromises with regard to women's rights. Tracing the development of family law in colonial and postindependence Morocco, Charrad explains that when the French issued a decree seeking to induce the Amazighen to turn to French courts rather than to Islamic ones (the so-called Berber Decree of 1930), tribes long resistant to the sultan's authority reacted to this attack on their religious allegiances by recognizing the Islamic family law of his courts as a legitimate replacement for their customary kinship laws: "Islamic family law legitimizes the extended male-centered patrilineage that has served as the building block of kin-based solidarities within tribal groups in the Maghrib. It supports the patriarchal power not only of husbands, but also of kin, over women."[32] In order to solidify national unity following independence, King Mohammed V reaffirmed his commitment to conservative rural interests by supporting the implementation of conservative family law based on Shariʿa.

Holding up an earlier period of productive anticolonial struggle as a standard of discursive identity, Mernissi proffers an alternate tradition against which to judge and validate gender relations in present-day Morocco. Thus legitimating recent socioeconomic developments and the resulting transformations in gender relations, she attempts to script out of existence the determinative weight of that other postindependence history. The dialogue that Mernissi opens is therefore not only with the "West" but also with Moroccans' own recent and more distant definitions of self-identity. Insisting on the discursive foundations of that identity, she also purposefully insinuates that this dialogue is already long underway, close to its goal of ensuring the social and political equality of women and men. Fatima's mother and the other modernizers of the Mernissi household, as well as her maternal grandmother, see nothing but progress for women in the future, sweeping aside the criticisms of those who in the 1980s and 1990s increasingly decried Morocco's modernization or critical lack thereof. *Dreams* therefore presents such phenomena as the entry of more and more women into universities and the workforce as an expression of the Moroccan self rather than as a concession to foreign ideals. Fatima even affirms that code switching is eminently Moroccan: "The idea of being able to swing between two cultures, two personalities, two codes, and two languages enchanted everyone!" (180). For the duration of its narrative, at least, *Dreams* instantiates this reality.

Fictional Selves, Mirrors of Reality

We might say that in place of the autobiographical pact, Mernissi avers the primacy of another pact: that between the storyteller and her audience, so perfectly exemplified by Shahrazad. In order to uphold Shahrazad's pact, Mernissi must prevail over her readers' convictions of the absoluteness of their knowledge, of others and also of themselves, by entertaining and inspiring them. Nowhere is her method more evident than in a footnote that appears in the revised French version of *Dreams*. In a reflection on her narrative project worth citing at length, Mernissi first confirms that she has taken liberties with both history and self-representation and then discloses some of her motives for so doing:

> This version of the facts concerning the demand for independence and the relation among the nationalists, the king, and the French Protectorate is, as one may suspect, not historical. The account is that of my mother, who is a fictional character, as is the child who speaks, who is supposed to reflect myself. If I had attempted to recount to you my childhood, you would not have read more than two paragraphs, because my childhood was flat and prodigiously boring. Since this book is not an autobiography, but a fiction in the form of tales told by a seven-year-old child, the version of the events of January 1944 told here is that which remained in my memory—the memory of what illiterate women recounted in the courtyard and on the terraces.
>
> Complicating things further, one must also remember that the version of the events that I presented coincided with a literary packaging that I needed in order to seduce my readers.[33]

Here Mernissi explicitly breaks the autobiographical pact she seems to establish in the opening lines of *Dreams*, but she does so only in a footnote and only for French-speaking audiences, who she may presume possess a stronger grasp of Morocco's colonial and anticolonial history. A safeguard against accusations of untruthfulness, crass commercialism, or collusion with Orientalism, this note but underscores what close readers of *Dreams* have already perceived: this memoir is not about Fatima Mernissi but instead about the ways in which one might continue to transform the rules of representation to legitimate new ways of being female and Moroccan. When filled with self-doubt, Fatima eschews categorical judgment and foregone conclusions and seeks out motion: "I knew that if you moved around, your mind worked faster, because you were constantly seeing new things that you had to respond to. And you certainly became more intelligent than someone stuck in a courtyard" (186).

Comparing *Dreams* with Assia Djebar's novel *L'amour, la fantasia,* Anne Donadey remarks that Mernissi's style is "much more conventional, beginning with 'I was born . . . ,' whereas Djebar's follows a non-chronological, exploded structure."[34] Although Donadey proceeds to establish certain similarities between the two works, the ostensible conventionality of Mernissi's style merits closer scrutiny. Linear, concluding with Fatima's realization that she has crossed the boundary into adolescence, and straightforward in its use of language, *Dreams* more or less follows the formula of the Bildungsroman. Still, while postcolonial adaptations of this genre often leave their protagonists on the brink of a great journey (entry into a colonial school in the metropolis or capital, uprooting from a rural milieu, descent into poverty or access to new resources), Fatima's coming of age consists of a decisive realization that she has become a young woman, a fact that her male cousin Samir insists must separate them. Rather than beginning a journey across a boundary, then, Fatima encounters a new obstacle. Anxious, a Fatima now more than ever conscious of the frontiers that divide the world asks Mina how she can ever hope to ascertain where she stands. Mina's words conclude the memoir: "If you can't get out, you are on the powerless side" (242). If one continues to believe in the autobiographical pact, *Dreams* reads as a conventional, affirmative tale of Fatima Mernissi's personal triumph in escaping from the harem. One of the lessons of *Dreams*, though, is that real power resides not just in the ability to get out but also in understanding where boundaries come from, what they are made of, and therefore how to manipulate them. Mernissi's tales of childhood do not struggle to offer an accurate representation of personal or political history. Instead, they strategically manipulate the rules of personal and historical representation in order promote self-articulation on the margins, in between Europe and the Islamic world, tradition and the modern, the local and the global.

Under cover of the engaging tale of Fatima's childhood, Mernissi contemplates more explicitly than in her previous work the myriad ways in which, according to Smith, "[w]oman has remained unrepresented and unrepresentable," without assuming, however, that self-representation can ever be complete.[35] Instead of offering readers the full story of Moroccan women's lives, Mernissi thrusts the burden of the women's unrepresentability back onto readers by subtly underscoring her characters' improbability. The tales of the Mernissi women concern fictional figures on the boundaries of the possible, offering a glimpse into an absence at the center of Moroccan, but also by extension readers', identities. Yet by seeming to confer speech on such figures, who until now seemed to lack the means and authority to voice their stories, *Dreams* entices readers with the hope that this absence may be overcome. For Fatima and the other independent-minded women of the Mernissi household—who speak in plain language but with the perspicacity of historians, political analysts, philosophers, Sufis, religious authorities, and sociologists—are characters in whose reality we very much want to believe. It is indeed tempting to impute to them a real existence beyond the pages of *Dreams*. Yet to do so would be to reduce Mernissi's project to one of self-legitimation.[36] Having conducted countless interviews with Moroccan women both educated and illiterate, urban and rural, publishing some as free-standing interviews and including bits of others as unconventional data in her academic works, Mernissi seems keenly aware not just that the reality of these women, as well as her own, cannot escape mediation through representation but also that this reality, this legitimacy, is the product of mediation. Without mediation, her narratives make clear, these women have no public voice, no influence, their existence conveniently silenced in political and public discourse.[37] This observation that artistic and political representation go hand in hand is, of course, one of the cornerstones of postcolonial studies.[38] In *Dreams*, however, Mernissi's accomplishment is to stretch the boundaries of the intelligible and legitimate that much further by using her tales to create in readers a desire to hear more.

Legend has it that after 1001 nights . . .

Yes, *Dreams* is largely an engaging fiction. Yet Mernissi's fantasy world is much simpler and more reflective of everyday existence in the real world than Shahrazad's representations are. The changes she envisions for Moroccan women are not the far-fetched products of wishful thinking but the result of observations of an existing potential for change. Indeed, history bears her out: In 2004, Morocco amended its Code of Personal Status, abandoning the principle of a wife's obedience to her husband for that of equal rights and responsibilities. The new code raised the legal age of marriage from fifteen to eighteen, introduced divorce by mutual consent while making it more difficult for husbands to divorce at will, placed tight restrictions on the practice of polygamy, and affirmed the right of mothers to custody of their children in the event of divorce or widowhood. This will surely furnish premises of new tales.

3 ∞ A Story without a Face

Reality is something within us, it shifts, it is elusive.
What upsets me the most, what irritates me, is
when would-be writers try to practice realism, to
relate man's little troubles. That's not realism.
Absolutely not. What is crucial is to be equal to this
madness, to this sort of delirium of reality. Reality is
DE-LI-RI-OUS. In unhappiness or happiness, delirium is
what matters. That's why in my books there is always
a sort of breakaway, a flight toward the imaginary.
There is a universe, how should I say, that escapes
everything.

—*Tahar Ben Jelloun, interview by Thomas Spear*

LTHOUGH THE STORIES of *The Thousand and One Nights* are potentially infinite in number, circular in their repetitiveness, and replete with feints and excrescences, they nevertheless maintain
certain narrative conventions, chief among them the teller's control of
an ultimately linear story. Various characters within the tales may be the
subjects of their own stories, but their very act of self-representation
already reveals a certain mastery over past and present. For as they tell
their stories, the narrators take fate into their own hands. In the story
the "Porter and the Three Ladies," for example, the visitors commute
the death sentences their rash questions have brought on them by relating the past actions that have guided them to this impasse; reliving
their misfortunes and misdeeds through the reflective distance of the
tale, they break through it.[1] By contrast, Shahrazad fixes her telos from
the outset. Each night's tale prolongs her life by an additional day,
nights and days working together to gradually rehabilitate the image
of women in the king's eyes. In Moroccan writer Tahar Ben Jelloun's
remarkable novel *L'enfant de sable (The Sand Child)*, however, the desired
outcome, even the subject, of the story is anything but certain.[2] For
building on what Mernissi deemed the insolent lesson of Princess
Budur—that the difference between the sexes is but a matter of dress—

55

Ben Jelloun's novel proposes the even more daring message that sex itself is a construct in need of radical reimagining. Challenging all that appears given, scrutinizing every essentialism, *The Sand Child* recounts the life of a familiar being who is nonetheless as indeterminate as the *Nights*, his/her origins obscured by the many similar characters who have preceded, her/his future inconclusive. Who possesses the authority to tell such a story? How can it possibly be told?

The Sand Child promises to relate the story of a Moroccan child born female, yet raised from birth as a male. Ahmed, so named by a father desperate for a son after the birth of seven daughters, embraces his destiny. Although he is conscious that his female body belies his male role within his family and patriarchal Moroccan society, his lived masculinity is more than a disguise; while the novel's first narrator stresses that he has been broken by burdens of secrecy and guilt, he continues to submit that Ahmed is a *man*. For his part, this narrator is a figure of folklore, a traditional, public storyteller of the kind rarely seen anymore since the arrival of the television era, even in that last refuge of the storyteller's craft that is, or was, Morocco. Yet this storyteller is only the first in a long sequence of storytellers who gather Moroccan crowds about them in the unnamed plaza of an anonymous Moroccan city that recalls the famous Jemaa al Fna of Marrakech. Each storyteller claims to possess the secret of Ahmed's identity and to master the true art of storytelling. As in the *Nights*, some insist on their personal ties to Ahmed's family, while others favor the more literary approach of reading from a journal they authenticate in various ways. One after another, they add to the already-told tale, filling in the details of Ahmed/Zahra's life while introducing new variations into it. Like all good storytellers, they endlessly defer the revelation of the secret they claim so intimately to know. In the meanwhile, unexpected characters enter and exit this narrative shot through with references to social, economic, and occasionally political realities in Morocco: scholars and experts concealed among the members of the audience, a storyteller who strangely resembles Jorge Luis Borges, and a character from the European recensions of the *Nights*. Both radically imaginative and materially urgent, the story of the sand child slips through the fingers of each storyteller, communicable only through its common loss.

In its exploration of the difficulties in telling a tale intimately bound up in the indeterminate future of a postindependence nation's being and consciousness, *The Sand Child* broaches issues of representation and identity that haunt not only Ben Jelloun but the entire field of post-colonial studies. Since receiving the preeminent French literary prize, the Prix Goncourt, in 1987 for *La nuit sacrée (The Sacred Night)*, billed as a sequel to *The Sand Child*, Ben Jelloun has drawn a great deal of criticism for pandering to Westerners' preconceptions of the Arab world.[3] As many North African writers do, Ben Jelloun writes in French, crediting that language with affording him greater freedom to speak of socially and politically taboo subjects, as well as an opportunity to play with meaning and narrative.[4] Yet *The Sacred Night* provoked vehemently critical responses for wholly different reasons. Unlike its precursor *The Sand Child*, it indulged in numerous scenes of violence against women, even subjecting the protagonist Zahra (formerly the Ahmed of *The Sand Child*) to female genital mutilation, a practice not current in the Maghreb. Ben Jelloun, his position as a vocal critic of human rights abuses complicated in the eyes of many by his long, privileged residence in France, found himself facing accusations of promoting, among other things, self-orientalization, chauvinism in the guise of feminism, and neocolonialist writing strategies.[5] These allegations once again call attention to the exemplary self-performance required of postcolonial writers both abroad and at home.[6] On the one hand, such claims reveal how much evaluations of so-called postcolonial work depend on criteria of self-display that rely on essentialist formulations of gender, ethnicity, race, and even culture, and on the other, they expose the particularly complex set of sociopolitical and moral obligations incumbent on any writer who today wishes to facilitate the circulation of stories between the global South and the global North.

While Ben Jelloun's later novels, beginning with *The Sacred Night*, do seem to lose much of the nuanced complexity of his earlier work in their sometimes hasty treatment of topics much in the European news, *The Sand Child* proposes a subtle, self-reflexive meditation on the evolving functions and responsibilities of the writer who inherits the storyteller's craft in postindependence times.[7] The first of his novels to reach international audiences, it draws readers with its initial focus on the figure of Ahmed, a woman obliged to live as a man in a society that denies women all agency. Yet while it seems to offer the kind of glimpse of Muslim women that has long interested audiences abroad, *The Sand Child* maintains a steady emphasis on those who mediate Ahmed's impossible, yet vitally important, tale. As they vacillate between fidelity to their subject matter and the obligation to meet the demands of their audience, these storytellers become characters in a story that frames the tale of Ahmed/Zahra. In their postures of self-promotion and self-abnegation, their appeals to their audiences' good faith and coengagement, the storytellers of Ben Jelloun's novel substitute for the spatial and temporal distance inherent to the printed page an engaged immediacy, a fluid give and take among subject, audience, and storyteller. Doomed to break down, this illusion derives its power from the self-consciousness of its fictionality. For as Ben Jelloun retells an oft-repeated, widely traveled story through the mediation of his storytellers, he initiates an ever more delirious play of fiction that elaborates Moroccanness as an ability to reject a realism that binds one to conventional identities.

Anachronisms in a rapidly modernizing world, the storytellers of *The Sand Child* emblematize the folkloric Morocco that lures tourists (and readers) despite their hints at the subversiveness of their tale. Willing to their story a revolutionary power, each one yet inevitably loses his way, almost a caricature of those storytellers whose renewed agency Frantz Fanon describes in an addendum to his famous essay "On National Culture":

> From 1952–53 on, the storytellers, who were before that time stereotyped and tedious to listen to, completely overturned their traditional methods of storytelling and the contents of their tales. Their public, which was formerly scattered, became compact. The epic, with its typified categories, reappeared; it became an authentic form of entertainment which took on once more a cultural value. Colonialism made no mistake when from 1955 on it proceeded to arrest these storytellers systematically.[8]

Through their skilled revival of the epic, these storytellers breathed new life into Algerians, developing the imagination until "the existence of a new type of man [was] revealed to the public."[9] Yet while the first storyteller in Ben Jelloun's novel summons his audience to join in his adventure through a collective invocation of Ahmed, the "new man" on whom they call incarnates ambivalence: "Welcome, O being from afar, face of error, innocence of the lie, double of the shadow. O long awaited, much desired one, we have summoned you here to belie destiny. You bring joy, but not happiness; you raise a tent in the desert, but it is the abode of the wind; you are a city of ashes; your life will be long, a trial for fire and patience. Welcome!" (25).[10] Like the subject of their tale, the storytellers of *The Sand Child* lead a tenuous existence in the wake of a Moroccan independence that neglected the emergence of a new way of being. Before they are able to enunciate Ahmed's story properly, they fall victim to a project of modernization absurd in both its unsuitability to local ways of life and its ignorant destruction of a prime tourist attraction: "In fact, the storyteller, like the acrobats and other vendors of strange objects, had to leave the grand plaza that the municipality, at the instigation of young technocrat urbanists, had 'cleaned up' in order to build a musical fountain from which, every Sunday, jets of water spurt to the pulsating Bo-Bo-Pa-Pa of Beethoven's *Fifth Symphony*" (135).[11] Despite this "progress," however, the storytellers have managed to create, if not a new man, at least others in their image. New storytellers emerge from among the former audience members to expose the many resonances of Ahmed's tale. Thus ultimately following in the footsteps of Borges rather than Fanon, Ben Jelloun blurs the distinction between narrating subject and narrated object in such a way that *The Sand Child* makes a spectacle of its telling, withholding even the promise of a triumphant resolution in order to command a meticulous attention to its composition.

A Body Devoured by Narrative

But let us return to the beginning. Or rather, the conclusion that serves as the point of departure for so many questing storytellers. Ostensibly, Ben Jelloun's novel is a tale of transvestism carried too far, with profound implications for that basic category of identity that is gender— or is it sex? Scholars have discerned in the story of Ahmed/Zahra allegories of bicultural or nomadic postcolonial identities, a critique of Islam's influence on the psyches of its adherents, a condemnation of colonialism's impact on gendered social relations, a commentary on the gender insubordination at the root of national identity, and a reflection of a culturally specific, postcolonial, gender theory.[12] All of these meanings are indeed in play in *The Sand Child*, yet just as no storyteller succeeds in proclaiming his or her version of Ahmed's tale the definitive one, the novel leaves itself open to conflicting claims of interpretive authority. Privileging Ahmed or Zahra, each developing a different relationship to his or her tale, the storytellers fail to deliver a definitive story, leaving readers to divine the significance of the secret purportedly at its center. So, what is the nature and motive of this protagonist, whom the storytellers allege self-authors his/her tale in such a manner as to make it unreadable?

Ahmed/Zahra is no simple transvestite, nor does he/she qualify as a hermaphrodite or intersex child. Ahmed is a woman. Or is he? Born the eighth daughter of a man absolutely persuaded that only the birth of a son can ensure his social status and posthumous legacy, Ahmed is designated male before he even sees the light of day. Several weeks prior to his birth, his father takes aside his long-suffering, fearful, pregnant wife, compliments her on her obedience, and informs her, "The child you will bring into the world will be a male. It will be a man; his name will be Ahmed even if it is a girl! I have arranged everything, foreseen everything" (23).[13] Prior to the father's announcement, the narrator of this section reminds his presumably Muslim audience of their religious laws, which accord only a third of an inheritance to women. Under the Shari'a law adopted by the Moroccan state, the successful business of Ahmed's father would essentially devolve to his greedy brothers—delighted at the reproductive "misfortunes" of their sibling—were he to fail in producing a male heir. Thus, Ben Jelloun seems partly to exculpate the father by indicting the Moroccan state for promoting such desperate acts of madness. Initially, then, *The Sand Child* seems to target the religious foundations of Moroccan society, painting a portrait of women's monolithic oppression (their silencing, effacement, and utter dependency on men) in a society where rigidly codified gender relations prevent the evolution of women as full citizens in their own right. Alternately oppressor and victim, Ahmed's father follows to its conclusion the perverse logic of this society, his decision reflecting his absolute faith in the very system that victimizes him.

There is more, however. When the narrator suddenly introduces the colonial context, the subterfuge of Ahmed's father in making his daughter pass for a boy begins to read as one Moroccan man's effort to reaffirm a masculinity under attack by the colonial system. Zealously propagating his own lie, or seemingly taken in by it, Ahmed's father publishes the following birth announcement in the newspaper, appending a photograph of himself: "A boy—may God protect him and bring him long life—was born Thursday at 10 a.m. We have named him Mohamed Ahmed. This birth portends fertility for the land, peace and prosperity for the country. Long live Ahmed! Long live Morocco!" (30).[14] Although only men possess an identity in the world into which Ahmed is born (witness his father's inability even to remember the names of his daughters), the colonial situation denies an identity to the colonized as a whole, male and female alike. In his excessive and unexpectedly nationalistic birth announcement, Ahmed's father purports to throw off years of emasculation by literally fabricating a son out of what is for him thin air. He confers an identity on himself by thus willfully creating his son, for good measure doubling the traditional male name Mohamed in Ahmed and implying, for those in the know, that such radically affirmative actions ensure Morocco's future. Yet once again, Ahmed's father only reifies existing categories of gender and the values of passivity and activity, lack and self-sufficiency, affixed to each. He yokes Morocco's future independence, and his own, to a foundational deception reliant on the maintenance of the present sexist social order, pinning all his hopes on a single performance of virility that his son Ahmed will not be able to repeat. The destiny of postindependence Morocco, it seems, rests on a sleight of hand.

Although the narrators of the novel for the most part frame the father's aberrant, if almost understandable, decision as a horrible repression of his child's innate "femaleness," Ahmed experiences no such sense of injustice. Indeed, he persists in defining himself as male, startling even his father with the depth of his scorn of women and all things feminine. Unlike Princess Budur, whose story inspired the women of the harem in Mernissi's *Dreams of Trespass*, Ahmed does not see his masculinity simply as a means of survival. It is an end in itself. Thus in a passage in which Ahmed confronts his menstrual blood for the first time, what occurs is not an insight into a hitherto repressed female identity but a confrontation with the materiality of a body that does not conform to social and scientific definitions of masculinity—and that body's rapid reinterpretation into a male order of experience.

> I am the architect and the dwelling; the tree and the sap; myself and a male other; myself and a female other. No detail, whether from the outside or from the bottom of the grave, should come to perturb this rigor. Not even blood. And one morning blood stained my sheets. Imprints of a fact about my body, wrapped in a white sheet, to shake the tiny certainty, or to give lie to the architecture of appearance. . . . It was certainly blood. The resistance of the body to the name; a splash from a tardy circumcision. It was a reminder, grimace of some buried memory, the memory of a life that I had not known and which could have been mine. Strange to be thus the bearer of a memory that had not been accumulated in lived time, but given unbeknownst to one and all. (46)[15]

Ahmed quickly subordinates his blood to male experience by qualifying it as the splash of a tardy circumcision. Offsetting the doubts it provokes are his success in growing a beard and his failure to develop breasts, signs of the triumph of his masculine mind over his female body. Yet the last few sentences of the passage indicate that while Zahra, the woman, is at no point essentially present in Ahmed's being, her absence somehow remains palpable enough to suggest the possibility of another order of experience.[16] It is this vacillation between a perception of sex as just as malleable as gender and anatomy as a tenacious reminder of destiny that maintains the hope that Ahmed will carry his perverse logic so far as finally to place into crisis the very social order that gave birth to him.

Again and again, Ahmed presents his masculinity as a personal choice, an act of his sovereign will. Yet his story bears out Judith Butler's caution that while sexual identity may be performatively constructed, it is hardly a simple matter of will or choice: "At stake is a way to describe this deeper and perhaps irrevocable sense of *constitutedness and constraint* in the face of which the notions of 'choice' or 'free play' appear not only foreign, but unthinkable and sometimes even cruel."[17] Indeed, Ahmed is no radical in his masculinity, for societal and cultural norms absolutely dictate the form of its expression. There is nothing delirious in his self-constitution, which instead scrupulously adheres to convention, the aberrant (because not read as male) biological functions of his body only intensifying the constraints on his male being. Choosing to perceive as open doors the restrictions placed on his performance of masculinity, Ahmed willingly assumes the roles of both jailor and detainee when he takes over from his father as architect of his own dwelling: "Not only do I accept my condition and live it, but I like it. It interests me. It grants me the privileges that I would never have known. It opens doors for me, and I like that, even if it then locks me in a glass cage" (50).[18] Nevertheless, unable to take any norm of masculinity for granted, Ahmed suffers or benefits from a heightened perception of gender's "unnaturalness." He confesses that while he sleeps, necessarily renouncing his conscious mastery of his body, he experiences sensations of suffocation and vertigo and approaches the void. He thus revels in the limitations everywhere evident in his waking life, craving the constraint that Butler identifies as constitutive: "[C]onstraint is not necessarily that which sets a limit to performativity; constraint is, rather, that which impels and sustains performativity."[19] Yet Ahmed's very self-mastery portends his undoing, by taking him to what seems to be the limits of performativity.

Wary of any physical contact that might shake his own and others' confidence in his maleness, Ahmed nonetheless determines to marry, for only marriage can confer on him full membership in his society.[20] While his decision highlights the queerness of his existence, it does so in such a way that this queerness ultimately challenges only his own existence, though not in the most obvious way. At first, Ahmed's horrified family, whose livelihood continues to depend on the maintenance of his maleness, fears that he has fallen prey to the short-sightedness of his father in his fervor to perfect himself. Sex is at stake here: the act would reveal the attribute, expose the radical incompatibility of sexual identity and body. Sex, however, is not the source of Ahmed's downfall, for despite the anxieties of his family, he has carefully anticipated the threat that his duties both to consummate his marriage and to procreate would pose to him. Selecting an epileptic and handicapped bride, his cousin Fatima (whose family is only too happy that she has found any husband at all), Ahmed bets that her physical shortcomings will divert all attention from his own physical "abnormalities."

Fatima keeps her end of the unspoken bargain, but her silence is rooted in neither gratitude nor submissiveness. Like Ahmed, Fatima rejects her female, and handicapped, body as determinative, yet does so not by refashioning it but by seeking to divest herself of embodiment altogether. Rebuffing the social role Ahmed holds out to her like a reward, she wraps herself in solitude. For Fatima, her newfound social position as "wife" merely buys her the opportunity to immerse herself in the writings of mystics, to seek to dissolve the material in the immaterial. It is her very lack of resistance to his social designs that profoundly shakes Ahmed's confidence in the masculine self he has thoroughly embraced:

> Little by little, I was overcome by scruples and insomnia. I wanted to get rid of Fatima without harming her. I set her up in a room well removed from mine, and I slowly began to hate her. I had just failed in the process that I had planned and set in motion. This woman, because she was handicapped, revealed herself to be stronger, harder, more rigorous than I had foreseen. Though I wanted to use her to perfect my social appearance, it was she who knew better how to use me and who almost dragged me into her profound despair. (79)[21]

Fatima's unexpected response, or lack thereof, certainly challenges Ahmed's estimation of women. Yet her particular form of refusal to participate in a society that rejects her as even less than a woman no more challenges the fundamental assumptions of this society than Ahmed's maleness does. Her study of mysticism brings her no closer to a joy of existence. If anything, her character implies that the popular mysticism still strongly represented in Moroccan Sufism has turned inward toward spiritual renewal, away from political causes, in the face of postindependence political, economic, and social stagnation and injustice.

Not until just before her death does Fatima evince any sign of the kind of ecstatic love, or elevation of the spirit, that grants insight into the design of the world and permits its transcendence.[22] Even then, her revelation is but a bleak parody of that elevation of the spirit. Several days before she succeeds in definitively freeing her soul from the materiality of her body, Fatima infuriates Ahmed one night by slipping into his bed and caressing his female sex. A short while thereafter, she relays her stark message to him:

> I have always known who you are, and that is why, my sister, my cousin, I came to die here, near you. We were both born leaning over the stone at the bottom of the dry well, on a sterile land, surrounded by gazes without love. We are women before being infirm, or maybe we are infirm because we are women. . . . I know our wound. . . . It is common. (80)[23]

Fatima's grim assessment of their lives negatively echoes Ahmed's birth announcement, lifting the veil on the futility of his as well as her existence. She renounces any possibility of agency, apparently overwhelmed by the complexity of the symbolic violence that has grown in conjunction with the material destitution of their land. While his hatred of her bears witness to his sense of some complicity in the desolation of his and Fatima's country, Ahmed nonetheless does not embrace her despair. Abruptly discovering in himself another dupe, rather than the master, of his self-narrative, he declines the part of tragic victim that Fatima in turn offers him. Instead, he begins a process of self-narration that departs from the script he had so successfully followed and begins to make of his life an exemplary and cautionary tale.

Composing Oneself

Once again, we return to the beginning that presaged Ahmed's end. After Fatima's death, the storyteller explains, Ahmed, beset by self-doubt and infirmity, secludes himself and begins to write "confused or unreadable things." This moment in Ahmed's life corresponds to the storyteller's initial account of his character and his autobiographical impulses:

Since there had been a rupture between him and his body, a kind of fracture, his face had aged and his gait had become that of a handicapped man. Nothing remained for him but refuge in total solitude. This had permitted him to spell out all that had preceded and to prepare for his definitive departure toward the territory of supreme silence. (10)[24]

Broken, but nonetheless still a man, Ahmed cannot, nor does he seem to desire to, erase years of will and habit. Rather, he now contemplates how he/she may separate a self from all that has been, a self that is not a woman, for his society still dubs femaleness an infirmity, or a man, who affirms himself only by dominating a female other. In the immediate aftermath of his face to face with Fatima, his other and likeness, Ahmed searches for the most fundamental element of identity: "I have lost the language of my body; anyway, I never possessed it. I should learn it and begin first by speaking like a woman. Like a woman? Why? Am I a man? I have a long journey ahead of me; I must go back over my steps, patiently, and rediscover the initial sensations of the body that neither head nor reason control. How to speak? And to whom will I speak?" (96).[25] Having lost all his bearings—his sense of self and with it his understanding of those others against whom he had always measured himself—Ahmed turns in circles. He frantically declares his commitment to an essential language of the body and then abruptly suggests that, without an interlocutor, without the opportunity to enter into a dialectic of self and other, he can never find himself. The more he seeks definitively to spell out what preceded in conventional terms, the more Ahmed's writing becomes "confused and unreadable," the more it runs up against a symbolic order by which he cannot represent his experience. For the fiction of masculinity he had so carefully maintained persists on his body that he has begun to read differently. The seeming incompatibility of the two call for the invention of a radically imaginative self-narrative, for a delirium of self-representation.

Truly at this moment, when Ahmed has withdrawn from all personal contact and secluded himself in his room to revisit all that has come before while awaiting death, there is nothing for the storytellers to tell. Ahmed's story folds back on itself, the only possible continuation another repetition of a tale the audience already knows. Broken and confused, Ahmed seems destined to remain a recluse until his imminent death, communicating only via letter with an anonymous correspondent who functions as his conscience. The storyteller implausibly possesses Ahmed's replies as well as the letters he has received, but he reads there only Ahmed's utter renunciation of the most familiar and deeply ingrained marks of identity. After Fatima's death, Ahmed writes: "Know, friend, that the family as it exists in our country, with the all-powerful father and women relegated to domestic work with a small bit of authority that the male concedes to them, the family, I repudiate it, I wrap it in fog and I no longer recognize it" (89).[26] Maintaining as it does inequality between the sexes and inculcating gender roles accordingly, the family constitutes the primary source of identity in Ahmed's society. Tellingly, he lampoons the language that for many years gave Moroccan husbands the right to summarily and legally divorce their wives in his repudiation of the very concept of the Moroccan family as it exists in his lifetime. Ahmed's remarks only confirm that there is no saving his narrative by looking to the past, to so-called traditional ways of life and narration. Although the avowed goal of the storytellers is to initiate their audience into the secret of Ahmed's being, this secret cannot be resolved in any return to presumed prior certainties but rather resides in the very crisis of personal and collective narrative with which they grapple.

Not incidentally, *The Sand Child* thus explores the failure and decay of both social and literary narratives that have only reified the circumstances they once promised to overcome. If the aim of anticolonial movements was total liberation for all, Ahmed's postindependence breakdown and the rigid grimness of the world in which he lives out his final days delineate the failure of this revolutionary narrative. Other narratives, including those that encompass militant religious extremism, resigned idealization of a past golden age, spectacular commercialism, and strict socialist realism, mingle in Ahmed's tale as the storytellers cast about for a guiding thread or the glimmer of a resolution. None finally proves suitable in itself, but as storytellers test variations of one and the other, the limitless quest for a future for Ahmed's story becomes a critical end in itself, the secret of transformation and survival. Meanwhile, the multiple storytellers, at times desperate for an audience, at a far remove from the populist heroes of Fanon's optimistic essay, and reduced to less than folkloric icons of Moroccan culture, raise a critical question about their own function, and that of the postindependence writer, once the ideal of the revolutionary man of culture has faded from the horizon, modernization has brought new entertainments that usurp those of the past, and advocates of tradition have denounced them for their decadence.

As a postindependence writer who holds university degrees from France, is a psychologist by training, writes in French, and frequently acknowledges in his work his debt to European as well as other non-Arab writers, Ben Jelloun seems particularly open to allegations of decadence and nonrepresentativity.[27] Yet works like *The Sand Child* undermine the validity of such claims by exposing their dependence on a fantasy of rigid and impermeable boundaries between Occident and Orient, the West and the Arab world. Weaving others' fictions of the Orient into his novel, perverting or recuperating them, Ben Jelloun harnesses and claims for Moroccans the imaginative power to which Morocco and the Orient have given rise around the world. Still, as Cynthia Running-Johnson reveals when she studies the implications of Ben Jelloun's stated debt to Jean Genet in one of his later, nonfiction works, the politics of such "postcolonial" boundary crossing are incredibly fraught ones: "Genet may facilitate Ben Jelloun's initiation of his connection with his Maghrebi origins, but one continues to feel the force of Western values in Ben Jelloun's essay."[28] While Ben Jelloun may credit Genet with reintroducing him to his Moroccan roots, European readers are less likely to credit Ben Jelloun with reacquainting them with their so-called Western origins. Although his work seeks to unmoor the imaginary dividing line between East and West, Africa and Europe, readers consistently work to reinstall these boundaries, by reading Ben Jelloun as a *Moroccan* author, or not. It remains that while Borges and Genet drew praise for the cross-cultural influences in their work, the same is not true for the postcolonial Ben Jelloun. In his case, as well in that of many authors in the wake of colonialism, Orientalism, and economic globalization, regional particularism is assumed to dominate their aesthetics. The storytellers in *The Sand Child* assess the negative repercussions of this imposed obligation as they seek to craft a story that pays tribute to the particularity of Morocco's past, yet does not bind its future to predetermined limitations and outcomes.

Counting Ahmed/Zahra, who is the author of the journal on which many of the storytellers rely, seven storytellers narrate *The Sand Child*. They see Ahmed/Zahra through six "doors," indicated by the chapter titles "The Door of Thursday," "The Door of Friday," "The Door of Saturday," "Bab El Had," "The Forgotten Door," and "The Walled-Up Door," and up to a seventh, "The Door of the Sands." Fraught with symbolism, the seven doors of *The Sand Child* evoke not only the seven ancient gates of the city of Marrakech, famed for its storytellers, but also the mystery attached to this number since ancient times. Leading the audience through "doors" that each add another dimension to Ahmed/Zahra's story, the storytellers evoke the seven levels of meaning described by many works of Islamic mysticism. Yet the opening of another door does not necessarily signal progress toward enlightenment, as readers familiar with the *Nights* will recall. Within the story of "The Porter and the Three Ladies," for example, the third dervish recounts how his blissful sojourn in a marvelous palace filled with stunning women and unheard of wealth was abruptly curtailed when, unable to stifle his curiosity any longer, he opened the forbidden hundredth door. Retold with many variations and sometimes with seven rather than one hundred doors, this much circulated tale even became the subject of a popular colonial movie, *La septième porte* (The Seventh Door) (1946) filmed in both a French and an Arabic version for audiences on both sides of the Mediterranean.[29] In *The Sand Child*, the seventh door leads— But I am getting ahead of myself.

Maktūb (Mektoub)

The first storytellers who take up Ahmed's tale brandish a book to establish their intimate, authoritative familiarity with his/her life. Asserting that it is the journal Ahmed composed just prior to his death, the storytellers prevent the members of the audience from directly accessing its content. Rather, they proclaim the terrible nature of the tale within and promise to convey its unbearable secret in moderate doses to the curious. The first storyteller proclaims himself an avatar of the book, one who has learned its contents at the cost of great personal sacrifice; appropriating the language of revelation, he promises his audience a cautionary tale that will lead them toward enlightenment:

> This book, my friends, can neither circulate nor be given. It cannot be read by innocent souls. The light that emanates from it dazzles and blinds eyes that carelessly come to rest on it, unprepared for it. This book, I have read it; I have deciphered it for such souls. You cannot accede to it unless you cross my nights and my body. I am this book. I have become the book of the secret; I paid with my life to read it. Once I arrived at the end, after months of insomnia, I felt the book incarnate itself in me, for such is my destiny. (12–13)[30]

With his language verging on the blasphemous, the storyteller introduces himself as a kind of prophet prepared to aid his followers in uncovering transformative truths. He proceeds to draw on the multiple significations, religious and secular, of the word *bāb* (a chapter as well as a door or gate), as if promising them an initiation into higher truths. While urging his audience to entrust themselves to his guidance, the storyteller also implicates his listeners in Ahmed's drama by informing them that they already possess keys to these seven doors but do not know how to employ them. After he dismisses the audience with these enigmatic promises to tell and resolve for them a tale with which they are already intimately familiar, they depart in silence. The storyteller has assured his audience that the tale harbors the power to transform them and their reality but also that their reality has the power to disclose the transformative truth of the tale. At this moment, the intrigue is compelling, but the nature of the tale to come is no clearer.

As if to guarantee further his listeners' engagement with his version of the tale, the storyteller calls on them to contribute to it. In order that his test of their attentiveness not be perceived as an admission of ignorance or a lapse of skill, he informs them that the book contains blank pages just when it should address Ahmed's adolescence, that potentially rebellious stage of life. Immediately, several members of the audience comply with the storyteller's request. One proposes that the adolescent Ahmed finds himself torn between the truth of his body and his filial duty; another, that Ahmed experiences no doubts, confident in his social conditioning. Still a third declares that the truth is much more complex and subtle, that Ahmed's father continues to control his son's development carefully, sheltering him from any contact with women and femininity. Yet another dismisses this last speaker's claim and confronts everyone present: "Are we capable of inventing him? Can we dispense with the book?" (42). A fifth focuses everyone's attention on the storyteller: "Since you say you have the proof in that book you're hiding, why not give it to us. . . . We'll certainly see if this story corresponds to the truth, or if you have invented everything" (42–43). These voices show that the members of the audience form no picturesque or homogeneous assembly. Split between confidence that they possess the elements of the story necessary to guide it to its conclusion and trust only in the authority of the written word, not one of these figures really targets the ideologies that inform the order of the society in which they live. Neither, however, do they fully place their faith in their guide, the storyteller. Observing this, he squelches the minirebellion by hastily turning back to the book. It seems, however, that this interlude may have introduced an irreparable, and potentially productive, split between himself and his narrative, a split that offers a glimpse of other permutations that Ahmed's story might assume.

For the time being, the audience attributes the final word on the story to its presumed author, Ahmed, conferring not just authority but also responsibility on him. Thus localizing and delimiting Ahmed's story, they resist exploring their complicity with it. And the storyteller seemingly exploits their resistance, promoting their continued reliance on his interpretive skills. Soon, however, a second storyteller easily dismantles the first storyteller's pretences to authority. He introduces himself as Fatima's brother and, therefore, an eyewitness to many of the events of Ahmed's story rather than a mere interpreter of its textual traces. Furthermore, he debunks the first storyteller's account of his all-consuming immersion in the text of Ahmed's life by identifying himself as his predecessor's informant. Taking over the narrative for a few pages, he then produces another book, the real journal, he claims: "Here it is; it is covered with a newspaper from the period; you can read the date. . . . Doesn't it coincide with the date of his death?" (70). While the first storyteller concealed his book in a piece of black silk and carried with him the pens and inkwells of a public scribe, this new storyteller wraps his book in a newspaper that announces the facts of the story and arrives without any writing implements. He, it seems, will report the facts of Ahmed's tale without literary pretense.

Diverting the audience's attention from the shakiness of his facts, he immediately denounces the first storyteller as a charlatan who has read Ahmed's story from "a very cheap edition of the Qur'an" (70). An immutable point of reference, the direct word of God, the Qur'an cannot be materially altered; it broaches no accommodation for the evolution of the Arabic language. On it and the voluminously documented tradition literature, or *hadīth*, which records the pronouncements of the Prophet on matters not treated by the Qur'an, reposes not just the Islamic faith but also an entire legal, social, and political edifice. By accusing the first storyteller of perverting a very cheap edition of the Qur'an, however, the second storyteller seems to imply less that the given text is somehow defective or the copy careless than that his predecessor's approach to the tale makes but a show of respect and devotion to the religious principles on which their society is founded. Paradoxically, this second storyteller then proceeds to praise the first man's courage and deem his tale worthy of standing as an account of Ahmed's life. Somewhat obliquely, this second narrator thereby promotes the view that not just his predecessor's but also his society's interpretation of Islam is flawed, thereby producing such figures as Ahmed. Yet the second storyteller avers himself neither reporter nor religious purist. Instead, employing a metaphor of critical distancing, he enjoins his listeners to climb with him onto a high terrace in order to explore with him at their leisure the underpinnings of the artifice that is Ahmed's life.

Yet in spite of his charismatic promises, this storyteller fails to master the tale to the satisfaction of his audience. Listeners dwindle after he relates that Ahmed has perverted a verse of the Qur'an, suggesting the limitations imposed on criticism and artistic license in his country. Addressing his remaining audience, the storyteller confesses that the very givens of Ahmed's story slip away as he attempts to read them, the syllables and verses of his journal awakened, rearranged, and purged by the forces of nature that are the wind, the dawn, and insects. At this impasse, he interjects an appeal not to nature but to artifice:

> Fragmentary, but not devoid of meaning, the event attacks my conscience from all sides. The manuscript I wanted to read to you falls to pieces each time that I attempt to open it and to deliver it of its words, which poison so many birds, insects, and images. Fragmentary, it possesses me, obsesses me, and brings me back to those of you who have the patience to wait. The book is thus: a house where every window is a neighborhood, every door a city, every page a street; it is an illusion of a house, a stage set where the moon is constructed from a blue sheet stretched between two windows and a lit bulb. (108)[31]

Embracing the artificiality of Ahmed's story, the storyteller develops the metaphor of the book as abode, only to undermine it simultaneously, thereby foregrounding the absolute contingency of Ahmed's story. The book, he informs his audience, is an abode that cannot provide real shelter but offers vistas onto the neighborhoods, cities, and streets of the country. Yet these, too, like the house, are but mediated reflections. Owning up that the story he relates is as much an urgently necessary illusion as a faithful reflection of reality, the storyteller accomplishes the unexpected: he moves the story out of its previous stalemate and on toward an unforeseen denouement. After the storyteller enjoins the audience to occupy this stage set with him, he begins a new chapter in Ahmed's life, the chapter that narrates his transformation into Zahra. Once again narrating in the first person, the storyteller reads of Ahmed's decision to remove the bandages from his (or is it now her?) breasts and to leave behind the house of his youth to make his/her way in the world. Not really a woman, no longer a man, Ahmed finds a place for herself in a carnival sideshow, where she performs as a man impersonating a woman, taking the name Zahra. There, on the fringes of society, placing her-/himself on display as neither man nor woman but as a being in whom biological identity and illusion are indistinguishable, Zahra/Ahmed finds a measure of acceptance and respect.

Like many tales in the *Nights* but with a quite different outcome, Ahmed's life story plays on the notion of the written as *maktūb*. This word, from the root *k-t-b*, on which are formed the Arabic words for *writer, writing, book, record, bookseller, office,* and so forth, also signifies fate; in popular parlance, to say something is *maktūb* means it is preordained.[32] In the *Nights*, characters who try to defy their fate find themselves fulfilling destiny in unexpected ways; when the third dervish in the tale of "The Porter and the Three Ladies" vows, for example, to protect the young man whom astrologers have foretold he will kill, he nonetheless kills the young man in the course of a freak accident. While many characters in the *Nights* seem to prevail against destiny by surviving orders for their execution, they effect the lifting of these unwritten orders by revealing the marvelous and intricate ways in which destiny has already traced their lives. Their stories are written down for all time as further lessons that the means and permutations of destiny remain infinite and ungraspable. In *The Sand Child*, by contrast, Ahmed has lost sight of fate and attempts to uncover what was written for him/her before his father's intervention by composing a journal that seeks to unwrite what has already transpired. Yet the words in the presumed journal, if indeed there are any, only leave him at an impasse. Nor does biology impose itself as destiny, unable as his/her physical body is to revert to its "nature" in the wake of a life lived otherwise. *Maktūb*, or fate, instead exerts its influence over Ahmed/Zahra in the guise of the social milieu into which he/she is born. Together, the storytellers imply that this agent of destiny, however, can and must evolve in order to create an alternative to the opening of the seventh door, the door of fate, which always leads those tempted by it back to the place from which they set out, much the worse for wear.

Accountabilities

If by joining the carnival sideshow, Zahra/Ahmed in many ways avoids participation in a social order she has renounced, she also fails to dispute the ideology that underpins that order. Living on the margins, among the marginal, her/his performance is but a momentary diversion for those in search of the sensational, and her/his confidence soon falters before guilty recollections of the injustices Ahmed perpetrated on his sisters, mother, and Fatima. Having seen Ahmed up to this point of growing remorse, the second storyteller now abruptly vanishes, swept away by the modernization of the plaza. An anonymous narrator explains that this storyteller has died of sadness, the manuscript clasped in his arms; his unclaimed body was donated to the medical school, and his personal effects, among them the book, were burned. Nearly nine months after the second storyteller's disappearance, in an unrenovated café on the fringes of the plaza, three members of the former audience, Salem, Amar, and Fatouma, take to heart this narrator's declaration that "a story is made to be told until the end" (136). Salem, the son of a former slave, pursues the story with an account of sexual brutality that results in the violent deaths of all the principal characters. Amar, a former schoolteacher, rejects this denouement as but an expression of perverse, sublimated desires. In Amar's version of the tale, Ahmed wanders for some time in a Morocco wracked by social problems, before embarking on a boat headed for the end of the world; finally, Ahmed transforms his journal into a critique of the condition of Moroccan women, writing from the balcony that he has in reality never left, surrounded by works about love from the golden age of Islam. Salem and Amar take up storytelling in the face of their ever more definitive banishment to the margins of society, yet neither of their tales succeeds in opening up Ahmed's story onto a universe of others' stories. They as well are left turning in circles.

The two men debate for a time regarding the relative merits of the fates, violent or idealist, that they confer on Ahmed, breaking their deadlock only when they look to the silent member of their trio, an aged woman named Fatouma. Rather than taking sides, she remarks only on the social aberration that her own presence in a café with two men represents. Enumerating her many social transgressions (she has no children, has left her family, and has traveled alone), she tests the two men's commitment to social reform by inviting them to visit her in the room she occupies at an orphanage. When they arrive the following evening in this space that recalls the isolation of Ahmed's room, Fatouma prefaces her tale with an invocation not of Ahmed or Zahra but of her ideal audience: "Men! There is a piety that I love and seek out; it is the piety of memory. I appreciate it because it asks no questions. I know this quality is in you. Thus, I will anticipate your queries and calm your curiosity" (163).[33] Charging them to remember rather than to ask questions of her, Fatouma counsels the two men to look to themselves for the secret of Ahmed's story. Like the previous storytellers, she begins where her predecessor left off, in this case on the balcony where Amar had left Ahmed to dream up his adventures. Where her predecessors declared themselves dominated and obsessed by Ahmed's tale, however, Fatouma employs it as a parable of her own life, narrating in the first person and declaring: "I have thus learned to be in the dream and to make of my life an entirely invented story, a tale that remembers that which really happened" (168).[34] Gathering the fragments of Ahmed's story, Morocco's social history, and her own experiences into a fiction that reflects her hopes and desires, Fatouma critiques her culture and society but also begins to shake its determinative grip.

Of all the narratives, Fatouma's is the least linear and the most unresolved. She begins by recounting an imaginary pilgrimage to Mecca, which quickly takes on the character of a lived event, one that induces her to reject her stable life on her return home and to wander disguised as a man. But this last measure, undertaken for the sake of greater liberty, brings her to a dead end:

> And then everything stopped; everything froze: the instant became a room; the room became a sunny day, time an old skeleton forgotten in this cardboard box; in this box there are old mismatched shoes, a handful of new nails, a Singer sewing machine that runs all by itself, an aviator's glove taken off a dead man, a spider fixed at the bottom of the box, a Minora razor blade, a glass eye, and the inevitable mirror in bad shape and which has rid itself of all its images. Moreover, all these objects in the box are only from its own imagination; since it has extinguished itself, since it has become a simple piece of glass, it no longer gives objects. It emptied itself during a long absence. . . . I know at present that the key to our story is among these old things. . . . I don't dare rummage for fear of having my hand ripped off by the mechanical jaws that, despite their rustiness, still work . . . , they are not from the mirror, but from its double . . . , I forgot to mention it. Well, I didn't forget, but avoided it out of superstition . . . , so what. . . . We won't leave this room without finding the key, and in order to do that it will be necessary to evoke, if only by allusion, the double of the mirror. (166–67)[35]

Here, as throughout the novel, words are transformed into objects, this time into a box of junk, souvenirs of obscure and unknown pasts devoid of function or meaning in the present. Certainly, the useless mirror indicates the breakdown of Ahmed's and Fatouma's selves once they have lost the ability or will to reflect maleness and masculinity. At the same time, the passage inverts the mystic metaphor of the world as a mirror that everywhere reflects God, as if the loss of the mirror's silvering connotes utter spiritual desolation, and the survival of only some industrial detritus emphasizes Morocco's material poverty. In support of such a reading, Fatouma adds a short while later what she has witnessed: "the moving away of my country: the men and History, the plains and mountains, the prairies and even the sky. Remain the women and kids" (167). Exposing the room (and, by extension, the nation) that shelters them as a prison, Fatouma nonetheless insists on the presence of the key to their liberation among the discarded items in the room. That the unseen key lies *among* these old things suggests that the future of this story that is now thoroughly their own depends on their capacity to recombine the things in new and unpredicted ways in order to capture the popular imagination again. To do so, they will need to revalue all that has been left behind so as to avoid the trap that also lies among the objects.

Obliging Salem and Amar to face the impossible enigma of the present, Fatouma cautions against the temptation to seek refuge in the timeless ideal conjured by what she terms the "mirror's double," a luminous garden evocative of paradise, which gives onto "the sea that swallows and carries away all the stories that are born and die between the flowers and roots of plants" (167–68). Natural, complete, and eternal, while the mirror is industrial, broken, and antiquated, the garden promises ease, freedom from need, and transcendence, while the broken mirror represents hardship, penury, and the manmade. The garden seduces with a promise of forgetfulness, but Fatouma warns that it is but a mirage induced by the desolation of the everyday, one that lulls into resignation those drawn to it while shredding them in its rusty mechanical jaws. Pursuing her narrative, Fatouma explains that eventually she recognized her male disguise as an expression of "contempt of the other" and that, throwing off the costume that reinforced the very social order that had oppressed her as a woman, she joined in street protests with the impoverished and the orphaned. Wounded by a soldier's bullet and cared for by the poor, she eventually found a home in the room where she now sits with Salem and Amar. Her story, then, offers no conclusion, no resolution—whether spectacularly violent or dreamy—to the enigma of Ahmed's life. Rather, it demands continuity. It shows that to the violence of the present must respond not a beautiful, pleasing tale but one that seizes imaginations, implicates its audience in its twists and turns, and leads them always to new places.

One More—and Another

"I am a man of few words and great generosity, and I must relate to you the stories of my other brothers, in order to prove it to you."[36] So speaks the barber to the caliph in Husain Haddawy's translation of the *Nights'* "Story of the Hunchback," intent on defending himself against an accusation of garrulousness by relating in detail the misadventures of all six of his brothers. His brothers, of course, all suffer roughly the same fortune; their foolish actions result in financial and physical ruin and dependency on their seventh brother, the barber, also known as the Silent One. Successful in staving off his execution by these stories but nevertheless sent into exile, the barber moves to China, where he continues verbosely to profess his wisdom, good sense, and humanity. There, the now very old barber finds favor with the king through an unexpected twist of fate. Composed of intricately nested stories within stories, "The Story of the Hunchback" indicates not only how fates may be subtly transformed in the course of seemingly endless repetition but also how travel does not so much distort stories as promote unexpected and welcome turns in them. In the course of her narrative, Fatouma proffers a somewhat heavy-handed reminder of the travels and endurance of Ahmed's tale: "My story is ancient . . . , it dates from before Islam" (168). Though her words are meant to emphasize the origins of the story in an oppression of women fostered by culture rather than religion, she repeats a point made often in the course of *The Sand Child*, namely, that Ahmed's story is but a particularized variation on an obsession expressed in many popular tales of transvestism. Early in the novel, a member of the audience declares that Ahmed's story reminded him of the fierce warrior Antar, alleging that death revealed this legendary figure to be a woman in disguise.[37] Seizing on this addition to the ancient epic poem, the storyteller describes an incident in which the undisguised Antar humiliated and enraged her male lover by pretending to sodomize him. This, of course, echoes the story of Princess Budur, though with a more menacing twist.

Near the conclusion of *The Sand Child*, a shadow of the faraway Argentinean writer Jorge Luis Borges, avid student and falsifier of the *Nights*, suddenly appears at the table of the three friends in this

Moroccan café, bringing from afar yet another version of Ahmed's tale. Introducing himself as a character from a story within a story, he offers falsehoods rather than pieties:

> The Secret is sacred, but when it becomes ridiculous, it's better to rid oneself of it. . . . And . . . you will no doubt ask me who I am, who sent me, and why I arrive thus in your story. . . . You're right. I'll explain to you. . . . No. . . . Know simply that I have spent my life falsifying or altering the stories of others. It doesn't matter where I come from, and I wouldn't know whether to tell you that my first steps left their imprint on the oriental or the occidental bank of the river. (171)[38]

Pure contrivance, this character brings not resolution but only more intrigue. An outsider to the Morocco of the three acquaintances, he is unencumbered by personal experience of that country's recent history and culture and thus by the limitations they might pose on fictions generated there. He arrives in the midst of the acquaintances not to return his stories to their origins but to remind them of the inspiration he took from Arabo-Islamic art and culture and how he remade that art and culture in the image of his imagination. Further entangling art and reality, the Argentinean storyteller affirms that his creations have again doubled back to make him a character in his own fictions.[39] In these closing pages of *The Sand Child*, then, he impossibly perverts Ahmed's origins by relating a multilayered tale in which his/her doubles figure everywhere. Taking a page from the Borges story "The Zahir," where that term, which designates "surface," took on the form of a coin circulating in Buenos Aires, the blind man recounts how his memory of this Argentinean *zahir* was awakened by his receipt of a *battène*, an Egyptian coin. The name of this coin, he specifies, signifies the other side of *zahir*, the "interior," or that which "one has buried within oneself" (176). This *battène* (a transcription of the term *bāṭin*, better defined as "concealed") is stamped with the image of a man on one side and with that same likeness as a woman on the other. In Islamic mysticism, the surface (*ẓāhir*) can aid the follower in approaching that which is concealed (*bāṭin*), but in this fiction within a fiction the "interior" is externalized in a rare coin, symbol of worldly wealth, that yet retains its value only as long as it remains in circulation, neither of the two likenesses on its surfaces more interior or apparent than the other.

To complicate matters even further, the blind man explains that he was given this coin by an unknown woman whose simultaneously masculine and feminine voice is that of Tawaddud, a character in the later recensions of the *Nights*.[40] A slave girl, Tawaddud saves her dissolute young master from utter ruin by urging him to sell her to the caliph Hārūn al-Rashīd for a large some of money. She merits her asking price by outperforming a series of the caliph's top advisers with her incomparable knowledge of religious law, *ḥadīth*, the Qurʾan, medicine, astronomy, and philosophy and her skills at chess, backgammon, music, and singing. Burton claims that Tawaddud's discourse exemplifies the state of the above sciences in the "Shāfiʿī School," qualifying his decision to include it in his translation of the *Nights* as a proof of his superior erudition: "Lane (ii636) omits this tale, 'as it would not only require a volume of commentary, but be extremely tiresome to most readers.' Quite true; but it is valuable to Oriental Students who are beginning their studies, as an excellent compendium of doctrine and practice according to the Shāfiʿī School."[41] All Burton's pedantry, Orientalism, and competitiveness converge in this note, which, despite his well-known misogyny, positions him as the Tawaddud of his time.[42] For the storytelling double of Borges, himself an avid student of Burton's *Nights* and the falsifier of an episode or two from that collection, the masculine quality of Tawaddud's voice seems indeed to result from an echo of Burton's voice. Yet very unlike Burton, the blind man situates the interest of his tale in its artificiality, its irreducible fictiveness. He seeks not to have the final word but to underscore the indeterminacy of his story's origins and limits, its openness to innumerable appropriations.

Informing the blind man that while she resembles his own fictions, she is not one of them, the imaginary double of Tawaddud summarizes a predicament strangely parallel to Ahmed's:

> You alone are capable of understanding why I am here at this moment. I am not one of your characters; I could have been one, but it is not as a silhouette full of sand and words that I present myself to you. . . . That which I seek is not the truth. I am incapable of recognizing it. It is not justice either, for that is impossible. There are verses in this Book [the Qurʾan] that function as law; they do not attribute right to women. That which I seek is not forgiveness, for those who could have given it to me are no longer here. And yet, I need justice, truth, and forgiveness. (179–80)[43]

Unable to fashion a resolution worthy of his interlocutor's needs, the blind storyteller admits that he failed her, obliging her to persist in her being. Haunted by her face, the last he saw before going blind, and by a dream, the storyteller relates a confrontation with an invisible presence, now woman, now man, now human, now phantom, with whom he struggles for his life in the Alhambra. Uncertain that he ever emerged from this struggle to the death, the blind storyteller begs his now very large audience to reveal to him his fate. After momentarily suffering their silence, he adds, evoking Shahrazad: "Everything was accomplished by a woman who conceived of the exorbitant, the impossible, the unthinkable. There are the first glimmers of the Secret" (197). His is a story that undermines its own authority and throws all its elements into question. Unsettling his audience by obliging them to look to the past and move forward at the same time, it disperses the storyteller's authority among them, demanding of them that they reinvent themselves in the measure of the fictions they claim.

This overwhelming injunction, to invent anew justice, truth, and forgiveness, is in the novel's final word placed before the audience the blind storyteller has gathered. At the very end, the long-lost second storyteller reappears only to confess that he is a professional storyteller who fabricated Ahmed/Zahra's story on the basis of a tale told to him by an Egyptian woman. While he earlier held up his notebook as Ahmed's own and definitive word, he now claims that its writing has been erased by the full moon, taking with it his memory and liberating him from the clutches of the story. Thus divested of his obsessive obligation, he deposits the notebook, along with ink and pen holders, in front of the assembled and announces his definitive departure. Once again, the final door, the door of the sands, leads us back to the beginning, as if the entire adventure has not occurred. Yet, as always, enough traces of the passage of time persist to assure us of the reality of the experience and to intensify our regrets for our imprudent behavior. Some marks of the effaced writing do remain on the pages of the notebook, indicating that the slate has not been entirely wiped clean, that all possibilities are not equally open. Yet, with the disappearance of the writing vanishes not just the promise of a much needed, immediate resolution but also the notion that the future is already given. That, perhaps, was the conviction that drove Shahrazad. Like her, the unknown, genderless, still silent members of this audience have listened to many a story, all of which have left their traces, the foundations of an inexhaustible variety of tales to come.

What to make of this story offered and then withdrawn? Through his many doubles, the storytellers, Ben Jelloun entices those readers in search of an ethnographic performance of Moroccan authorship and then, through a radical foregrounding of fictionality, turns such a project to ridicule. He makes of himself, Tahar Ben Jelloun, an author produced by the past stories, fictions, and even lyrics to which he was granted access. If *The Sand Child* at first seems to exploit the topic of sexism in the Islamic world, it does so to reveal the artificiality of those constructions of gender that underpin it, withholding a definitive image of Muslim women as victims by refusing, symbolically at least, to have the final word. Ben Jelloun's oblique likening of himself to Shahrazad would qualify as outrageous were it not that in the final pages of his novel he confers not just on the audience within but on all his readers the critical agency of Shahrazad. Not to be taken lightly, this agency insists that vigilant acts of invention born of attentive re-readings must always also be rewritings.

4 ∞ *La fantasia réclamée,* or Voice Incorporated

IN THE MINDS OF READERS, storytelling characters provide a contrast to the solitary writer. They embody connectedness with one's audience and the voice of the (disenfranchised) masses, and for many they offer exoticism and the promise of the fantastic. Ben Jelloun's storytellers twist and refute these expectations in recounting the tale of a character neither here nor there, always in search of a means of expression appropriate to his/her being. Yet their own corporeal identity is for the most part straightforwardly male. The one woman who temporarily assumes a storytelling role does so only to emphasize how little weight her words carry and how anomalous and scandalous her presence is before a public audience. Indeed Shahrazad, despite her iconic status, tells her stories in private, under the cover of darkness, and to a single man, her husband. And, of course, to her sister and accomplice, Dinarzad. The often overlooked relationship of the two sisters is fraught with complexities, for without Dinarzad's convenient, prearranged prompting, Shahrazad would never have had occasion to deploy the power of her stories. Dinarzad's discreet presence, her disembodied request from beneath the bed, effectively legitimates Shahrazad's voice. At the same time, Shahrazad places Dinarzad in harm's way; should her project fail, her younger sister would be the king's next victim.

The lives of Shahrazad and Dinarzad therefore hang on intertwined threads, each indebted to the other for every day of survival. Night after night Dinarzad's voice furnishes Shahrazad with the key to their salvation; night after night Shahrazad draws inspiration from fear that her sister may come to bodily harm if she falters. Algerian writer and filmmaker Assia Djebar explores this charged sisterly obligation in her 1987 novel *Ombre sultane*, translated into English as *A Sister to Scheherazade*.[1] There, Isma, an educated, emancipated, French-speaking narrator, relates the tale of Hajila, an uneducated, lower-class, fatherless woman who defies her upbringing and social expectations by slipping unveiled out of her new husband's apartment to explore the streets of Algiers. *A Sister to Scheherazade* is no joyful celebration of women's solidarity, however; rather, it holds up for scrutiny the darker dynamics of power in sisterly relationships. Like Shahrazad, Isma initially places Hajila in harm's way, arranging her marriage to a man she herself divorced because of his violent, alcohol-fueled, jealous rages. She thus consigns Hajila to an unfamiliar life in a modern high-rise, where Hajila cooks for the man, who barely notes her presence, and raises his two children, who speak only French. Unlike Shahrazad, Isma leaves her "sister" to fend for herself, not intervening to protect her from rape and beatings at the hands of her new husband. Isolated, Hajila begins to flout the restrictions others place on her body but remains largely mute both inside and outside the apartment. Instead Isma, anonymous (her name means, simply, "name") yet ever-present, relates Hajila's daily escapes as a foil for recollections of her own freer, amorous relationship with her former husband. When at the novel's end Isma surreptitiously passes a copy of the apartment key to the now-pregnant, recently beaten, and again cloistered Hajila, she does not offer her the means to a certain liberation. The key only opens the apartment door; in a world still ruled by men, a voiceless woman like Hajila has few options for survival other than begging and prostitution.

Interestingly, Isma views herself throughout the novel not as Shahrazad but as Dinarzad, fearing that she has failed to wake her sister in time to save both their lives. She ponders the fragility of Shahrazad's stratagem, its absolute dependence on Dinarzad's vigilance:

> What if her sister, whom she had installed as a precaution under the bridal bed, had fallen asleep? What if the sister had thus relaxed her guard and the sultan's bride for one night had been delivered up to the executioner, waiting in broad daylight, with his axe? . . .

> Yes, what if Scheherazade were to be continually reborn, only to die again at every dawn, just because a second woman, a third, a fourth, did not take up her post in her shadow, in her voice, in her night?[2]

In *A Sister to Scheherazade*, Isma has not quite failed to support Hajila's project of tentative independence, but she abandons her before Hajila has found a voice with which she might defend herself. At the novel's end, Isma takes her daughter and returns to her ancestral home to take up the veil, real or symbolic, determined to forge new ties with the circle of women whose censorious influence she always escaped. Hajila, for her part, seems to have rejected Shahrazad's solution, the status that motherhood would confer on her, by throwing herself into the path of a moving car. She lives, Isma implies, but aborts the fetus she is carrying. No satisfactory conclusion is in sight, as Hajila is left behind to wander the streets of the capital, stripped of all previous social ties. In this story of modern-day sisters who fail to live up to the example set by their mythical ancestors, Djebar revisits a problem that not only marks the legacy of Shahrazad but also dominates all of Djebar's work since her return to writing after a thirteen-year silence. That theme—how Algerian women might together raise their voices against the darkness in order to reclaim their bodies in the light—surfaces in a particularly nuanced and forceful way in *Women of Algiers in Their Apartments* and *Fantasia, an Algerian Cavalcade*, the two works that precede the publication of *A Sister to Scheherazade*.[3]

Already a successful novelist at age twenty-one, Djebar was rebuked for the apparent lack of political engagement in her first novel *La soif* (*The Mischief*), published in 1957 in the midst of the Algerian war for independence.[4] Although she responded by shifting the focus of her later novels more toward the national struggle and away from the lives and loves of privileged Algerians, Djebar reflects many years later that she broke through to her real voice only when the topic of erotic fulfillment intruded into the last of her youthful novels, *Les alouettes naïves:*

> At first, I thought that this private stuff did not belong in there; it was going off in a different direction from the rest of the book, depicting mutual erotic fulfillment right smack in the middle of a war story. I think now that, at bottom, even though I *thought* I was writing as far away from my own self as possible, my fiction had suddenly caught up with me. I could not help it. My life as a woman tripped me up.[5]

Significant in this statement is Djebar's new consciousness of the political stakes of narrating her existence as a woman so soon after the independence that had promised new freedoms to Algerian women. In the interval between the publication of *Les alouettes* in 1967 and her return to writing in 1980, the socialist yet military-based, postindependence government of Algeria, which had proclaimed Islam the national religion and Arabic the national language, set the stage for the promulgation of the repressive Family Code by neglecting to codify reforms governing the status of Algerian women.[6] As critics advocating democracy, a more representative socialism, recognition for Algeria's non-Arabic speaking populations, and legal, political, and social equality for women were increasingly silenced, Djebar explicitly began to meditate on the possibilities and pitfalls of representing Algerian women in a mode and language deemed ever more alien to Algeria. Beginning with her collection of short stories *Women of Algiers in Their Apartments* and more urgently in her 1985 novel *L'amour, la fantasia (Fantasia: An Algerian Cavalcade)*, Djebar's work foregrounds the multiple obligations of the postcolonial woman author, who is both a part of and outside the collectivity that she publicly represents. In each case, the narrator's bilingualism draws her into a search for an elusive language in which she can triumphantly embody herself, rejecting the role of victim yet without glossing over the suffering of her sisters.

Night Watch

In "Forbidden Gaze, Severed Sound," her epilogue to *Women of Algiers in Their Apartments*, Djebar turns to Eugène Delacroix's famous 1834 painting of the same name in order to illuminate the moment of Algerian women's separation from their bodies.[7] Not the first harem scene painted by a European, Delacroix's painting nevertheless drew special authority from the artist's firsthand glimpse of this domestic arrangement that so fascinated Europeans; he created his *Women of Algiers* from drawings he made while visiting the private quarters of the wives of a former Turkish official in Algiers. The painting depicts three seated women—two of them engaged in conversation while one reclines in the foreground—and a black servant, who looks back over her shoulder at the women as she exits the scene.[8] For Djebar, a "mute and unformulated uncertainty" permeates the image, suggestive of the radical changes wracking the recently conquered Algiers of 1832 that Delacroix visited (*Women* 135).[9] In Djebar's eyes, Delacroix's painting does not merely bear witness to a dynamic moment in Algerian history during which the relations of Algerian men and women to their society, culture, and bodies, and to each other, hang in the balance. She also examines how the painter's presence alters the reality he claims to represent, a project she will pursue in *Fantasia* as she reworks the records that soldiers, painters, and writers left of their sojourn in her native country. Thus, when she inquires of Delacroix's fidelity to his material—"This heart of the half-open harem, is it really the way he sees it?" (*Women* 135)— her concern is less with the mimetic quality of the work than with calling attention to the uncertainty that this image still provokes. For in breaching the forbidden space of the harem, Delacroix stole the images of these long-mysterious Algerian women, leaving behind what must have been to him their unintelligible voices.

Djebar remarks that the intrigue of Delacroix's painting lies in the peculiar eloquence of the women's silence: "Evoke, one and a half centuries later, these Bayas, Zoras, Mounis, and Khadoudjas. Since then, these women, whom Delacroix, perhaps in spite of himself, knew how to observe as no one had done before him, have not stopped telling us something that is unbearably painful and still very much with us today" (*Women* 136). This seemingly positive engagement with Delacroix's, and later Picasso's, work has earned Djebar some criticism from feminist scholars; Winifred Woodhull, for example, claims that Djebar privileges the vision of Algerian women that these artists elaborate: "[D]espite the political importance granted women's *speech* throughout Algerian history, the genius of the masters holds sway over women's *gaze* and directs their future efforts to free themselves."[10] Yet the issue is far more nuanced than Woodhull's remark suggests. For Djebar turns to these stolen images of Algerian women not as a guide to the future but as manifestations of the initial promise of dominant discourses of Algerian women's emancipation—and as illustrations of their failure. Weighty with the presence of its subjects, Delacroix's painting fleetingly captures the reality of Algerian women and ensures their subsequent confinement to obscurity, violating as it does the taboo of the women's visibility without granting them the subjectivity that would enable them to emerge from the harem definitively. Picasso's *Femmes d'Alger dans leur appartement*—a series of paintings in homage to Delacroix, in which Djebar discovers a felicitous juxtaposition of women in motion and at rest—captures the optimism that permeated the years just after the declaration of the Algerian war of independence in 1954, that same optimism that Frantz Fanon invoked in his essay "Algeria Unveiled."[11]

Yet Djebar looks back on Picasso's work as if to underscore just how unfulfilled its promise remains. The Spaniard's reworking of Delacroix's static, confined female figures was not able to grant Algerian women the political representation they so needed in order to take control of their own movements. His pictorial language, like that of Delacroix, also eventually fails Algerian women, exposing them in a way that contributed to their silence.

Thus Algerian women's first entry into a European language, pictorial in this case, entails a silencing veiled by a deceptive exposure. Citing Delacroix's personal traditionalism in a footnote, Djebar notes that he sought not to bring women out of the harem but rather to celebrate this institution: "It is beautiful! It is straight out of Homer! The woman in her women's quarters busy with her children, spinning wool or embroidering splendid fabrics. That is woman as I think she should be!" (*Women* 153). Delacroix's unabashed sexism did, however, allow his painting to convey something about these women's lives that might have been masked by painters more critical of the harem. In Djebar's eyes, his *Femmes d'Alger* opposes some resistance to their objectification because of the way they occupy their bodies and their apartments in seeming indifference to the painter's presence:

> The whole meaning of the painting is played out in the relationship these three [women] have with their bodies, as well as with the place of their enclosure. Resigned prisoners in a closed place that is lit by a kind of dreamlike light coming from nowhere—a hothouse light or that of an aquarium—Delacroix's genius makes them both near and distant to us at the same time, enigmatic to the highest degree. (*Women* 135–36)

These Algerian women do not present themselves to viewers but exist elsewhere for themselves and one another. The painting thus offers Djebar, an Algerian woman writing in French over 150 years after its completion, a fleeting look at a community of women embodied through a dialogue among themselves.

For Djebar, Delacroix intuits the repercussions of his gaze when he revisits the theme—but not the source—of *Femmes d'Alger* fourteen years later in a painting of nearly the same name.[12] This second *Femmes d'Alger* "better brings out the latent sense of the painting," she observes, by distancing the viewer from the women to emphasize their isolation. The women on the canvas have lost the veneer of self-presence that intrigued Djebar in the earlier work: "They remain absent to themselves, to their body, to their sensuality, to their happiness" (*Women* 137).

Already, the women have been reduced to pawns in the battle between colonizers and colonized. Like Fanon in his work on the veil, Djebar emphasizes that the advance of colonialism in Algeria imbued the harem with additional signification as a site of resistance to precisely the kind of appropriating gaze that Delacroix seems to cast on its inhabitants.[13] But while the strict invisibility of Algerian women may have frustrated the colonizers' efforts at winning Algerians over to their way of life, it resulted in an ossification of Algerian culture that eroded women's agency: "Thus, while outside an entire society partitions itself into the duality of the vanquished and the victorious, the autochthons and the invaders, in the harem, reduced to a shack or a cave, the dialogue has become almost definitively blocked" (*Women* 141). In this frozen society, the space that women once very much occupied becomes a simple prison from which women seek to escape in the only way possible, by pretending neither to see the walls that confine them nor to hear their echo, by absenting themselves from their bodies.

Less remarked by critics than Djebar's reinterpretation of Delacroix's and Picasso's *Femmes d'Alger* is her brief treatment of Algerian women's oral culture as a record of women as active spectators. Describing a "song of Messaouda," a call to arms that emerged from an 1839 battle between tribal groups with opposing loyalties in the Franco-Algerian conflict, she suggests that women were critical participants in the early confrontations among tribes spawned by French attempts to extend their control beyond the capital of Algiers. Extrapolating from the traditional lyrics that sing the young girl's praises, Djebar credits to Messaouda the victory of her tribe, faithful to the celebrated emir ʿAbd al-Qādir (Abdelkader), who united Algerian tribes in opposition to the French. Of the song, she writes: "a variation, certainly, on heroism and tribal solidarity, but above all here the establishment of a correspondence between a body in danger (through completely improvised movement) and a voice that calls, challenges, and scorches. In the end, it is a delivery from the temptation to cowardice and enables one to discover a victorious outcome" (*Femmes* 157).[14] Women's participation in early battles, their bodily confrontation with the enemy, Djebar claims, promoted a creative development of the relation between women's bodies and their voices. Once the French conquest of Algeria became total, however, any such creativity vanished: "In the oral culture of Algeria, primarily in the thoroughly occupied small towns, there develops the almost unique theme of the wound, which comes to replace the lively unpredictability of the expression of ironic desire, in poetry, in song, and even in the patterns of the slow or frenzied dances" (*Women* 141). In *Fantasia*, then, Djebar's project becomes the creative excavation, with any archaeological tools she finds at hand, of this dynamic relation between Algerian women's bodies and their voices.

Although the lyricism of Djebar's language is largely lost in the translation, the compelling tactility that has become the hallmark of her writing in *Fantasia* and beyond already marks this epilogue, as if to reactivate the creative forms of resistance stifled in the aftermath of Algeria's definitive colonization. Like Mernissi, Djebar specifies that in the postindependence era the voicing of women's burden of oppression no longer suffices. Instead, Algerian women must once again craft expressions of desire, new movements of and for their bodies that will urge them and their fellow Algerians on to seemingly impossible accomplishments. Still, where Mernissi presented a narrator self-assured in her guilelessness and strategically confident in the progress of history, Djebar produces fractured narratives related by fragmented, self-doubting, and flawed narrators. For her, Algerian women were not able to fashion themselves anew in the struggle for independence, in large part because of the taboos that were thrown up around women's bodies. She attributes, albeit somewhat obliquely, the silencing of the triumphs of Algerian women to a sense of shame that results from the objectification of the female survivors of torture and rape as symbols of defeat. Despite the public outcry on both sides of the Mediterranean raised against the torture and rape of Algerian women combatants in the war and the more recent revelations that many ordinary Algerian women also suffered this fate, Djebar notes that Algerian women of the postcolonial period have failed to celebrate their sister combatants as triumphant heroines.[15] Unless Algerian women can create new languages of embodiment to displace motherhood as the only sanctioned form of recognition for women's bodies, Djebar's work everywhere presciently cautions, the victory of Algerian independence will return to them as a defeat.

Djebar therefore looks further back in time than Mernissi for the creative vitality that may furnish women with the means to establish a discursive continuum and enable them to reinvent the present and future. It must be emphasized, however, that if Djebar and the narrators of her subsequent works recover some hope from the encounters and battles that accompanied the arrival of the French in Algiers, they do not yearn to replicate their ancestors' lives. Countering the impulse to romanticize the existence of those women as seemingly untouched by modernity, a romanticization against which Gayatri Spivak has cautioned, Djebar casts her narrators' escape into the uncertain light and noise of the colonizers' language as irreversible and necessary.[16] Whereas the harem women of the disgraced former Turkish official found themselves translated by Delacroix into a language that did not accord them any subjectivity, Djebar masters the language of the conqueror in such a way that she makes palpable its absencing of the Algerian women to whom colonizers once offered it as a lifeline. For, she demonstrates, not only does the French language harbor its own sexism, but also the expressions of desire that it legitimates remain alien to those whose bodies and voices have been differently socialized. Djebar therefore cautions that a young Algerian woman cannot escape the harem simply by turning to the couple idealized in French culture: "[D]istancing amounts to shifting the location of her muteness: she exchanges the women's quarters and the old community for an often deceptive one-on-one with the man" (*Women* 148). This line encapsulates a critical stage in the personal story of Djebar's narrator in *Fantasia*, a stage at which she explores the possibility of forging a community of women that does not lead back to the harem. There, her narrator positions herself not as a guide but as a modern-day Dinarzad seeking to awaken her sisters to speech.

Waking

In *Fantasia*, Djebar thus searches desperately for a Shahrazad to transform again the existing representations of women at home as well as abroad. If in *Women of Algiers* she writes relatively conventional short stories featuring women of different backgrounds during the war of independence and its aftermath through the late 1970s, in *Fantasia* she introduces a French-educated, writer-historian narrator whose life story resembles her own and who self-consciously mediates the stories of other Algerian women's lives. This narrator, who intersperses autobiographical reminiscences of her education in languages and cultures (an *éducation sentimentale*, if you will) and narrative scenarios of the conquest and liberation of Algeria with interviews of rural women who lived the war of independence, emphasizes throughout her inability to tell the very stories of other Algerian women's lives that are her subject matter. In the epilogue to *Women of Algiers*, Djebar declares: "Only in the fragments of ancient murmuring do I see how we must look for a restoration of the conversation between women, the very one that Delacroix froze in his painting" (*Women* 151). Near the end of *Fantasia*, she performs this kind of restoration by juxtaposing women's voices in an innovative composition. There, however, Djebar's narrator still oscillates between the conviction that she is helping to give her interviewees back to themselves by spurring this conversation and the fear that she is further alienating them from their communities: "Your voice is caught in the trap; my French speech disguises it without clothing it. I barely brush the shadow of your footstep! . . . Torch-words that light up my companions, my accomplices; from them, they separate me once and for all. And beneath their weight, I am expatriated" (*L'amour* 161).[17] Carrying the weight of a bloody colonial history, the French language acquires a materiality that prevents the narrator from embodying herself fully as an Algerian woman. Through the opacity of that language, which nonetheless frees her body from seclusion and permits her voice to enter the public domain, she struggles to encourage other voices to take possession of and transcend a double legacy of violence. This task requires of her the formulation of an ethical, nonappropriative relation to others, a sisterly vigilance. But the paradigmatic storyteller to whom she could cede center stage has yet to emerge, and she, writing in an enemy tongue, necessarily always falls short in her endeavor.

Benefiting from a skillful English translation that succeeds in conveying the intimate texture of Djebar's writing, *Fantasia* has gained wide readership and become a mainstay of women's and postcolonial studies courses.[18] Nonlinear in structure, lyrical and *recherché* in its language, and critical of postindependence narratives of progress, Djebar's novel indeed exemplifies the "fractures caused by colonization and gender inequality" that Donadey contends dominate work at the intersection of feminist and postcolonial studies.[19] *Fantasia* has thus generated a respectable body of critical work, with some scholars, such as Woodhull, criticizing the pessimism of the novel's conclusion, in which the narrator announces her premonition of a new era of violence against women: "Yes, in spite of the tumult of my people all around, I already hear, even before it arises and pierces the harsh sky, I hear the death cry in the *Fantasia*" (*Fantasia* 227).[20] Yet if Woodhull contends that Djebar does not allow for non-Eurocentric models of subjectivity, Clarisse Zimra praises Djebar's counterappropriation of the French language: "She uses the colonizer's language against the colonized's own gender code, showing it for what it is, an argument *ad feminam*."[21] Meanwhile, John Erickson argues that in *Fantasia* Djebar transcends the "ideological limitations" of French to open up a linguistic space that allows for a "dialogical engagement" of Algerian women with history, and Jarrod Hayes discovers a subversive gender theory at work in Djebar's complex manipulation of language: "There is no natural body behind the veil waiting to come out, no body outside language. . . . In her writing, unveiling involves taking on another veil."[22] It is this very multiplicity of meanings that intrigues in Djebar's writing, for as she struggles to incorporate women's voices, she fabricates a maze of incipient narratives and sometimes contradictory significations.

Djebar's narrator concludes the first brief chapter of the novel—a quick summary of her desire's evolution through a forbidden exchange of love letters, a subsequent courtship, and the erotic fulfillment of marriage—with a symbolic explosion of narcissistic self-assurance: "I blew the space within me to pieces, a space filled with desperate voiceless cries, frozen long ago in a prehistory of love" (*Fantasia* 4–5). The scattered fragments of this explosion become the chapters of the novel, in which the narrator delves into the histories that mold her particular relationship to the languages of Algeria, to other Algerian women, and to herself. Although Donadey credits Djebar with establishing a subversive, female *isnād*, or chain of authority, the narrator of *Fantasia* is also acutely attentive to the misreadings of intention and authority (fatal and felicitous) that writing in the French language (that all writing) generates.[23] Just as happens to the women of Delacroix's painting, Algerian women's entry into the terrain of French writing bespeaks their imminent disappearance. As she considers how language is tested by the bodies that it seeks to delimit and that fashion themselves through that language, the narrator foregrounds an experience of disembodiment as the common thread that binds her to Algerian women past and present. The novel thus comprises a kind of quest for an *écriture féminine* that does not depend on an essentialized experience of the female body, for a writing of desire that would permit her and her Arabo-Amazight sisters to embody themselves, yet not limit the forms that embodiment might take.

Although the title of *Fantasia* again evokes a painting of Delacroix's— this time his *Fantasia, ou exercices militaires des marocains* (1832)—the novel's concern lies rather with the consequences of a particular instance of this "equestrian entertainment of Arab horsemen" referenced in the novel's epigraph.[24] Taken from nineteenth-century painter Eugène Fromentin's travel narrative *Une année dans le Sahel (Between Sea and Sahara: An Algerian Journal)*, this epigraph inscribes the death cry of Haoua, or Hawā, an Algerian woman struck dead during a *fantasia* by the mount of a spurned lover.[25] Fromentin infuses something of his emotion into his description of the event: "A heart-rending cry arose—I can hear it still as I write to you—then the air was rent with screams, then pandemonium broke loose." Here, this cry, uttered by a woman whom Djebar later dubs the first Algerian heroine of a French-language story, announces not triumphant presence but rather the permanent departure that is death. Yet it reaches Djebar's narrator as an urgent reminder of still-untold tales. In the penultimate chapter of *Fantasia*, itself entitled "Fantasia," Djebar returns to Fromentin's account of his 1852 visit to Algeria, revealing how the elegant painter was more than a transparent spectator in this recently conquered land: "This consummate draughtsman, who excels in hunting scenes, portrays our ancestors surrounded by this soft glow and makes them seem the sad accomplices of his melancholy" (*Fantasia* 224). More important still, she suggests, is his ignorance of the provocation of his own presence, which culminates in the death of Hawā, who openly received a Frenchman after rejecting the warrior of a tribe that had steadfastly opposed the French, to the point of its decimation. Instead of inscribing Hawā's desire (and perhaps his reciprocation of it) in his language, Fromentin transcribes only her proclamation of her mortal wound. Daring to inhabit her body by transgressing the prescribed boundaries of behavior, Hawā, whose name, perhaps not incidentally, means "intense desire, love madness," ultimately found no language to receive her.

By rewriting the tale of Hawā's death, Djebar attempts to forge a new space for Algerian women's existence in the French language, putting herself in the position of the friend to whom Hawā purportedly spoke these final words: "Oh, my friend, I am killed!" (*L'amour* 253).[26] The full emergence of Hawā's presence in and through the story has been prevented, because no one has yet taken up her words, permitting instead the *fantasia*, otherwise futile in its enactment of the gestures of victory in this time of decisive defeat, to silence her: "And this is what is really tragic about the *Fantasia* that Fromentin resurrects: gesticulation of a lost victory, elevation of bodies to the sun in the speed of the cavalcades" (*L'amour* 253).[27] The horsemen take refuge in a mythology of valor, turning to self-defeating acts of revenge. When they trample to death a woman who had approached those wielding the tools of representation that would become so decisive in shaping the French and Algerian identities during the ensuing period of colonization, they turn their backs on the possibility of forging new tools of victory. Over a century later, Djebar's narrator comes too late to save the Shahrazad that Hawā might have been. Through the tale of Hawā's effacement, however, Djebar issues a call to yet unknown Shahrazads, urging them to seize any tools of representation available to them.

H. Adlai Murdoch discovers in *Fantasia* a model for creating a particularly postcolonial subjectivity: "Djebar writes woman as object of desire into woman as desiring subject, drawing on the alienation and desire for recognition which are the legacies of a colonialist discourse."[28] Yet long before she reinvents Hawā's story, the narrator of *Fantasia* ponders the contingency of subjectivity and the ensuing impossibility of recognition, by confronting the illusory plenitude—the promise of self-realization—that her maternal tongue seems to hold out to her. At the outset of the novel, she details a self-loss occasioned by the French language, through which she had gained access to love and sensuality, apparent gauges of self-possession withheld from her in a sex-segregated Algerian culture. Awakening one day from a pleasure long perceived as stolen to a new awareness that her "love" marriage was in fact "arranged" by her access to French education, she finds that she has lost her voice:

> Memory purges and purifies the sounds of childhood; we are cocooned by childhood until the discovery of sensuality, which washes over us and gradually bedazzles us. . . . Voiceless, cut off from my mother's words by some trick of memory, I managed to pass through the dark waters of the corridor, miraculously inviolate, not even guessing at the enclosing walls. The shock of the first words blurted out: the truth emerging from a break in my stammering voice. From what nocturnal reef of pleasure did I manage to wrest this truth? (*Fantasia* 4)

Startled, the narrator discovers that the promise of immediacy and plenitude, of self-fulfillment, has relocated to the mother-tongue of dialectical Arabic, now outside her reach. Her stammering suggests a loss of linguistic self-mastery, a slippage that exposes to her the self-separation at the heart of the French language in which she had fashioned herself. Yet the trick of memory (*mutilation de la mémoire*) that cuts off the narrator's route back to her self proves impossible to circumvent or repair in the chapters that follow. There, she discovers dispossession as constitutive of all language, though in a particularly acute and some-times literal way for women. Eventually, she calls for women to reinvent a language of desire that broadens their possibilities for self-expression while remembering the dispossession that always lurks beneath it.

Sounding Inscriptions

Analyzing how body and language intersect in the ethical theory of Frantz Fanon and Emmanuel Levinas, Ewa Ziarek remarks, "[T]he obverse side of the linguistic constitution of the body is the incarnation of language, which renders this constitution incomplete, indeterminate, and thus not only open to transformation but also exposed to radical exteriority."[29] This is to say that the self is never immediately apprehensible except through language, a language that elaborates rather than simply describes, and that as a physical function language also quite simply depends on the body. As a result, self-possession is always fragile and contingent, acutely so for those with gendered and raced bodies. In a chapter in which she confesses her coldness to any written expression of passion, whether in French or classical Arabic, the narrator of *Fantasia* evinces the profound link between her body and any writing addressed to her as well as her obligation to deny as taboo any writing that alludes to her physicality and thereby invokes quite literally the law of the father. For if her French-teacher father granted her the rare opportunity to study, he also forbade her to receive correspondence from male classmates. It ensues that writing has for her become a way to engage, yet master by recusing, her body's forbidden desire: "I did not write to lay bare my soul, not even for any thrill, even less to express my ecstasies; but rather to turn my back on them in a denial of my body—with an arrogance and naïve sublimation of which I am only now aware" (*Fantasia* 59). Recalling the furor generated by words written in the harem, words that permit something of the body to slip outside its enclosing walls, the narrator again clings to writing as a potential form of self-determination. Instead of sealing herself up in the women's quarters, she seeks a way to reconfigure written language so as to make possible the recognition of selves always wrestling with embodiment as necessary self-expression and taboo, as liberatory and a potential dead end.

Throughout all three parts of *Fantasia*, then, Djebar both thematically and stylistically contemplates the possibility of initiating a language that acknowledges the slipperiness of one's own self-possession while widening rather than narrowing the possibilities of embodiment for others. She concludes her meditation on love letters, received and sent, by establishing the parameters for a new kind of love letter, one that takes the form of a simultaneous exposure of the writer's desire and the qualities of an other who remains ungraspable in his or her fullness:

> To write *facing* love. Illuminating the body to help lift the taboo, to unveil. . . . To unveil and simultaneously keep secret that which must remain secret, so long as the lightning flash of revelation does not intervene.
> The word is a torch; to brandish before the wall of separation or retreat. . . . To describe the face of the other, to maintain his image; to persist in believing in his presence, in his miracle. To reject a photograph, or any other visual trace. The word alone, once written, arms us with serious attention. (*L'amour* 75)[30]

Here, the narrator contemplates the possibility of an inscription of the other that might transform the weapon that formerly annihilated into a tool of redoubled attentiveness. Because she must battle with the signification of the French language that has emerged in Algerian history, her own love letter remains abstract, a tentative approach offering up neither her self nor her other. As beyond reach as such a respectful approach to one's love through an enemy language may seem, however, the narrator does tender a few examples in the first two sections of her novel: one, a postcard from her father addressed to her mother, quietly braves the taboo against naming one's wife in the public domain and is reciprocated when her mother utters her husband's name in conversation with women; another, a commander's remorseful report of his massacre of an entire Algerian tribe, describes "the enemy otherwise than as a horde of zealots or a host of ubiquitous shadows" (*Fantasia* 78). Each of these incidents violates a code of silence, Algerian and military, respectively, by carefully attending to a particular, material existence, female and native, long negated. At the same time, each piece of writing recognizes its limitations, lifting the veil on those beings without seeking to appropriate them.

While cataloging this mode of writing that would respect an embodied existence that defies the age-old dichotomy between mind and body, the above passage appropriates much of the imagery (of the lifted veil and the lightning flash of revelation, for example) of a mystic Arabic poetry that often treads a fine line between earthly and spiritual imagery.[31] Djebar thus seeks out a language of ethics while the poetic quality of her language also pays tribute to a respected Arabic-language tradition of women's elegiac poetry.[32] Yet all throughout *Fantasia*, Djebar reworks familiar Arabic and French genres—historiography, the novel, autobiography, the ethnographic interview, feminist theory, classical song forms, film, and poetry—in such a way as to place a renewed emphasis on how they enable or circumscribe the emergence of embodied subjects. More than a virtuoso display of postmodern bricolage (a literary *fantasia* in both senses of the word), however, Djebar's style presents itself as an urgent necessity. A prescient exploration of women's embodiment in the face of impending violence (the Algerian civil war of the 1990s), it embraces the dispossession inherent in language, French and Arabic, in the hope of defending against a resurgence of the women's literal disembodiment through untimely deaths.

Gayatri Spivak credits Djebar's works with increasing her awareness of how we are always possessed by history: "To an extent, the way in which one conceives of oneself as representative or as an example of something is this awareness that what is one's own, one's identity, what is proper to one, is also a biography, and has a history. That history is unmotivated but not capricious and is larger in outline than we are."[33] In this formulation as well as in her earlier article on *Fantasia*, Spivak, all too conscious of the stubborn persistence of the mind-body duality that has vexed feminist and race theorists, glosses over Djebar's insistence on the bodily inscription of history and identity, cautioning only against a "corporeal rhetoric" that equates women with body.[34] Thus in *Fantasia*, Djebar's task is not just to excavate the history of her identity in a general sense but also to explore the ways in which that history has shaped women's experiences of themselves as constituted in their bodies. Her narrator knows that Algerian women cannot begin the process of shaping future identities, of contesting the way in which their histories of identity, their biographies, are written without putting their bodies on the line. Shahrazad exposed herself like the warrior women whose tales Djebar relates throughout her novels, yet with a difference. Prompted by her sister, she spoke in a language she knew had carried orders for the execution of thousands of women and transformed its words into the tools of their reprieve and, one hopes, eventual salvation. While awaiting the executioner, she undertook the lengthy task of reconfiguring the king's view of women as bodies outside history, of women defined as transgressive physical drives. Her representations opened the king's eyes to the centrality of women in his history, his biography, past and especially future. Yet Djebar's very real Algerian ancestors have been less successful than their fictional precursor; accorded only the most limited and silent access to the realm of artistic representation, they have been effaced in the popular consciousness. Djebar took this lesson to heart in the midst of a growing unrest in her country that eventually resulted in the civil war of the 1990s, when extremists directed particular violence against journalists, teachers, and artists of all kinds.

Even as she works to represent Algerian women past and present, the novel's narrator knows that she is represented and dispossessed by the language in which she seeks to tell her story. Colonization may have transformed French into an Algerian language just as prior colonizations had made Latin and Arabic into North African languages, she notes, but none of these languages took root in Algeria without first pronouncing a death sentence on many of that land's inhabitants. In the first "historical" chapter of *Fantasia*, she therefore writes herself into Algerian history as a character—a physical yet immaterial presence—on the dawn of the day of the conquest of Algiers: "I slip into the antechamber of this recent past, like an importunate visitor, removing my sandals according to the accustomed ritual, holding my breath in an attempt to overhear everything" (*Fantasia* 8). Arriving too late to chronicle more than the absence of these women from historical record, she seeks to exhume the traces of such women who disappeared, through murder or seclusion, with the arrival of French in Algeria. These deaths and disappearances, largely uncounted because the victims did not speak the language in which the conqueror recognized subjectivity, haunt the French language for the narrator. At the same time, she suffers from the sentiment that she cannot reclaim for them a subjectivity in this language that always reinscribes their vanishing. Looking back on her novel as a project of self-constitution, she declares it a failure:

> Autobiography practiced in the enemy's language has the texture of fiction, at least as long as you are desensitized by forgetting the dead that writing resurrects. While I thought I was undertaking a "journey through myself," I find that I am simply choosing another veil. While I intended every step forward to make me more clearly identifiable, I find myself progressively sucked down into the anonymity of those women of old—my ancestors! (*Fantasia* 216–17)

Although she concludes this section by qualifying the French language as a "tunic of Nessus," that robe smeared with poisoned blood to which Heracles succumbed, and is drawn to an Algerian identity defined as oblivion, she resolves to fight anonymity on behalf of her ancestors. Their disembodiment from all history, French and Arabic, imposes itself as an obligation to persist in the writing of their and her history, in the elaboration of their collective biography, even if it speaks only of dispossession.

Complicating the narrator's sentiment of dispossession is her intimate sense that she has lost access to the immediacy of a still strong, dialectal women's language. At times, she reasons that her need for the "mother's milk" of this language exceeds Algerian women's need for her interventions on their behalf in a language so distant and foreign for them that they barely perceive its, and her, existence. For in their eyes, she, too, is disembodied—unveiled and incapable of uttering even the ritual ululations of celebration and lament. The cries that she works into her narrative are instead raw expressions of emotion outside the recognized parameters of women's expression. Time and again, the narrator of *Fantasia* longs for a return to the dialectal language of her youth, a language of love rather than of victimization, where, "[a]t last, voice answers to voice and body can approach body" (129). Yet the narrator recognizes that her taboo-laden native tongue attracts her only to underscore her dispossession: *"I shelter again in the green shade of my cloistered companions' whispers. How shall I find the strength to tear off my veil, unless I have to use it to bandage the running sore nearby from which words exude?"* (*Fantasia* 219). Her characterization of orality as maternal plenitude may lay Djebar open to charges of essentialism and even phonocentrism, but her narrator also recognizes that full self-realization in this orality is impossible, merely a mirage conjured by distance, for the oral language of Algerian women veils her as much as French does. She must of necessity translate herself and her companions between two languages, discovering in this indeterminacy a strategic advantage. Shahrazad's remarkable stories would never have survived to inspire others had not someone passed them on, verbally but also in writing, in whatever language she momentarily possessed. In the process, much was transformed, but a sense of purpose endured, the very indeterminacy of the tales ensuring their appeal to future generations.

Voice Incorporated

In part three of her novel, Djebar applies the term *fantasia* to a graphic collage authored in cooperation with long-anonymous women who helped to shape her biography. It is a collage that openly departs from the conventions of composition, mixing translations of rural Algerian women's oral histories with the narrator's reflections on her personal experiences of enculturation, her disembodiment and miscommunications, and her ruminations on the impossibility of reconciling written French with dialectal Arabic. Algerian women, initially anonymous, narrate their stories in chapters titled "Voice" and "Widow's Voice," followed by the narrator's revelation of their identities and circumstances. Donadey, following Soheila Ghaussy, observes, "The oral tradition enters into written history, and the written text inserts itself into the female, oral tradition."[35] Indeed, substituting for the aural quality of Algerian women's voices with the inadequate vocalized writing system of the French language, Djebar nonetheless strives to refashion the codes of language in order to set one history of identity in communication with another. In the resulting dialogue, the interlocutors would understand their others as integral to their own identity, yet inassimilable to it. Both pessimism and a hopeful urgency therefore permeate this section, which makes apparent how yesterday's war heroines subsist on the margins of 1980s Algerian society, silenced because their stories might trouble the virile myth of heroism that envelops the war of independence.[36] Tentative and circumscribed, Djebar's translation nevertheless permits the women's stories to endure for the time being, awaiting recognition from those who would catch some reflection of themselves or their circumstances in this partial record.

Recorded as well in these passages is how the narrator's personal invitation to speak permits Chérifa, who as a strong-willed young shepherdess joined the freedom fighters, to free herself momentarily from the silent drudgery of a life scrutinized by a mother-in-law, "who prowls around us, hoping to discover what the hesitating narrative reveals: what exigency in the story, what secret, what sin, or simply what is missing" (*Fantasia* 141). This is not the first appearance in *Fantasia* of those older Algerian women who police the behavior of their daughters and daughters-in-law, censuring voice and movement so as to ensure the sanctity of the harem. Because of the spying and disapproving presence of these ancestors determined to maintain the propriety of women's (self-)effacement, so different from those cunning old women who served as lovers' go-betweens in the *Nights*, the narrator rediscovers the advantage of transferring women's voices to another, intermediary language, a secret code as it were. In Chérifa's voice, however, she perceives the signs of another defeat as she wonders how long the much weakened woman's self-liberation will last: "Chérifa aging, in poor health, is housebound. As she sets her voice free for me, she sets herself free again; what nostalgia will cause her voice to fail presently?" (*Fantasia* 141–42). Chérifa's memories of her defiant former freedoms contrast sharply with her present life as a resigned second wife raising another woman's children. Nostalgia for her former strength, or perhaps even shame at a violation so taboo it was never spoken, threatens at any moment to silence her. Djebar thus records both Chérifa's voice and the circumstances in which she speaks, making of them both a source of inspiration and a cautionary tale, not for individual readers, but for the collectivity that is the Algerian nation. A tale of triumph, its loss signals the depth of Algeria's defeat in the postrevolutionary era.

The hope that others might in the future decipher and resuscitate Chérifa's story is not entirely naive, as the narrator's exchange with Lla Zohra, the mother of four *moujahidine*, shows. After Lla Zohra recounts her stories of the war, the narrator, in return, relates the tale of two Algerian dancers and prostitutes whose deaths Fromentin describes in his travel narrative, and in doing so she discovers with her cousin a new thread of common ancestry forged through words. Translating from the French into dialectal Arabic, from the conventions of nineteenth-century literary French into the storyteller's turns of phrase, she awakens the widow's interest in these two social outcasts as if they were her ancestors: "I, your cousin, translate this story into our mother tongue, and tell it now to you, sitting beside you, little mother, in front of your vegetable patch. So I try my hand as temporary storyteller" (*Fantasia* 167). Spivak finds in this scene an exemplary message for the postcolonial intellectual, "that to achieve autobiography in the double bind of the practice of the conqueror's writing is to learn to be taken seriously by the gendered subaltern who has not mastered that practice."[37] Lla Zohra's very subalternity, her lived experience of marginality, permits her to hear the story of the two prostitutes as part of her own history, even though she fought against the French with whom they were judged to be collaborating. Neither disapproving ancestor nor spy, she instead takes up the role of accomplice vis-à-vis the marginalized narrator. This narrator wonders that Fromentin did not fix the uninhabited bodies of the two dead prostitutes permanently on a canvas, leaving instead their elusive traces in a written account in which their descendants might find and reclaim them. As for herself, though taken seriously, she does not pretend to the role of communal storyteller, preferring instead to speak briefly in the darkness in order to prompt others to deploy their voices in turn. Interestingly, this momentary success as a storyteller earns her a physical embrace that recalls a childhood experience of plenitude as well as Dinarzad's presence in the nuptial chamber: "The nights I spent in Ménacer, I slept in your bed, just as long ago I slept as a child curled up against my father's mother" (*Fantasia* 167). For the time being, the king is absent; the stories are for the two sisters alone.

The narrator experiences a similar embrace on the far side of Algerian history when she comes across the inscribed words of a French woman. In the letters of Pauline Rolland, exiled to Algeria in 1852 for her participation in the revolution of 1848, Djebar's narrator discovers an almost tactile record of cross-cultural community forged in a common experience of dispossession.[38] In a lengthy, noteworthy passage, she reads one of Rolland's letters home to France as evidence of a foundational exchange between women on opposite sides of the Mediterranean:

> I met this woman on the terrain of her writings: she and I are now clasped in each other's arms, our roots entwined in the rich soil of the French vocabulary. I re-read these letters sent from Algeria: one sentence catches my eye, lovingly inscribed, covering Pauline's life: "In Kabylia," Pauline writes in July 1852, "I have seen women treated as beasts of burden, and others odalisques in a rich man's harem. I have slept at the side of the former on the bare ground, and beside the latter amid gold and silk. . . ."
>
> Affectionate words from a woman, pregnant with the future: they give off light before my eyes and finally set me free. (*Fantasia* 223)

The simple lines that Pauline writes to an anonymous destinary propose respectful attentiveness, a desire to approach other women by acknowledging how they live their bodies rather than by remaking those women in her image or possessing them. Her words encompass the diversity of women's material conditions in an Algeria not yet entirely "subdued," while expressing her society's own practices of physical effacement and silencing. Because she writes on the verge of death, a final disembodiment, rather than in a moment of triumph, Pauline writes alongside, rather than over, Algerians' own defeat. Embracing her through the words that record her own dispossession, Djebar designates Pauline an ancestor by example of Chérifa, Lla Zohra, and the other Algerian women who were willing to sacrifice themselves for independence only to suffer postindependence effacement. Pauline's letters—not detailed and complete, but suggestive and open—and her retroactive rehabilitation by feminist scholars outline for the narrator a future for the Algerian women whose voices she has captured so imperfectly. She is a forerunner of lives and words to come.

Yet the section dedicated to Pauline is but the antepenultimate chapter of *Fantasia* and precedes Djebar's darker account of Hawā's death. The very last chapter, innocuously entitled "Air on a *Nay*," evokes a landscape decimated by war and littered with dismembered corpses, the dying Algeria that Fromentin once described. From that landscape the narrator recuperates a macabre trophy, the severed hand of an Algerian woman that Fromentin had previously culled from the debris only to toss aside a short while later: "Later, I seize on this living hand, hand of mutilation and of memory, and I attempt to bring it the *qalam* [pen]" (*Fantasia* 226). In this image of the narrator's striving to reembody this hand through language, the language of its presumed murderer, in which it surely would never have imagined writing, Djebar encapsulates all the complexity of her endeavor. Though this section is heavily marked by violence, past and future, its tone is not entirely hopeless. The narrator's symbolic gesture shows how even death will not put an end to Algerian women's stories, that they will continue to seek out any means of expression by which to take possession of history, past and present. Moreover, by insisting that language, whether written or oral, is never definitively embodied, it relaunches the optimism necessary to any such endeavor. Recasting in positive historical terms the subversive power of literate women described in the novel's opening chapter, the narrator's grasp of her unknown ancestor's hand proclaims that she will continue to write against the containment of women in the harem or elsewhere. The awakening she attempts is more radical by far than that performed by Dinarzad, for it resolves to thwart her premonition of the coming death cry with a *fantasia* composed of a thousand women's stories. She steps into the part of Shahrazad in spite of herself.

5 ∞ Shahrazad at the Vanishing Point

A thousand and one nights had slipped away in these innocent entertainments. They had even helped to allay the stubborn prejudices that the sultan held against the fidelity of women. His spirits had softened; he was persuaded of Scheherazade's merit and great good sense. He recalled the courage she had displayed by voluntarily becoming his wife, unmoved by fear as she confronted the death she knew awaited her the following day, as it had the others who preceded her.

These considerations, along with the other qualities he had discovered in her, finally moved him to spare her. "I well see," he said to her, "lovable Scheherazade, that your little tales are inexhaustible: you've entertained me with them long enough; you've calmed my anger, and I renounce of my own volition, for your benefit, the cruel law I had dictated to myself. I restore you entirely to my good graces, and I want you to be regarded as the liberator of all the girls who were to be immolated for the sake of my just resentment." The princess threw herself at his feet, and kissed them tenderly while showing all the signs of the liveliest and most perfect recognition.

—*Antoine Galland,* Les mille et une nuits

Framing Fantasy

At the conclusion of the *Nights*, Shahrazad falls silent. In both the first European-language translation of Antoine Galland and the (in)famous English translation of Richard F. Burton, Shahrazad sheds her role of storyteller as one gratefully abandons a burdensome task.[1] Whether she has critically supplemented her verbal lessons by obedient and chaste behavior or by bearing three sons with astonishing discretion, the Shahrazad of the European-language translations at last submits with joy to a now more even-tempered King Shahrayar. Once she has altered the king's disposition toward women, she abandons the wiles—or, more positively, the shrewd intelligence—that permitted her to survive in order to return to more traditional wifely duties. The respectfully devoted Shahrazad of Galland's last night and the proudly silent, spectacularly attired, runway model Shahrazad of Burton's conclusion coalesce into two still-influential paradigms of Arabo-Muslim women: that of the submissive, silent wife and that of the exotic, highly sexualized harem beauty.[2] In the final word, both Shahrazads evince but a timid feminism that leaves them still the captives of a despotic system, beneath which they quickly vanish in the colonial era.[3]

This final glimpse of Shahrazad has been influential and lasting. It has facilitated the virtual effacement of the storyteller as speaking agent and her replacement by images of static harem beauties and silent (mysterious or oppressed) veiled women during the years of colonization and beyond.[4] Yet today more than ever, thanks to cultural globalization, artists and activists from the Islamic world have begun to superimpose alternate images of Arab and Muslim women over these older ingrained ones. In France, the country of the first European-language translations of the *Nights* and the chief colonial power in North Africa, aggressive challenges to such stock images by young people of North African descent have in recent decades begun to infiltrate mainstream music, film, literature, visual arts, and even television, leaving their imprint on politics.[5] The literary production of *beur* (French teenage slang for Arab) youth demolishes the myth of assimilation by exposing double standards and ingrained stereotypes as vestiges of a sometimes brutal colonial history many have tried to forget.[6] Directly or indirectly, these *beur* artists reject with finality the silent denouement imposed on Shahrazad, and even on King Shahrayar. They too, however, must remain constantly on their guard against renewed commodification and objectification of their images.

Most of the artists of this movement, which began in the 1980s, focus on the gritty day-to-day realities of youth in the housing projects of suburban Paris, Lyon, Marseilles, and Toulouse. They foreground lack of educational and employment opportunities, the desolation of suburban projects, gang violence and culture, the rising tide of Islamic fundamentalism, and the frustrations of young women negotiating the expectations of conservative, sometimes uneducated, working-class parents and "secular" French culture. By contrast, the *beur*-centric novels of Franco-Algerian writer Leïla Sebbar, who belongs to an older generation of immigrants and North African writers, reject the semiautobiographical, realist style and rap or hip-hop aesthetic of many *beur* works. Instead, they foreground the visual culture that has saturated all levels of French society, accompanying, absorbing, and refracting colonial history, anti-colonial wars, and economic globalization. Born and raised in colonial Algeria, daughter of an Algerian father and a French mother who were schoolteachers there, Sebbar moved to Paris shortly before Algeria's 1962 independence in order to study literature. Although a French citizen whose class background differs from that of many of her protagonists, Sebbar grew familiar with the immigrant youth culture of the 1980s and 1990s through her work with organizations such as *Sans Frontière*, a newspaper destined for a working-class immigrant readership, which attracted the participation of a number of North African intellectuals and artists. In her "Sherazade trilogy"—*Sherazade: Missing: Aged 17, Dark Curly Hair, Green Eyes (Shérazade: 17 ans, brune, frisée, les yeux verts)* (1982), *Les carnets de Shérazade* (The Notebooks of Sherazade) (1985), and *Le fou de Shérazade* (Mad for Sherazade) (1991)—she invokes the heroine of the *Nights* tales in order to reflect critically on the nature of subjectivity in and through a contemporary culture of representation.[7]

Sherazade, a teenager of Algerian descent raised in France, materializes against a backdrop of stock images of harem women, Muslim, African, and Caribbean immigrants, runaway teens, residents of housing projects, drug dealers, prostitutes, and the urban youth culture. Sebbar's three novels trace the limitations of visual media as a means to disrupt such formulaic reinscriptions of otherness. Mimicking in many ways the screenplays of French New Wave cinema, referring constantly to photography, fashion, and Orientalist painting, Sebbar's novels confront the objectification inherent in the medium of film as well as in the visual arts more generally without, for all that, employing a single visual image of their own (apart from the cover art selected by various editors).[8] As a result, each of the novels in the trilogy explores in a singular manner the power of words versus image in the visually saturated world of late twentieth-century France. As they mimic or allude to, rather than expressly reject, the power of the visual, Sebbar's novels position themselves as at once complicit in and resistant to self-reflexive, postmodern visual culture. Meanwhile, they forever foreshadow and then withhold any finalizing resolution to Shahrazad/Sherazade's story.

A young woman raised entirely in France, Sherazade speaks little Arabic, knows Algeria largely through childhood vacations and her parents' memories, and seems to retain of Islam only a sense of the physical gestures with which believers accompany their prayers. A few sentences sketch for readers the conditions of her existence prior to her flight to Paris, never fully explicating her motives. Although early on identified as North African or exotic by other characters, Sherazade differs from her peers primarily because of her interest in French colonial-era representations of Algeria and Algerians. These representations, which she at times carefully catalogs, ultimately tell readers little about her own character but much about what French consumers of culture would have made of women like her at various moments in French colonial and postcolonial history. Sherazade may appear less than perfectly French to many, but she possesses no sense of a real Algerian identity distinct from her French self. In the first novel, *Sherazade*, the eponymous heroine resolves to travel to Algeria, but the subsequent *Les carnets de Shérazade* reveals that she never makes it to that mysterious land evoked by her fading childhood memories. Moreover, when she finally does journey to the Middle East, Sherazade finds herself othered by virtually everyone she meets and all that she encounters. Sherazade, then, lays no claim to a national, cultural, religious, or linguistic identity that might resist Euro-American cultural, political, and representational hegemonies. Still, somehow always marked by the elusive category of ethnicity, this Sherazade, like her namesake, entertains and diverts by tapping into and contesting the presuppositions of her audience. In so doing, she exposes the failure of past social and political movements as well as the traps posed by an emerging identity politics that would validate itself through appearances rather than concrete forms of agency.[9]

Mixed Metaphors

In her three novels, Sebbar thus deploys and tests the kind of hybridity theory that marked postcolonial theory of the 1980s and 1990s. Untouched by the fundamentalist Islam that began to sweep through North African immigrant communities in the late 1980s when Marxism lost its power as a model of socioeconomic reform, the characters of Sebbar's novels briefly toy with the radicalism of the 1970s only to abandon it when they grow disillusioned with the few opportunities for self-expression it offers them.[10] Instead, many of them survive and even thrive by expressing themselves in ways those in positions of power expect of them. As is apparent in the following passage, which details the French bourgeoisie's interest in these youth, Sherazade and her companions consciously assist in the commodification of their own culture:

> They weren't required to have brilliant university careers or be well-connected. They were invited for themselves, for the charm and grace they exhibited when they danced and chatted, when they put themselves out to please. They knew how to be the life and soul of a party. They were good fun. The new [cultivated and aesthete bourgeois] circles, with their good education and excellent taste, were prepared to let themselves be exploited, for one evening, by these crazy, cocky, captivating young things, most of whom were born in the concrete jungle of the suburbs. They had nearly all been involved at some time or other in the petty crime or major criminal activities common in their native housing [projects]. They were fascinated by the outward signs of everything up-to-date, always attracted by anything flashy, but sufficiently critical to wear or use it with their tongues in their cheeks; they went in for anything that came directly from the USA, music, electronics, clothes, but were choosy and the label *"Made in USA"* was not enough. . . . These gangs of outlandish young things might herald a new craze; they mustn't be neglected, you never know, you must stay in the swing—and when your job involved display, the social comedy, society games, it was essential to keep your eyes open. (*Sherazade* 125–26)[11]

While this hybrid, immigrant youth wields a measure of social and economic power, they do so as consumers with a potential for being transformed into objects of consumption by those designers, photographers, advertisers, and marketing executives who seek them out at such parties. They resist conventional models of Frenchness only to favor a kind of North American-style globalization. Youth who desire to go further, to exceed their assigned roles as exotic, cutting edge, and entertaining by calling for social change or by challenging the rule of the marketplace, are quickly dropped from the scene and the pages of Sebbar's novels, with the possible exception of Sherazade.

It is not that Sherazade's companions, acquaintances, and squat mates pass unscathed through lives of penury and unemployment; some prostitute themselves or sell drugs to survive; others fall victim to overdoses, abuse, and despair. Still others are betrayed by their own success, abandoned once their looks fall out of fashion. The few successful among them prove adept not at controlling their own appearances but at creating a steady stream of demand for certain products of the entertainment industry or luxury goods, as is the case of Krim, the motorcycle designer hired by a Japanese firm. Again and again rejecting the scenarios in which others desire her to play a leading role, Sherazade more than any of the others seems to grasp that the sole power available to the youth is all show, at best guaranteeing individual success but not initiating any kind of fundamental social change. Yet Sherazade's interests do not turn directly to politics. Instead, while her friends endeavor to sabotage mainstream culture by producing a marketable alternative culture of fashions, rock music, designs, and visual art, she explores the "high" art of literature, museums, and opera, the culture of those in power, perhaps. When Sherazade does dabble in politics by briefly joining a revolutionary cell, she finds its members carefully scripting their acts according to influential artistic representations of revolutionaries, "playing" their roles for maximum recognition as well as visual effect. The breakdown of the cell appears predicated more on a clash of aesthetics than on ideological differences, or perhaps, Sebbar implies, they are the same thing. At the end of the first novel, Pierrot, the older and more traditionally Marxist leader of the cell, apparently commits suicide. His unexplained and absurd end owes much to Jean-Luc Godard's film *Pierrot le fou,* itself replete with references to famous paintings. Consequently, the first novel concludes by seemingly affirming the circularity of representation, rejecting with some finality the possibility of a radical break with the images of the past.

The cosmopolitanism of these young immigrants seemingly exemplifies a hybridity and use of mimicry that some postcolonial theorists have praised for its subversiveness.[12] Yet Pheng Cheah raises a critical point about agency when he chastises hybridity theorists for their embrace of "culture as nature's final end for humanity." Drawing a parallel between hybridity theory and the philosophies that informed colonialism, Cheah asserts: "[H]ybridity theorists subscribe to the same concept of normative culture as the old-style philosophical cosmopolitanism they reject: the understanding of culture as the realm of humanity's freedom from the given."[13] Sebbar's trilogy, by contrast, reveals only to what degree the characters of Sherazade and her peers are circumscribed by culture, how much they are culture's products, and how unyielding that culture is in spite of what initially appears to be their free play with it. For his part, Cheah contends that at best hybridity theories possess only a power to demystify, adding: "Any extrapolation from this negative use of hybridity to articulate a general theory of transformative agency inevitably exaggerates the role of signification and cultural representation in the functioning of sociopolitical life and its institutions."[14] Of course, Sherazade, unlike the migrants of whom hybridity theorists write, is a fictional character whose very point is to highlight the role of cultural representation in French social and political life. Not surprisingly, the fictions authored by immigrants who have indeed grown up working-class and in the housing projects paint a darker, more conflictual picture of *beur* life in France. Yet these too are commodified, by cultural enthusiasts who see in them either a touch of exoticism or the continuity of a tradition of French hard-knocks coming-of-age tales, but also by sociologists and politicians who find in them evidence of the failure of French policies of integration and a window into the sources of religious fundamentalism, delinquency, and violence.

What, therefore, sets Sebbar's trilogy of novels apart is an implicit reflection on their status as mere representations. That is, they present themselves as works of art, subject to appropriation in turn, yet with limited power to represent this generation of immigrant youth politically. By situating the action of the first two novels and, to some extent, the third within the context of the social movements and historical events of 1980s France, Sebbar renders the improbable adventures of the strong-willed, tight-lipped, teenage runaway Sherazade more probable. Yet as the novels increasingly draw attention to the limits of their own representational techniques, Sherazade's ever more fantastic adventures amplify both her fictionality and that of Sebbar's novels. The trilogy distinguishes itself from the works of most of the *beur* writers who emerged during the same period, not in its foregrounding of those populations designated liminal by French history and visual representations in film, on television, and in advertisements, but in the novels' insistence on their status as fiction. It is as if Sebbar disputes not just the positioning of the others of France but also the interpretation of their cultural production as ethnographic objects first and foremost. Her novels, then, deliberately scramble the boundaries between the commodification of hybridity within the narrative and the narratives as commodity.

Through the Looking Glass

Sherazade differs from her namesake in that Sebbar endows her with the consciousness that images speak louder than words. In a number of other ways as well, Sherazade stands apart from her ancestor: largely silent, she refuses to reassure or to stay put; she roams throughout

Paris, France, and the Middle East, eluding all admirers. At the outset of *Sherazade*, the young heroine encounters Julien, a young *pied-noir* (a person of European origin who made his home in colonial Algeria), computer scientist, and amateur Orientalist, who unflaggingly pursues her throughout the trilogy. Just as Sherazade bears little likeness to Shahrazad, refusing to tell the men in her life the stories that they so long to hear, so does Julien little resemble King Shahrayar. Although a somewhat predatory, older man, enamored of the odalisques of Orientalist paintings, Julien lacks the power to control Sherazade's movements or to demand that she account for them, and Sherazade largely leaves him in the dark, even as he acts as her guide to Orientalist art. In the second novel, the as yet untranslated *Les carnets de Shérazade*, Sherazade offers to slip into the role of her namesake by telling a French truck driver stories in exchange for transportation through France. Still, to Gilles, the truck driver, Sherazade's North African heritage matters far less than the fact that she is a runaway, a class of young women with which he has had too many negative experiences. Rather than a supremely skilled narrator, Sherazade emerges as initiator of a rather idealized dialogue that transcends ethnic and class distinctions, borrowing from identity politics in order to rise above them. Once again silent in *Le fou de Shérazade*, Sherazade travels throughout Lebanon and Israel, confronting apparently real violence (whether or not this is part of the film Julien and his friend are shooting remains unclear) in the face of which words seem to exert little influence. Spectacle does, however, and Sherazade once again finds herself a pawn in an infinitely refracted battle for the control of representations.

Combining short sentences and concise descriptions with a contemporary, even colloquial, language (but with little of the often perplexing *verlan*, or French teenage slang), Sebbar's novels convey the flavor of contemporary, urban adolescent life. While they incorporate abundant references to Orientalist art and literature, they do so in a manner of avowed familiarity with critiques of colonialism and Orientalism. Indeed, many readings of Sebbar's trilogy have centered on the main character's subversive, active engagement with Orientalist artifacts, whether written or visual, exoticism, and colonial practices.[15] Yet while the novels' approach encourages readers to assume a position of skepticism with regard to Orientalist imagery, their persistent mimicking of and references to film, in particular French New Wave film, reinscribe Sherazade's objectification. Sherazade's physical appearance, particularly her fetishized green eyes, occupies a central place throughout the narratives, as if she were the leading actress in a movie. Sebbar describes her actions and interactions almost as if writing a screenplay, relating how her main character appears to others but rarely conveying her inner thoughts, so that there is no psychological development of the character even across the three novels. Meanwhile, numerous *mises-en-abyme*, or scenes within scenes, in all three novels depict Sherazade and her friends confronting those who would objectify them. The ramifications of this filmic quality of Sebbar's trilogy have been largely ignored by critics, yet they exert enormous influence on how Sherazade continues to be read by many, sometimes wishfully, as representative of a Muslim-French immigrant youth, and this despite increasingly urgent evidence that many such youth, perceiving themselves as wholly alienated by both French and global culture, are turning to far more militant articulations of identity.

Motion Picture

The first scene of *Sherazade* might well have been written as a screenplay. A dialogue between Sherazade and Julien, it concentrates on Julien's impression of this young girl who has begun to fascinate him, offering readers a number of "visual" clues to her character. In this ostensibly asymmetrical dialogue, Julien remains physically invisible; indeed, the novels never dwell on his appearance. Here, then, not much is said, but a great deal is revealed:

> "Your name's really Sherazade?"
> "Yes."
> "Really? It's . . . it's so . . . How can I put it? You know who Sheherazade was?"
> "Yes."
> "And that doesn't mean anything to you?"
> "No."
> "You think you can be called Sherazade, just like that? . . ."
> "No idea."
> He looked at her, standing the other side of the high, round counter at the fast-food, unable to believe his eyes.
> "And why not Aziyadé?"
> "Who's that?"
> "A beautiful Turkish woman from Istanbul who Pierre Loti was in love with, a hundred years ago."
> "Pierre Loti I've heard of. Not Aziyadé."

"He dressed as a Turk and learned the Turkish language for her sake. He even went to live in the poor district of Istanbul to see her in secret. Aziyadé belonged to the harem of an old Turk. She was a young Circassian slave, converted to Islam."

"Why you telling me about this woman? She's got nothing to do with me."

"She had green eyes, like you."

"That's not a reason."

Sherazade was drinking her Coke out of the can. She wasn't listening anymore. Julien Desrosiers went back to reading the [classified] ads in *Libération*. (*Sherazade* 1–2)

Julien's Orientalist references clash with the setting of the fast-food restaurant in this conversation with Sherazade; globalized youth culture and Orientalist "high" culture confront each other. Sherazade's perfunctory responses to Julien's inept pickup lines suggest that the old codes of Orientalism are losing their grip. Indeed, Julien's reference to Sherazade's namesake and the brief summaries of the frame tale in all three novels propose that Sebbar's readers may themselves be unfamiliar with the *Nights,* much less such relatively obscure works as Pierre Loti's *Aziyadé.*[16] While Julien ostensibly tries to style himself as a contemporary of Loti, Sherazade expresses not the slightest interest in playing the role of Aziyadé. Meanwhile, the homogeneous setting of the fast-food restaurant accentuates Sherazade's indifference to Julien's propositions, suggesting that his references harbor few repercussions for today's youth. Their respective pre- and postconversation activities (listening to a Walkman, reading the classified ads in the newspaper) seem remarkable only for their lack of complex signification.

It seems as if any intrigue between the two characters might be over before it has begun. Yet the scene raises the question of whether the global capitalist culture emblematized by the fast-food restaurant and Sherazade's can of Coca-Cola really constitutes progress over the vestiges of colonialist representations apparent in Julien's questions. Several remarks and details in the scene reveal that the characters of Sherazade and Julien by no means represent mutually exclusive worldviews. Somewhat surprisingly, Sherazade avers some knowledge of Loti. Julien, for his part, may be a fan of Orientalist works, but his perusal of the classified ads in the far-left-oriented newspaper *Libération* suggests a commitment to progressive politics.[17] At the same time, his presence in the fast-food restaurant also gestures toward the demise of the leftist politics of the generation of '68 (those that inspired the founding of

Libération) in the face of an ever more rapid and comprehensive economic and cultural globalization. He seems to fantasize sacrificing all for Sherazade in a romantic gesture that resembles Loti's, yet in the almost sterile environment of fast food she hardly seems to possess the glamorous attributes he seeks. Is Sherazade a spokeswoman for globalization or an example of resistance to it?

In the French version, as in the English, the title *Sherazade* imitates a missing person's report, consisting of a brief, relatively generic, physical description of its heroine. Julien's conversation with Sherazade underscores her green eyes, the feature that again and again attracts the notice of those Sherazade encounters in the course of her adventures. The remainder of this three-page chapter, however, foregrounds just how semantically charged another aspect of Sherazade's appearance is for Julien. It introduces a series of narrative flashbacks that proceed from a certain cheap, inconvenient, red and yellow scarf with shiny tassels that Sherazade wears. Unlike her physical characteristics, this article of clothing reflects Sherazade's identity as she styles it; throughout the three novels she and her friends seek out, put on, and discard a variety of "looks" as their notions of themselves and their function in a given situation vary. For the Sherazade of the fast food, then, the cheap scarf, "favored by Arab women from the Barbès neighborhood and those fresh from the backwoods who haven't yet been attracted to the scarves sold at Monoprix stores that imitate designer label ones with muted colors and abstract designs," recalls a pride in roots that have themselves lost their authenticity in the wake of globalized mass production (*Sherazade* 2). Sherazade's "perverse joy" in wearing the scarf arises from the way it sets her apart, not just from the French, but also from those immigrants who seek to assimilate French culture in its cheapest manifestations, all while making a mockery of sumptuous Orientalist representations of the Orient. Less overtly militant and idealistic than the kaffiyeh, the Palestinian scarf, that Sherazade once wore, this scarf is nonetheless susceptible to a variety of economic and political significations.[18] All show, its mass-produced gaudiness roughly imitates the luxurious Eastern silk textiles that long fascinated Europeans, while its obvious cheapness betrays the contemporary poverty of its wearers.

Sherazade wears the scarf in tribute to those women who daily continue to live the consequences of colonial history, but her self-irony sets her apart from them. Julien, meanwhile, surprisingly becomes the ideal reader of this declaration of identity. In his reflections it grows apparent that he and Sherazade share more in common than first meets the eye and that their respective stories have already connected:

> She tied another knot in her scarf and it was only then that Julien thought of the picture he liked to linger in front of, all by himself, as no one ever stopped to look at these women . . . the *Women of Algiers*. That scarf with its debased Oriental appearance, too yellow and too red, and just to look at it you could sense the poor-quality synthetic fiber, because this girl tied it in front of him, like the Arab women in the little village of Oranie, in the courtyard and the schoolhouse where his father taught, in the *mechtas* where his mother took him when she went to nurse the women and children, Sherazade's hands, her fingers that pulled the ends of the scarf into a knot that would not come undone straight away and then as an afterthought making a double knot, these gestures moved Julien so much that he had to hold on to the edge of the table. (*Sherazade* 8–9)

Julien shifts now to the pictorial reference of Delacroix's *Femmes d'Alger,* still objectifying Sherazade. Yet he grasps perfectly the meaning of the scarf, and her gestures rather than her looks trigger his memory, suggesting that this is more than simple objectification. Indeed, Julien's reflections reveal that his ties to Algeria are as strong, and authentic, as Sherazade's.[19] Were it not for his French nationality he would be more Algerian than Sherazade herself, for he refers to Algeria as "back home" in a way that Sherazade, raised in France, never will.

Julien's memories of colonial Algeria stir up reminders of a history painful for many *pieds-noirs,* who after residing in Algeria, sometimes for several generations, were forced into exile in France following Algeria's independence. Early chapters in this first novel revolve around Julien's memories of his mother's work as a nurse and his father's profession of schoolteacher in colonial Algeria and their defiant activism on behalf of Algerian independence. These memories are not those of a colonist angered by the loss of his land or social station, by his exile and his erasure from French history; rather, they express regret at the loss of a potential identity that defied the elusive line between Occident and Orient, a line that Orientalist art generally reifies. Curiously, Julien inherited his first paintings of odalisques from his mother, a woman who was intimately acquainted with the harsh realities of Algerian village women's lives and who must have found in these works some expression of a lost idealism regarding Algeria. These images of a shadowy, feminized Orient thus evoke that (mythic) time before Julien's identity was fractured by exile. Indeed, Julien prefers the distant, dreamy, inaccessible (and fully clothed) women of Delacroix's *Femmes d'Alger* above all others. Sherazade, her scarf, and her gestures prompt Julien to recollect his past and in some ways hope to return to it. At the same time, her own fractured identity, as the text reveals again and again, suggests to Julien that together they will elaborate a new kind of postcolonial identity.

Unable to convince Sherazade to stay with him, Julien fixates on her image, obsessively photographing her, for example. The Sherazade of the first novel, however, is neither static image nor soothing story-teller but rather moving picture, a moving picture for all the men in her life who would like to script her actions but especially for Julien, who has the greatest power to do so. Like a fetish, she serves Julien's desire by enabling him to deploy his fantasy. Evaluating the usefulness of psychoanalytic constructs of fantasy for feminist film theory, Elizabeth Cowie emphasizes that fantasy operates by staging, rather than fulfilling, desire: "Fantasy involves, is characterized by, not the achievement of desired objects, but the arranging of, a setting out of, desire: a veritable mise en scène of desire."[20] Significantly, Julien never issues an ultimatum to Sherazade, never insists that she choose him and only him. On the contrary, he hovers attentively in the background, following Sherazade at a respectful distance throughout her adventures in the two subsequent novels. For the time being, he revels in any glimpse of her life that she offers him, enthusiastically proposing that she select her own poses for his photographs and that she coscript a film on which he is working. Julien's real need thus seems to lie not the possession of Sherazade but in the never-ending scenarios that she is able to represent for him, scenarios that challenge the paradigms of power, race, and culture that supported colonialism. Free to pursue her adventures, Sherazade exemplifies the possibility of transforming the colonial past and the colonial identities that trap Julien as well as her in a new, contemporary culture. In this manner, she re-members in the only way possible for Julien that sense of unfractured identity that he forever lost when his family left Algeria. By contrast, any attempt to constrain Sherazade's movements and affections would chain Julien to the colonial past and its divisive power dynamics. He would only confirm with finality his loss.

Consequently, Julien does everything possible to support Sherazade in her adventures, even leaving off his pursuit of her when she requests it. Yet in the final novel, Julien seems to betray Sherazade abruptly by falling in love with Yaël, a green-eyed Israeli woman descended from Algerian Jews. Foregrounding Yaël's own green eyes and ties to Algeria, Sebbar confirms Lacan's remark that "the phantasy is the support of desire; it is not the object that is the support of desire."[21] Julien himself muses as he looks over photographs he has taken of Yaël: "If Sherazade is alive, if he finds her . . . And now Yaël . . . It's enough to make him believe that he can't keep himself from living his fictions. . . . Or the contrary" (*Fou* 88).[22] Just as Julien fears that he is about to lose Sherazade and with her his sustaining fantasy, Yaël appears to revive it anew. By virtue of her physical features, Yaël acts as another fetish that enables Julien to represent an alternate constellation of identities that emerge from the colonial past, to live his fantasy of postcolonial Algerian identity in yet another way.

Already in *Sherazade*, however, Sherazade divines her function in Julien's life when she grows exasperated with the photographs of herself that Julien has posted throughout her apartment and rips them from the walls, methodically tearing the thick photographic paper into small bits as she informs him, "I'm sick to death of seeing my mug everywhere, you understand . . . you don't need me in the flesh after all" (*Sherazade* 169–70). For Anne Donadey, this scene exemplifies Sherazade's effective use of violence to counter the oppressive representations that men would make of her: "The Other's actual presence is in excess in the economy of colonial desire. Sherazade's violent act allows her to break through Julien's colonial unconscious."[23] Sherazade's destruction of some of Julien's photographs (she leaves those he has stored in boxes untouched) is, however, hardly parallel to an earlier scene to which Donadey compares it. There, Sherazade impulsively smashes a photographer's camera at a party when he orders her to pose as an exotic harem girl, in order, according to Winifred Woodhull, to realize a "fantasy of *possessing* the daughter of the powerful vizier sexually, while *dispossessing* her as a maker of cultural meanings."[24] By contrast, Julien photographs Sherazade in poses of her choosing, his very obsession with photographing her over and over revelatory not of a desire to fix her being but rather of a somewhat idealistic goal to contemplate all the possibilities of her becoming. Psychoanalytic theory has long shown us that the other's presence in the economy of desire is always excess. Sherazade's demolition of the photographs only fleetingly exposes the dimensions of a desire that far exceeds Julien's.

Because Yaël is an Israeli citizen and Sherazade in many ways more

French than Algerian, the Algerian identity for which Julien longs is indeed a fully imagined construction. Significantly, Julien never falls for a woman in whom Algerian birth, cultural, and legal identity completely converge. Instead, he seeks out women themselves denied access to the imagined fullness that coinciding legal and sentimental identities would confer. Like his own, Sherazade's national identity does not match her lived experience; although Julien was born in Algeria and spent his childhood there, he is legally French (Algeria did not exist as a distinct nation while Julien lived there, in what was legally considered a department of France), while Sherazade, who has spent almost her entire life in France, remains legally Algerian. Yaël, who was born and raised in Israel and whose Jewish parents would have been accorded French citizenship in colonial Algeria, faces identity politics of a different kind in a state that often denies the Arab origins of its citizens.[25] The two women thus also constantly reinscribe Julien's loss in more ways than one at the same time that they seem to represent its potential overcoming. As Slavoj Žižek explains of the fantasy scenario, "[T]he phantasmatic narrative does not stage the suspension-transgression of the Law, but *the very act of its installation*, of the intervention of the cut of symbolic castration—what the fantasy endeavors to stage is ultimately the 'impossible' scene of castration."[26] Indeed, Sherazade's reiterated but never definitive rejections of Julien reenact that moment in which a newly independent Algeria declared its state religion Islam and its official language Arabic, excluding those who, like Julien, were not Muslim. Yet in the strict sense, this declaration also excludes Sherazade, who speaks only a bit of dialectal Arabic, and certainly Yaël and her family.[27] In the scenarios he plays out with Sherazade and Yaël, then, Julien grasps at an identity—by turns national, sentimental, cultural, and ethnic—that must always remain just beyond his reach. In the end, the attainment of identity, one's full occupation of it, appears as no more than a play of representations, a fantasy that masks self-loss.

Sebbar's careful characterization of Julien's family as supporters of Algerian independence differs sharply from treatments that attribute to this population a darker nostalgia for colonial history. Benjamin Stora points out that as French citizens in colonial French Algeria, the *pieds-noirs* were perceived as a homogeneous group representative of French rule, regardless of the socioeconomic status, political convictions, and cultural, ethnic, and religious (Catholic, Protestant, Jewish) backgrounds that distinguished them among themselves. When they were "repatriated" to France in 1962, they initially received a rather cool reception from a population that preferred to forget the drawn out war in Algeria and those they held responsible for it. Nonetheless, on the whole the *pieds-noirs*, entirely cut off from an Algeria in which they had lived for generations, quickly integrated economically and socially into French society, sometimes embracing an extreme nationalism that pitted them against North African immigrants and their children.[28] An older, well-educated, financially secure male, Julien enjoys material and social privileges that anyway cast him as far more powerful than Sherazade, so that at times his obsession with her bears all the marks of *Lolita* with an "Oriental" twist. For readers, then, Julien easily slips into the role of villain, a predator who threatens Sherazade's nascent independence. Sebbar mitigates this impression by reversing expected roles somewhat: Julien's firsthand knowledge of Algeria and pictures of the Orient transmit to Sherazade something of the lives and experiences of preindependence Algerian women, positioning him, rather than her, in the role of native informant. Through this reversal of roles, both he and Sherazade continue to set out a larger social fantasy, one in which those who lost with the demise of colonial rule as well as those who were formerly oppressed by it join forces and assimilate together without violence into French society, contributing to its cultural richness and infusing it with new dynamism.

Julien's character reinforces a reading along these lines when he articulates his vision of multiculturalism to Sherazade: "'I do believe that France is becoming a multi-ethnic society. . . . Those of original French stock will become the new minority in a few decades,' Julien said with a laugh, 'and all because of girls like you'" (*Sherazade* 205). Still, in Sherazade's repeated, if indirect, refusals to cooperate with Julien's representational projects, Sebbar introduces a critique of such easy visions of a multicultural France. In his efforts to record Sherazade's adventures as exemplary, Julien resembles those royal judges within the *Nights* who decreed that their petitioners' stories be recorded for all posterity. Yet in both the first and last novels of Sebbar's trilogy, his efforts to visually transcribe Sherazade's exploits and fix her character do more to obscure Sherazade behind screens of fantasy. To argue that readers can distinguish the real Sherazade from Julien's fantasies, however, is but to fall prey to a romanticization of her otherness that the novels play on and undermine throughout. Sebbar therefore maintains Sherazade as a shadowy character of indeterminate nature, open as the stories of the *Nights* are to a host of appropriations. She depicts her heroine always in motion, in new contexts, and, finally, embedded in so many layers of representation as to defy even the remotest illusion of realism. The conclusion of the first novel in the trilogy implies that the only graspable attribute of Sherazade/Shahrazad is the legacy of what she has meant in French history and culture.[29]

Rewind

Just when nearly everything about Sherazade has been cast into doubt, the second novel of Sebbar's trilogy intervenes with a reassuring portrayal of an ultimately triumphal, up-to-date Shahrazad. *Les carnets de Shérazade* for the most part eliminates techniques of *mise-en-abyme* and metanarrative so prevalent in the first novel, also temporarily relegating the character of Julien to the background. It introduces French truck driver Gilles Rivière, a working-class French everyman, in the role of would-be leading man. Unburdened by complex fantasies and memories of irrevocable loss, Gilles is initially and sometimes amusingly unaware of the Orientalist legacy in which he becomes entangled through his association with Sherazade. While her name initially signifies nothing to him, her type, the runaway, is intimately familiar to and disliked by him. He therefore scrutinizes her conversation for any attempt to "lead him on" and remains poised to ditch her at the slightest provocation. A counterpoint to the urban, educated, neurotic Julien, Gilles harbors no intellectual pretenses, dreams rather conventionally of relocating to a tropical island, and makes no effort to record Sherazade's presence. In the "true stories" she relates to Gilles, Sherazade engages, in a contemporary and Western context, the themes that play a central role in the *Nights:* the inequality of the sexes in social and political life, real and symbolic violence, class and race. The growing friendship between Gilles and Sherazade illustrates how two groups, the working class and immigrants, share much and have much to learn from each other despite the increasing shift of the former (and even the latter) from the political left to a nationalist and often xenophobic extreme right.[30]

Those familiar with the outcome of the *Nights* know in advance that Sherazade will confound the truck driver's expectations and win his admiration and love. Indeed, she emerges clearly victorious in this novel, less concerned with her looks (although she avails herself of every opportunity to visit Orientalist paintings along the way) than with a sort of cross-cultural dialogue. Gilles reveals the complexity of his own cultural background as he and Sherazade retrace the path of the 1983 Beur March, an event that raised awareness among the general French population of the racism and discrimination faced by the children of North African immigrants.[31] As Sherazade prompts Gilles to reconsider his negative assessments of runaways, to wonder at the people and things he encounters along his route, and to reflect more critically on his country's history, they establish a kind of solidarity. Yet their solidarity does not elaborate itself on the basis of economic, political, or even social grounds. Instead, the solidarity of the immigrant Arab Sherazade and the working-class Gilles emerges through culture. As the novel progresses, Sherazade introduces an increasingly receptive Gilles to opera and the visual arts as well as to the music, pastimes, and fashions of immigrant youth. Culture thus functions in Sebbar's novel as a means of transcending difference, as an alternative to various groups' strategic employment of a common difference to create a coalition of interests. *Les carnets de Shérazade* thus presents its characters as primarily functions of culture, that fluid category that begins to usurp the older categories of religion, race, class, and national identity at precisely this period. Despite its greater adherence to the conventions of realism and its specific engagement of gender issues, then, this second novel of the trilogy presents Sherazade's journey as an exemplary cultural artifact, as the idealized rescripting of a less than ideal social history.

As they journey across France, Gilles gradually grows aware of the scenario in which Sherazade seemingly obliges him to play the role of sultan. When he confronts her, it is with mixed amusement and annoyance; he needles her by pointing out that she is not faithful to the role she has assigned herself even while he rejects the part of oppressor in which she has cast him:

> Sherazade stiffened in anger and clenched her fists. Gilles said that the woman in the *Thousand and One Nights*, he had read excerpts, he remembered her now, the one who told the stories to the despot, is a soft and flexible woman, not like her . . . aggressive. . . . If he couldn't joke . . . He wasn't obliging her to speak to him . . . to tell him stories; he wasn't going to rape her or kill her at dawn after a night of lovemaking. (*Carnets* 103–4)[32]

In these statements that he makes less than halfway through *Les carnets*, Gilles recognizes, despite himself, the enduring power of colonial representations of self and other that he initially believed did not concern him. Unlike King Shahrayar, he momentarily perceives himself through Sherazade's eyes as someone also defined by those pervasive representations that emerge from the juxtaposition of his profession, class, and gender. Thus, although less focused on the visual than the two novels that frame it, *Les carnets* as well underscores the difficulties in dislocating or altering dominant representations. Sebbar traces the power of return of all kinds of representations by examining how they shape present-day identity claims. Implicitly responding to those on the far right who look to the purity of a medieval France as represented by Joan of Arc, Sebbar places in Sherazade's mouth throughout the novel reminders of centuries of Arab presence in what is today southern France. Thereby evoking a legacy of cultural exchange that belies narratives of France's contemporary degeneration as a result of "foreign" influences, Sebbar also underscores just how reality and artistic representation are continuously bound up with each other. Finally, Sebbar effectively rewrites the conclusion of the *Nights* in two significant ways in this, her contemporary, adaptation of its framing narrative. First, dismantling the myth of the white male as neutral subject, she shows through Gilles that no one may presume to stand and act outside prevailing sociopolitical realities that are informed by and inform ideology. Second, instead of falling silent, Sherazade parts ways with Gilles, now rather in love with her, vanishing, presumably to continue her adventures.

Broken Frames

In *Le fou de Shérazade*, the final novel of the trilogy, Sherazade apparently ventures from France to the Middle East and back, her character as well as all those with whom she interacts exemplifying both perpetual difference and the possibility of conciliation. Sebbar blurs distinctions between Sherazade as autonomous character and Sherazade as a product of Julien's fantasy by relating throughout the novel the events of a film (which may or may not be directed by Julien and his friend) whose subject is the making of a film. As a result of this uncertain convergence of the reader's perspective with that of the long ambivalent character Julien, as well as a multiplication of intertextual references and *mises-en-abyme*, different degrees of representation become indistinguishable from one another, placing in question once again the role of artistic representation in the shaping of everyday realities. Any attempt to distinguish between the events (often wildly implausible) that befall Sherazade outside of the film and those staged events that she acts out for the film leads back again to the originary artifice of the novel, for to differentiate between the "real" Sherazade of the previous two novels and the Sherazade who is now a character in a film would entail choosing between two fictional representations on the basis of equally fictive criteria of accuracy. By thus stripping away every illusion of realism in this, the culmination of Sherazade's adventures, Sebbar appeals to her readers' complicity in a social fantasy as yet without resolution.

The definitive instability and uncertain future of the character of Sherazade within Sebbar's trilogy underscore how networks of representation mediate and even fabricate the public's understanding of reality both abroad and at home. *Le fou de Shérazade* addresses explosive political tensions in the Middle East and in France by exploring how those on all sides seek to manipulate media, especially visual media, for their own political ends. In this final volume, conflict is driven by and waged over and through visual representations transmitted in seconds around the globe. Throughout, Sebbar reveals how the media's constant presence and quest for images initiate and sustain the very events to which the media claim to bear witness.[33] In these final adventures, Sherazade figures as both object of representation and representing subject, sometimes both at once. Thrust into a milieu in which the stakes of representation—of the media and art as well as local politics—seem a matter of life and death, Sherazade, who on the basis of her study of visual art, film, and literature had envisioned herself triumphing in one role or another, finds herself involuntarily scripted into any number of quite different roles that confront her with an unanticipated, and overwhelming, polyvalence of significations. Adapted even less to this environment than to the France of the first two novels, Sherazade once again forges her path through visual, literary, and this time religious representations. In essence, then, *Le fou de Shérazade* revolves entirely around the reading, in every sense of the word, of Sherazade.

In *Le fou de Shérazade*, Sherazade's savvy blending of cultural influences denotes her as an outsider to all on a terrain where deadly battles are being waged over ethnic, religious, and cultural identities. In contrast to France, where multiculturalism is held up by some as a broadening of old notions of French identity, the Lebanon that Sherazade visits figures as a formerly vibrant multicultural nation abruptly fragmented by sectarian violence and the revindication of absolutist identities. Her playful hybridity holds little currency there, at best confounding the soldiers who take her captive almost immediately on her arrival. Bearing no resemblance to the noble freedom fighters of post-independence Algerian mythology, these drunken soldiers carry her off, planning to rape her, mocking her name and berating her for her unladylike presence in a grove of olive trees. When a seemingly more legitimate militia rescues her from this imminent rape, the very accoutrements of her various roles—the pistol, notebooks, books, and postcards of Matisse's *Odalisque à la culotte rouge*, with which she played at revolutionary, scholar, storyteller, and artist of the self—suddenly confer on Sherazade the unexpected, yet potentially deadly, fictive identity of an Israeli spy. Taking Sherazade hostage, the members of the militia eventually recognize the error of their judgment but are nonetheless unable to pin any other identity on her. Undeterred, their leader circulates her picture to newspapers and television stations as if she were an important hostage, employing this representation of her to counter those characterizations of the Middle East formulated by European media. Of course, in so doing he becomes complicit with the very images of his people as violent barbarians that he criticizes; although he plays the same game as the painters, photographers, and filmmakers that Sherazade has encountered by casting women as bearers of identities, positive or negative, he is much more roundly condemned for the practice. Ultimately, however, no nation's government claims Sherazade, and the militia sets her free, enjoining her to return to her (unspecified) country. The moment Sherazade exits her prison, she steps into the sights of a photographer of her acquaintance, into the very realm of mediated representation that is her character's only true home.

In this final novel, all the parallel narratives (an old woman's journey on foot to Paris in order to recover a centenary olive tree that the film crew has uprooted from her village and Julien's travels in Israel, where he encounters Yaël) are set in motion by Julien and a friend's endeavors to shoot a film about a suburban girl-gang leader, Zina, who is to be played by Sherazade. As is typical in many films of the French New Wave cinema, the subtexts overwhelm the narrative, and the story of Zina remains unrealized. Or does it? For Sebbar's novels draw connections between the often marginalized, immigrant inhabitants of suburban housing projects around Paris and the populations of the past and present Orients among which Sherazade moves, connections that resist symbolic resolution. While waiting for his star and lover to appear, for example, Julien suspends gigantic posters of Turkish baths, odalisques, and nude French women from the balconies of the housing project, provoking vehement reactions from the immigrant women and children who inhabit the project. Young boys attack many of these images, as well as those of the (post)colonial wars, with clods of dirt and spray paint, and the women drape their best veils over the nudes, veils that are then taken by the boys as their canvases. Defined by their actions, the boys appear alternately as culturally impoverished delinquents, macho fundamentalists, and frustrated visionaries, while their mothers seem in turn defenders of women against exploitation and ignorant cultural illiterates complicit in their victimization. In their juxtaposition of competing stereotypes of Arabs, which may seem negative to some and positive to others, these scenes do not take sides to promote one or the other representation. Rather, taking a page from film theory, they suggest how representations function to encourage identification and create meaning.[34]

While film theorists stress the particular qualities of film, however, Sebbar's characters remain confined to print, and Zina, the character Sherazade has been cast to play in Julien's film, never attains even that degree of realization. Conceived as a defiant composite of exotic and journalistic images, a triumphant inhabitant of a lawless urban jungle, Zina's character remains typed in a number of important ways. According to her author, she is to be a "gang leader, rebel, poet, unruly, adept with a knife, expert at karate (like his first [female taxi-driver] heroine), fearless, a fugitive from ZUPs [the development zones], hanging around housing [projects], basements, underground carparks, wandering the streets, as illusive and frightening as a war-leader" (*Sherazade* 236). Zina's name likewise brings together two separate connotations, both of which yet fail to break out of the mold of sexism; in Arabic, Zina (*zīna*) means "beautiful, embellishment, or adornment" but also "the sin of fornication" if read as the transliteration of a different root (*zināʾ*). In French, the distinction is an impossible one. Like the "aggressive 'hardwired' women in cyberpunk," whose ideological appeal Žižek analyzes, the character Zina brings together "contradictory ideological positions, the fetishized male fantasy of a non-castrated 'phallic' woman whose unleashed aggressivity poses a threat to the world, *and* a feminist rebellion against the brutal partriarchal system."[35] In Zina, these contradictions are multiplied by factors of race and class and their attendant fantasies, so that she symbolizes at once a threat to French national identity and the resolution of that threat. Those characteristics perceived as dangerous to the integrity of French sociocultural life when they appear in her male counterparts lend her the appeal of a woman who rejects the victim status often assigned by French society to Muslim women. In the process, she loses the very religious and ethnic identity that positioned her as a threat in the first place. Yet Sebbar's twist is to impede Zina from materializing even on a symbolic level, from emerging as a character in her own right.

Instead, there is only Sherazade, who, while sometimes occupying the place of symbolic solution to irresolvable antagonisms, contrasts strikingly with Zina in her self-conscious staging of fantasy scenarios. In the first novel, for example, she adapts a Zina-esque stance toward her radical squat mates' "revolutionary" feminism:

> She was playing with Basile's .38. The shot went off smack into the left eye of Che Guevara, whose poster had been yellowing for months on the wall. Basile yelled out and snatched the .38 out of Sherazade's hands.
> "Wait, I was going to have a go at the other . . ."
> "What other?"
> "That one, next to Marx . . . I know his face. You see him everywhere."
> "What? Bob Marley!"
> "You're crazy, completely crazy!"
> "What the hell! They're all dead. . . ."
> Pierrot and Basile exchanged glances, taken aback. Sherazade always disconcerted them.
> Sherazade turned to Pierrot: "And now, don't ever call me a [chick] again or I'll do you in." (*Sherazade* 45)

Assimilating the two revolutionary if distinct philosophies of Che Guevara and Bob Marley, united in their opposition to Euro-American material, cultural, and spiritual colonization, Sherazade symbolically declares their time over. In her sights and in those of the populations she represents, Che and Marley have lost their oppositional force and become simply two commodified symbols among others. Yet Sherazade's symbolic resolution is itself all show, for her own militant posture is just that, a role she has learned from the rebel heroines of any number of films. No manifestation of militant feminism, this scene instead delivers a series of clichés, presenting Sherazade as well as Basile and Pierrot as new composites of hackneyed images. Just as we are about to cheer Sherazade's transformative agency, Sebbar again foregrounds her fictionality, leaving social and symbolic antagonisms not merely unresolved but increasingly complex.

In the last pages of *Le fou de Shérazade*, this effect is redoubled and finalized. Throughout the novel, other characters, including her mother and siblings, have been preparing for Sherazade's victorious return home as a film star. Although their expectations are thwarted over and over, not least when Sherazade's image appears on television as a hostage during her sojourn, this homecoming seems gradually to be coming together in the final pages of the novel. The various narrative threads of the novel all lead to the courtyard of the housing project of Sherazade's youth as Arab horses are led onto the set in preparation for a *fantasia*; Yaël, the green-eyed Jewish woman, appears disguised as a horseman from the Algerian South; and the old woman in search of her transplanted centenary olive tree arrives and settles in its shade, the dove that has guided her perched on her shoulder. Few of these details speak to the character of Zina as Julien's friend had conceived her back in the first novel of the trilogy, and the content as well as the form of the much discussed final scene of the film about to be shot remains shrouded in secrecy. Whose vision is represented in this scenario within a scenario purportedly scripted by Sherazade? Sherazade arrives discreetly, remarked by the other characters only when she embraces the woman beneath the olive tree. As the cameras begin to roll, the scenario is again comprehensively transformed: Sherazade and Yaël act out a meeting between an Israeli and a Palestinian journalist in Beirut, the Arab in the role of the Jew and vice versa. Together, they recline on the terrace of a half-ruined mansion with its elderly proprietor and her loyal Egyptian servant, mimicking with important differences, as Donadey remarks, the scene that Delacroix fixed in his painting *Femmes d'Alger*.[36] The elderly woman has just compared the journalists to escaped odalisques, to modern-day odalisques in wartime, when several mortar shells fall into the garden and onto the terrace, demolishing a scene as real as any throughout Sebbar's trilogy and killing all but the servant, who is left screaming at the destruction.

Sherazade's mother and sister rush to the scene in the wake of the bombing. Shaken, her mother cries out and is reassured by her other daughter, Meriem, their dialogue concluding these tales of Sherazade:

> "My daughter! Sherazade! You've killed her! My daughter is dead . . .
> Sherazade, my girl! Answer me . . . They've killed you."
> Meriem shakes her mother, who is sobbing:

"Imma! Imma! You're going mad! Sherazade isn't dead. It's the film . . . Your daughter is alive . . . Imma, don't cry; your daughter's alive . . . Look at her; she's not dead. Imma, Sherazade is alive, alive . . . alive." (*Fou* 203)[37]

The ellipses, which are present in the text, punctuating Meriem's reiterated declaration that Sherazade lives, banish any possibility of drawing a final distinction between the different levels of fiction at work in Sebbar's trilogy. Even to pose the question of Sherazade's survival places us in much the same position as that of Sherazade's mother, who seems naively unaware of the distinction between representation and reality. In conclusion, Sebbar's novels refuse to confer any closure on the social fantasies—of a defiantly multicultural, hybrid society; of transnational, interreligious, and interethnic dialogue—that they have set out for readers. Yaël and Sherazade as journalists who have swapped religions and ethnicities conjure up visions of an understanding and tolerance born of dialogue and openness to the other's experience. Their sudden annihilation in the very moment when it seems that the fiction will offer a resolution of all the conflicting narrative strands and images the novels have elaborated suggests that agency for change lies elsewhere. Like Shahrazad's stories, Sebbar's trilogy relates improbable and entertaining tales that ultimately prompt her readers to reexamine the relation that they perceive between the fictions that entertain them and the world in which they live.

Like Shahrazad, Sebbar attempts to mediate her audience's conviction that "seeing is believing" by showing them the power of words to convey invisible nuances of meaning and intention. Throughout, her Sherazade trilogy demonstrates how representation as art, activism, and business is both guided by and able to harness and shape fantasy, desire, and ideology. As her choice of medium indicates, however, Sebbar's novels impute a demystificatory power to verbal representation. Whether intentionally or not, her engagement of visual media and film not only targets contemporary offshoots of Orientalism but also critiques the prominent role that media, whether Western or Arab, play in shaping reality and fueling conflict. In the characters of the young Arab boys who have been raised in the insular world of the housing project and who have begun to identify fiercely with a people they have never met and a place of which they know only the names of battle sites, Sebbar foreshadows the emergence of the alienated religious extremists who have increasingly captured the attention of world audiences. To the sensationalist images of visual media, Sebbar opposes self-reflexive tales that nearly exhaust the potential scenarios of desire, past and present, to which a character like Sherazade might give rise. Unlike the visual scenarios in which Sherazade refuses to participate, however, her stories culminate never with a promise of self-realization or transcendence but rather with the installation of a loss with which characters and readers alike must come to terms.

Meriem's insistence on Sherazade's survival closes the scene, the novel, and the trilogy. Her words also urge Sherazade to raise herself once again, phoenixlike, from the ashes. In the years since the conclusion of *Le fou de Shérazade*, Sebbar has not revived her heroine, perhaps suggesting that the unending stories of Sherazade/Shahrazad necessarily exceed the representative abilities of a single writer or storyteller, perhaps indicating that it is time for someone new to reauthor Shahrazad again. For although she shows us one facet of the legendary heroine's legacy, Sebbar declines claims to "authentic" authorship. The evidence is there throughout the novels: several times characters who speak Arabic tell Sherazade that the French have dropped a syllable, the most suave, from her name. Yet Shahrazad, a name with Persian overtones, contains no extra syllable but rather an audible *h;* the extra syllable is a European interpolation. Thus Sebbar's Sherazade is not a more faithful translation of Shahrazad but a radical fiction born in the sociopolitical and cultural climate of 1980s France. Her tales do not ascribe any revolutionary transformative agency, whether political or literary, to either herself or her namesake. Shahrazad's strategy was never one of violent, sudden foundational change. Rather, stepping into an urgent situation, Shahrazad began to tell stories without urgency, stories that strove to alter the conditions that created the initial exigency. Sebbar follows her lead, attracting our attention in new ways to the fact that Occident and Orient are irrevocably intermingled, that Sherazade and Shahrazad are fictions with many authors, and that their lessons are for all, not merely for King Shahrayar.

Epilogue ∞ Reading, Listening

AT THE END OF THE 1970s, Moroccan writer Abdelkebir Khatibi spent a sleepless night committing to paper "Nuits blanches," a series of meditations presented as the thousand and third night.[1] A compendium of the scholar's reflections on the lingering fascination that *The Thousand and One Nights* continues to exert over the so-called Western and Arab worlds, his nights are metaphysical rather than literary in their objective. In them, Khatibi isolates and traces the implications of what he deems the guiding principle of the *Nights*, "tell a beautiful story or I will kill you" ("Nuits" 11).[2] He offers his words as an extension of his tired body during a night of frenetic wakefulness, inaugurating his one thousand and third night with a premise he dubs unheard of and outrageous: "And what if to die meant precisely to say no to this supreme principle, for us, the decadent Arabs of today, to say no. What if dying for us (in the beyond of morality and metaphysics) meant this unheard-of negation, still unspeakable: never again another Scheherazade?" (11).[3] By saying no to Shahrazad, "never again to this narrative and this death, this torn hymen, and this sleepless night" (11), Khatibi proposes once and for all to reject the gaudy and seductive Orient of which Orientalism has made Shahrazad the paradigmatic representative.[4] More crucially and according to the strategy

129

of double critique that he has outlined elsewhere, however, he also rejects a circular conception of time that he terms particularly Arab, that is to say Islamic, a conception of time that promises eternal life after death, thus freeing the (male) believer from a confrontation with death and sexuality.

To say "never again another Scheherazade" is not to dismiss Shahrazad. Rather, Khatibi exhorts readers to attend to her carefully: "[T]ake the time to love Scheherazade in the theoretical, highly theoretical, scene that she has immediately already set in motion" (12).[5] Khatibi nonetheless cautions that such attentiveness must resist the temptation to embody Shahrazad, arguing that women in a patriarchal society are forced to ensure their own annihilation and thus can possess no existence proper.[6] In the frame story of the *Nights*, King Shahrayar takes the logic of patriarchal society to self-defeating extremes: after he witnesses his symbolic death when he sees his wife take her pleasure with a slave, his social inferior, he imposes a literal death sentence on the women he suddenly perceives as threats to his social existence. No longer reassured by each successive bride's sacrifice of her virginity, he puts her to death the following morning, reasserting each time his primacy. Shahrazad's intervention, according to Khatibi, reintroduces into the narrative "the labor of death" that the king had thus hoped to elude. She, as woman, speaks as death and in the face of death, compelling him to confront in turn his own symbolic as well as literal death: the loss of his authority through his wife's betrayal and the death of his line. As she speaks, Khatibi specifies, her act of narration opens a precarious space between death and life, a time set apart from the normal cycle of night and day, a hallucinatory time that escapes totalization. She thus exists only in the *futur antérieur*, in that slippery time somewhere between the present that is the telling of the tales and the unknowable future of their conclusion.[7] The injunction "never again another Scheherazade" becomes for Khatibi a means to destabilize thoroughly the (patriarchal) order by which Arab thought and life have been structured, thereby making possible the existence of women in the present.

Terribly seductive, this theory of Khatibi's. And it is emblematic of a critical historical moment that also saw the publication of Edward Said's *Orientalism*, with its groundbreaking critique of a Western scholarship and politics that constructed the Islamic world as Oriental other in order to legitimate the Western self.[8] Khatibi's work takes the repercussions of Orientalism seriously, examining its lingering influence on the thought of the postindependence Islamic world. Resisting the temptation to oppose a more accurate representation to the distorted reflections of Orientalism, Khatibi turns instead to contemporary French philosophy in order to challenge a particular tradition of what he deems "Arab thought," or Islamic influenced philosophy, theology, and literature.[9] As he does elsewhere, in "Nuits blanches" Khatibi uses as his jumping off point a work co-opted by Orientalists, presenting it as the repressed other of Arabo-Islamic thought. Taking up Shahrazad's tale, he accentuates there the sexual anxieties that structure the unfolding events, targeting a theologically based thought that in 1979, in the wake of the Iranian revolution, was fueling a new religious extremism.

Enacting a passionate, sexual embrace of the heroine of the *Nights*, Khatibi foregrounds the sex act as a necessary embrace of death, an affirmation of life in the here and now in opposition to anticipation of self-realization only in the beyond of eternal life. Yet despite its declared affinity with deconstruction and poststructuralism, Khatibi's work also evinces a debt to the thought of Freud and Hegel in its more Orientalist applications. Today—when the effects of different histories of colonization, of struggles and wars for independence, of shifting political relations within and among Arab and Islamic countries, of different schools of Islam, of widely varying political models and resistance movements, and of the effects of economic globalization are swept aside by characterizations of a monolithic, innately violent, and misogynistic Islam—Khatibi's collapse of centuries of Arab and Islamic philosophical, theological, historical, and literary production into an undifferentiated "Arab thought" that promotes violence against women seems especially troubling.[10] For as the authors in this study show, there is now more than ever a need for not just one but multiple Shahrazads, to address all manner of rulers.

Surely, in turning almost immediately to the perspective of King Shahrayar, Khatibi reenacts the very repression of women he criticizes, dismissing centuries of women's activism and words. Shahrazad's agency in his narrative vanishes when her voice in the end is entirely subordinated to a patriarchal model of feminine sexuality. Although she may escape execution, then, Khatibi's Shahrazad does not, for all that, live. As Khatibi recasts her death and life as a foil for, and thus as entirely contingent on, the self-realization of men, he imposes a conclusion on the *Nights* that does not essentially differ from that on which its European translators insisted. The principal problem, though, resides in a detail of the premise from which he sets out, in the "tell me a beautiful story or I will kill you" that Khatibi designates as the supreme principle of the *Nights*. A supremely authoritative injunction, the command could come only from the all-powerful king Shahrayar or one of his doubles in the stories. Yet not even in the most orientalizing version of the *Nights* does Shahrazad speak at the behest of the king. Always, it is Shahrazad who takes the initiative, fearless in the face of death. King, judges, and sultans are all men of action, desirous of witnessing the execution of justice, of seeing the effects of their governance. To them, Shahrazad says: Listen. In her gesture of storytelling lies the simple principle that seeing alone cannot be equated with understanding. Shahrazad and the storytellers who are her doubles within the tales thus teach these commanding rulers and dispensers of justice that the essential will only escape them unless they stop to listen and wonder.

In 1996, in the midst of a period of Algerian massacres that seemed to arise from a suspension of logic that surpassed King Shahrayar's, Assia Djebar revisited the *Nights* tale "The Three Apples." In a story entitled "La femme en morceaux" (The Woman in Pieces), Djebar recalls the fate of that ailing young merchant's wife, mother of three sons, whose husband so loved her that he spared no trouble or expense to procure for her the out-of-season apples for which she had expressed a craving.[11] On the husband's return with three precious apples, the young woman seems to have forgotten her desire, for she leaves them untouched. Then, one day, her husband spots a black slave passing by his shop, holding aloft one of these same apples. Inquiring of the slave where he has obtained this rare fruit, the merchant learns that he has received it from his mistress, whose cuckold of a husband traveled far and paid dearly in order to obtain it for her. Returning home in a rage, the merchant discovers that one of the three apples is indeed missing; when he questions his wife, she responds that she has no idea what has become of it. Convinced that he has been wronged, the husband pounces on his wife and beheads her. Her mutilated body he wraps first in a veil and then in a carpet, placing it in a basket and then in a wooden chest, casting it all into the Tigris. There, the caliph Hārūn al-Rashīd and his vizier Jaffar discover the chest, setting in motion the search for the young woman's murderer and the story. In the meantime, the eldest son of the jealous merchant confesses to his father that he had stolen the apple that morning and that in the marketplace a black slave had taken it from him, laughing at his entreaties for its return.

Djebar's version follows this story for the most part faithfully, intensifying the sorrow of the caliph who discovers the beautiful young woman's body in the chest and according a place to the thoughts and emotions of the young woman before her murder. Significantly, Djebar hints that the young woman's physical decline and her craving results from an undeclared pregnancy, one unwanted by the exhausted, isolated young woman, dependent on her husband and father, cut off from any form of female companionship. In the *Nights*, the fate of the nameless young woman is forgotten as soon as Jaffar discovers that the slave who is to blame for her misfortune is one of his own servants, and he begins to relate a story of even more elaborate coincidence in an effort to spare his servant's life. In the end, Hārūn al-Rashīd frees the slave and makes the repentant merchant one of his companions, according him one of his "choice" concubines. Justice, it seems, is left undone for the anonymous woman, not because the caliph fails to execute her murderer(s), but because her own tale remains unheard, forever silenced. By contrast, in Djebar's story the young woman's tale is transformed into the subject of a young Algerian high school teacher's French lesson, which results in the teacher's own execution and beheading, in front of her class of literature students, by militant extremists. The Baghdad of Hārūn al-Rashīd and the Algiers of 1994 merge in this tale, which urgently foregrounds the need to recall the dismembered body of the woman silenced before she is properly heard, to seek out and revive her missing voice.

In Djebar's hands, this story becomes a refutation of the endings that have so often been imposed on the *Nights*. Severed from her body and placed on the teacher's desk, the young teacher's head continues to speak. Unlike the sage Duban, who figures in one of the opening stories of the *Nights*, this young teacher possesses no book of poisoned pages with which to exact justice on her executioners, already departed anyway. In the stillness that follows her death, she instead employs her fading voice to relate the conclusion of the *Nights*. In her version, Shahrazad begs for and receives Shahrayar's mercy on behalf of the three sons she has born him. Yet coming as it does on the lesson of "La femme en morceaux," in which prolific reproductive capacities are no guarantee of a life lived happily ever after, this conclusion resonates with a cruel irony. Once she abandons her voice, Shahrazad risks becoming as anonymous as the young woman of the story of the three apples, an innocent victim of a violent rage fueled by cruel coincidence. For her

part, the young teacher, Atyka, though married, seems to have no children. Instead, a classroom of bilingual students listens enraptured to
her lessons, adding their analyses in Arabic and French, at once audience and interlocutors. In the aftermath of her execution, one of these
students, a young man, hurries up to the head, from which her fading
voice issues its final words, and demands to hear the conclusion, the
entire conclusion. Afterward, he claims that the teacher's final words
are no longer Shahrazad's but her own and that they exhort the students to pursue the tales: "The night, it is each one of our days, a thousand and one days, here, in our city, in . . ." (213).[12] It is with the quest
of this same young man, who looks from the Algiers of the mid-1990s
to the Baghdad of Hārūn al-Rashīd for the lost voice of his beloved
teacher, for an explanation for her death, for justice, that Djebar concludes her narrative.

If Khatibi's refrain, "never again another Scheherazade," is seductive
for its evocation of a transformed society in which women, no longer
subject to sanctioned violence, share equal social status with men,
Djebar's tale reminds us that this time is not yet here. As horrifying
massacres, as well as everyday, less spectacularly visible violence, continue to erase women's stories throughout the world, it indeed seems
as if the time for Shahrazad to sleep recedes further and further into
the future. Taking as its source the very real massacres, many in the
classroom, of schoolteachers who defied Algerian extremists' orders to
cease teaching, Djebar's tale reminds her readers of the renewed high
stakes of what has sometimes been dismissed as entertainment, as mere
literature. Evoking a continuity of repression, but also of resistance,
across centuries and geographical expanses, the story is both pessi-
mistic and hopeful. Women have often been brutally silenced, it shows,
only to have their stories taken up again by self-appointed successors
determined to find for them an audience.

Many—translators, editors, and writers—have attempted to impose
a definitive conclusion on the *Nights*, to seal Shahrazad's fate once and
for all. Yet simultaneously, others have resisted closure by foregrounding the infinite possibilities and porous boundaries of Shahrazad's words.
Both those who seek to put in place an authoritative version of the
Nights and those who stress the open-endedness of the tales alike seem
drawn by a certain power of words, spoken but also written, that Shahrazad embodies. Simply by making others listen, Shahrazad is able to
change the course of a government. In the hands of others, her story

and stories alternately reinforce boundaries between seemingly separate worlds or break down barriers between cultures; indeed, it would not be going too far to say that by engaging the attention of the powerful, these tales contribute to the fates of entire peoples whose images they shape and reshape.

To her father, the vizier, certain that his daughter's self-assumed mission was suicidal, Shahrazad says, listen to my determination. To the king, self-assured in his justice, Shahrazad whispers, listen to this tale of intertwined circumstances so fabulous your justice could not imagine them. And last but not least, to the virgin awaiting an uncertain fate beneath the conjugal bed, to her sister, Dinarzad, Shahrazad gestures, listen and you will learn of the power of words to alter the course of destiny. Decades after the advent of a poststructuralism that revealed the arbitrariness of the signs that compose language, the foundational absence or lack from which language arises, the contingency of words, we are still listening. For at the heart of storytelling, journalism, writing, filmmaking, scholarship, and teaching there still lies the hope that words wield power over understanding, perhaps over the very course of history—if only someone is listening.

Acknowledgments

LIKE THE BARBER'S TALE, the process of researching and writing this book seemed at times to be endless. For valuable institutional support, I thank Temple University, which provided a research leave in the fall of 2002, as well as a summer research fellowship in the summer of 2003. It also gives me special pleasure to thank all those colleagues and friends, regrettably too numerous to list here, who have had a hand in shaping this book and my ideas and in supporting me throughout the writing process. In particular, I am grateful to Ewa Ziarek for her insightful criticism and support from the time of the book's conception through the long process of its maturation. Lourdes María Alvarez provided exuberance, unfailing patience, and intellectual and emotional support, not to mention assistance with translations, without which this book would never have been what it is today. I especially thank Walid Saleh for introducing me to the Fairuz song from which the epigraph for the book is taken and for his entertaining reminders that stories worthy of the *Nights* continuously play themselves out everywhere around us. The judicious and supportive comments of the two anonymous readers for the University of Minnesota Press proved enormously helpful to me during revisions; any remaining flaws and inaccuracies are entirely my own. Although this work did not have its origins there, I thank my teachers and mentors at SUNY at Buffalo—Rodolphe Gasché, Carol Jacobs, Anne Tomiche, and especially Henry Sussman—for showing me that no story is ever final and there are always multiple ways of telling it. For their timely words of encouragement, I thank Françoise Lionnet and Kalpana Seshadri-Crooks.

I am grateful to my colleagues and students at Temple University for providing me with an energetic environment conducive to scholarship as well as teaching, most especially to Susan Wells, Sally Mitchell, Sheldon Brivic, Paula Robison, and Shannon Miller for their comments on portions of the manuscript, as well as sage advice on the process. I thank my research assistants, Joel Nichols, Mouloud Mansouri, and Patrick Farrell, for their dedication to tracking down bits of seemingly random information. The editorial team at the University of Minnesota Press involved in the production of this book (Doug Armato, Heather Burns, Richard Morrison, and Laura Westlund) has been a model of support and encouragement for which I am exceedingly thankful. I am grateful to Robin Whitaker for her skillful copyediting. For their friendship and shared stories, I thank Ziba Rashidian, Nadia Sahely, and Joseph Clarke.

Finally, for her great generosity, wisdom, patience, and daily encouragement, I thank the (temporarily) silent one. I dedicate this book to my parents, Eric and Marian Gauch, for their unwavering confidence in my ideas and work, for their unhesitating support, and for their timely impatience to learn what comes next.

Notes

Preface

1. The title *A Thousand and One Nights,* or rather "a thousand nights and a night," is the literal translation of the Arabic *Alf Layla wa layla.* The title *The Arabian Nights,* more commonly employed in English renditions of the work, imputes an ethnographic component to the tales. For an illuminating discussion of the origins of each title, see Muhsin Mahdi, *The Thousand and One Nights* (Leiden: E. J. Brill, 1995).

2. Mahdi dates this Syrian manuscript to the fourteenth century and discovers in it ultimately the source of all later European-language collections as well as of Arabic editions from the colonial era onward. In the same manuscript Robert Irwin finds references to fifteenth-century events and, although he supports many of Mahdi's findings regarding the retroactive forgery of Arabic versions of some tales, expresses reservations about its status as source text. Mahdi, *The Thousand and One Nights;* Robert Irwin, *The Arabian Nights: A Companion* (London: Allen Lane, Penguin Press, 1994), 54–62.

3. Quoted in Irwin, *The Arabian Nights,* 49–50. The bracketed modifications to the quotation are Irwin's. Galland, a noted Orientalist who had assisted Barthélemy d'Herbelot in the production of the vast *Bibliothèque orientale ou dictionnaire universel contenant généralement tout ce qui regarde la connaissance des peuples de l'Orient* (Oriental library or universal dictionary generally containing all that concerns the knowledge of the peoples of the Orient), would certainly have had access to this well-known work.

4. Eva Sallis argues that various early European translations of the *Nights* deformed Scheherazade's character by diminishing her intellectual qualities in favor of physical qualities she never possessed in the early Arabic manuscripts. See Sallis, *Sheherazade through the Looking Glass* (Surrey: Curzon, 1999).

5. Ibn al-Nadīm writes of a "Shahrazad" simply "of royal blood." In his account, she is assisted in her stratagem by the king's head of household, Dinar Zad. In a reference from historian al-Mas'ūdī's *Murūj al-dhahab* (Meadows of Gold), Shahrazad is a vizier's daughter who possesses a slave named Dinazad. In the frame story to the European "translations" of the *Nights* and in Galland's fourteenth-century manuscript, Shahrazad is a vizier's daughter, and Dinarzad is her blood sister. For al-Mas'ūdī's reference, see Irwin, *The Arabian Nights*, 48–49. As the preceding indicates, Dinarzad's name is rendered in a variety of ways across different translations. I have chosen to follow Haddawy's lead in my own discussion.

6. Fatima Mernissi, *Scheherazade Goes West: Different Cultures, Different Harems* (New York: Washington Square Press, 2001).

7. Fedwa Malti-Douglas, *Woman's Body, Woman's Word* (Princeton, NJ: Princeton University Press, 1991), 11.

8. For one discussion of the marginality of the *Nights*, see Abdelfattah Kilito, *The Author and His Doubles: Essays on Classical Arabic Culture*, trans. Michal Cooperson (Syracuse, NY: Syracuse University Press, 2001). Although this view persists, largely because the *Nights* remains the most accessible work of Arabic literature in Western eyes, in the Arab world it remains a controversial work, generally sold in cheap, unattributed editions.

9. Chandra Mohanty, "Under Western Eyes: Feminist Scholarship and Colonial Discourses," in *Dangerous Liaisons: Gender, Nation, and Postcolonial Perspectives*, ed. Anne McClintock, Aamir Mufti, and Ella Shohat (Minneapolis: University of Minnesota Press, 1997), 258.

10. Gayatri Chakravorty Spivak, "Can the Subaltern Speak?" in *Marxism and the Interpretation of Culture*, ed. Cary Nelson and Lawrence Grossberg (Urbana: University of Illinois Press, 1988), 271–313.

11. Irwin, *The Arabian Nights*, 63–102.

12. Abdelfattah Kilito, *La langue d'Adam et autres essais* (Casablanca: Les Éditions Toubkal, 1999), 79. My translation.

Introduction

1. The principal Arabic editions of the *Nights* are as follows: Calcutta I (1814–18); Cairo I, or Bulaq (1835); Calcutta II (Macnaghten edition, 1939–42); Breslau (Habicht edition combined with Fleischer edition, 1825–38, 1842–43); and Leiden (Mahdi edition, 1984).

2. Muhsin Mahdi's work on the Syrian manuscript that inspired Antoine

Galland's translation revealed that the favorite tales of Aladdin and Ali Baba were in fact the fabrications of translators. See Mahdi's *The Thousand and One Nights*, 72–86; and Irwin, *The Arabian Nights*, 54–62.

3. For two detailed histories, see Mahdi, *The Thousand and One Nights;* and Irwin, *The Arabian Nights*.

4. Ferial Ghazoul, *Nocturnal Poetics: The Arabian Nights in Comparative Context* (Cairo: American University in Cairo Press, 1996), 2–3.

5. I discuss one possible inspiration for this conclusion in my preface.

6. Mahdi, *The Thousand and One Nights*, 6.

7. In her study of the *Nights*, Eva Sallis traces the transformation of meaning that occurs in Turkish folktales translated into French or English and then readapted again into Turkish. Unfortunately, she does not extend the implications of this analysis to her reading of Shahrazad. Sallis, *Sheherazade through the Looking Glass*.

8. Jorge Luis Borges, "The Translators of the *Thousand and One Nights*," trans. Esther Allen, in *The Translation Studies Reader*, ed. Lawrence Venuti (London: Routledge, 2000), 42.

9. "Is it not portentous that on night 602 King Shahriah hears his own story from the queen's lips?" Borges, "The Translators," 47.

10. "Si l'on veut bien se souvenir que ceci se passe en terre d'Islam, et à une époque où subsistent dans le monde entier toutes les formes de l'esclavage, on demeure confondu par l'audace de vues, l'absence de préjugés qui ont permis au narrateur arabe d'assigner à la femme un rôle que notre moyen âge n'a jamais entrevu et que notre XXe siècle n'envisage qu'avec bien des réticences." Marie Lahy-Hollebecque, *Le féminisme de Schéhérazade, la révélation des Mille et une nuits* (Paris, 1927), reprinted in Aboul-Hussein Hiam and Charles Pellat, *Cheherazade: Personnage litteraire* (Algiers: Société Nationale d'Édition et de Diffusion, 1981), 81. All translations from French, unless otherwise noted, are my own.

11. Fatima Mernissi, *Dreams of Trespass: Tales of a Harem Girlhood*, photographs by Ruth V. Ward (Reading, MA: Perseus Books, 1994), 15n.

12. Ghazoul, *Nocturnal Poetics*, 95.

13. Fedwa Malti-Douglas, *Woman's Body, Woman's Word* (Princeton, NJ: Princeton University Press, 1991).

14. In the original English text of *Dreams of Trespass*, Mernissi has recourse to Burton's translation; in the French translation of her work, she praises Muhsin Mahdi's excellent Arabic version of the work and excuses herself for falling back on a French translation of the Burton in order to remain true to her original. In *Scheherazade Goes West*, she employs Haddawy's translation of the Mahdi manuscript. Fatima Mernissi, *Rêves de femmes*, trans. Claudine Richetin with Fatima Mernissi (Paris: Albin Michel, 1996), 233n.

15. Ghazoul, *Nocturnal Poetics*, 96.

16. "Elle écrivait sur les milieux arabes et juifs de l'Afrique du Nord des romans et des contes à intrigues passionnelles et sombres vengeances ou encore des contes rappelant l'ambiance merveilleuse des *Mille et une Nuits.*" Jean Déjeux, "Elissa Rhaïs, conteuse algérienne (1876–1940)," *Revue de l'Occident Musulman et de la Méditerranée* 37, no. 1 (1984): 47.

17. Ibid., 47.

18. Ibid., 61.

19. Paul Tabet, *Elissa Rhaïs: Roman* (Paris: Grasset, 1982).

20. In his preface to a recent reedition of Rhaïs's novel *Le sein blanc,* Tabet describes his father: "He writes in the shadows, quasi-sequestered in turn; and on the body of this woman, whom he loves, whom he detests, he each night inscribes words, books, that he offers to her like so many tragic versions of the mask and the pen." ("Il écrit dans l'ombre, quasiment cloîtré à son tour, et sur le corps de cette femme, qu'il aime, qu'il exècre, il grave chaque nuit des mots, des livres, qu'il lui offre comme autant de versions tragiques du masque et de la plume.") Paul Tabet, preface to *Le sein blanc,* by Elissa Rhaïs (Paris: L'Archipel, 1996), 10.

21. To be sure, Déjeux speculates, Rhaïs may likely have required the services of a secretary—Raoul Tabet, the nephew of her second husband—to correct her grammar and misspellings; she may not have written all of her own works, and her adoptive son may have been her lover and authored a few later novels published under her name. Déjeux, "Elissa Rhaïs," 73–74.

22. In his preface to *Le sein blanc,* Tabet surmises that the reversal of sex (and religious) roles has fueled public outcry over his revelations (14).

23. Emily Apter, *Continental Drift: From National Characters to Virtual Subjects* (Chicago: University of Chicago Press, 1999), 129.

24. Fadhma Aith Mansour Amrouche, *Histoire de ma vie* (1968; Paris: La Decouverte, 2000); *My Life Story: The Autobiography of a Berber Woman,* trans. Dorothy S. Blair (London: Women's Press, 1988). In order to convey the nuances of the French, I have retranslated the quoted passages.

25. *Amazight* is the politically correct term for the people long called Berbers by the French. The Kabyle are a specific subgroup of the Amazight peoples, living in what today is northeast Algeria and in Tunisia. Jean Amrouche, Fadhma's son, was celebrated throughout France as the poet of Kabyle identity, renowned for his translations of the Kabyle songs he had heard from his mother's lips. Taos Amrouche became the premier performer of these songs and authored several novels, becoming the first Algerian French-language novelist. See Jean Amrouche, *Chants Berbères de Kabylie* (Paris: Éditions L'Harmattan, 1986); and Taos Amrouche, *Jacinthe noire* (1947; Paris: Éditions Joëlle Losfeld, 1996).

26. "Je viens de relire cette longue histoire et je m'aperçois que j'ai omis de dire que j'étais toujours restée 'la Kabyle.' . . . Aujourd'hui, plus que jamais, j'aspire à être enfin chez moi, dans mon village, au milieu de ceux de ma race,

de ceux qui ont le même langage, la même mentalité, la même âme supersti-tieuse et candide, affamée de liberté, d'indépendance, l'âme de Jugurtha!" Amrouche, *Histoire de ma vie*, 195.

27. After Algerian independence in 1962, Arabic became the official lan-guage of Algeria.

28. "Algériennes, Algériens, témoignez pour vous mêmes! N'acceptez plus d'être des objets, prenez vous mêmes la plume, avant qu'on se saisisse de votre propre drame, pour le tourner contre vous!" Kateb Yacine, introduction to Amrouche, *Histoire de ma vie*, 15.

29. Gisèle Halimi and Simone de Beauvoir, *Djamila Boupacha* (Paris: Gal-limard, 1962).

30. Benjamin Stora recounts how the War of Algeria was never named, French authorities preferring to employ euphemism after euphemism rather than acknowledge the gravity of the situation and recognize the will of the Algerian people. Benjamin Stora, *La gangrène et l'oubli: La mémoire de la guerre d'Algérie* (Paris: La Découverte, 1998).

31. The chapter that concludes Halimi's account of Boupacha's case is enti-tled "Ce livre reste ouvert . . ." (This book remains open . . .). In it, she recounts the ongoing refusal of military officials to furnish crucial pieces of evidence (photographs).

32. Two letters that Boupacha wrote to her supporters, reproduced in the book, bear witness to this. Halimi and Beauvoir, *Djamila Boupacha*, 99 and 150.

33. Deniz Kandiyoti summarizes this quandary when she observes, "Women, who were also participants in nationalist movements, felt compelled to artic-ulate their gender interests within the parameters of cultural nationalism, some-times censoring or muting the radical potential of their demands." Kandiyoti, "Identity and Its Discontents: Women and the Nation," *Millenium: Journal of International Studies* 20, no. 3 (1991): 440.

34. See Mounira M. Charrad, *States and Women's Rights: The Making of Post-colonial Tunisia, Algeria, and Morocco* (Berkeley: University of California Press, 2001).

35. For one Algerian woman's perspectives on what came to be called the Algerian civil war, see Zouligha, "Challenging the Social Order: Women's Liberation in Contemporary Algeria," in *Rethinking Fanon*, ed. Nigel C. Gib-son (Amherst, NY: Humanity Books, 1999).

1. Silent Reflections

1. Malti-Douglas discusses at length the play of desire in the *Nights*, cred-iting Shahrazad with inculcating in King Shahrayar "a new pattern of desire which, when transposed to the terrain of sexuality, can be seen as a more female approach to pleasure." Malti-Douglas, *Woman's Body, Woman's Word*, 21.

2. The most famous of these powerful figures is the historical Hārūn al-Rashīd (764–809), ruler of Baghdad at the turning point of the ʿAbbāsid caliphate. He figures in many *Nights* tales as a passionate, though sometimes cuckolded, lover and a popular ruler, always curious to learn more about the private lives of his subjects. For more on his historical role, see the *Encyclopedia of Islam*, 2nd ed., s.v. "Hārūn al-Rashīd."

3. A. S. Byatt, introduction to *The Arabian Nights: Tales from a Thousand and One Nights*, trans. Sir Richard F. Burton (New York: Modern Library, 2001), xiv.

4. Such works, especially paintings and illustrations, are far too numerous and sometimes ephemeral to reference here. Nevertheless, two recent adaptations of the *Nights*, one for television and one for the stage, exemplify the fascination of European and North American audiences with Shahrazad's person. A lavish film originally broadcast as a television miniseries modifies details of the frame story so as to feature more prominently Shahrazad. In it, King Shahrayar has been driven to homicidal paranoia after an assassination attempt by his brother, who covets both Shahrayar's throne and his unfaithful wife. An amateur psychologist of sorts, the beautiful Shahrazad obtains the material for her nightly stories during daily visits to a master male storyteller. *The Arabian Nights*, VHS, directed by Steve Barron (1999; Santa Monica, CA: Hallmark Home Entertainment, 2000). Meanwhile, in Mary Zimmerman's recent adaptation of the *Nights* for the stage, Shahrazad not only narrates the stories but also plays parts within them and sometimes shadows the narrators who are her doubles within the various tales. In this way, she is rarely out of audience's sight. Mary Zimmerman, *The Arabian Nights: A Play* (Evanston, IL: Northwestern University Press, 2005).

5. As Burton informs readers in the preface to his *Nights*, "He will not think lightly of my work when I repeat to him that with the aid of my annotations supplementing Lane's, the student will readily and pleasantly learn more of the Moslem's manners and customs, laws and religion than is known to the average Orientalist, and, if my labours induce him to attack the text of *The Nights* he will become master of much more Arabic than the ordinary Arab owns." Burton, preface (1885), xxxv–xxxvi.

6. The work in this vein perhaps best known to European and North American audiences is Naguib Mahfouz, *Arabian Nights and Days*, trans. Denys Johnson-Davies (New York: Anchor Books, 1995). Ferial Ghazoul offers a concise reading of the allegory Mahfouz proposes in *Nocturnal Poetics: The Arabian Nights in Comparative Context* (Cairo: American University in Cairo Press, 1996).

7. As is the case with the vast majority of African films, films by North African directors seek funding from a combination of private and public sources at home and abroad, frequently from Europe and often France. This has long been an issue of concern to filmmakers seeking to protect the artistic and

ideological integrity of their work. For extended discussion of this issue, see Manthia Diawara, *African Cinema* (Bloomington: Indiana University Press, 1992); and Imruh Bakari and Mbye Cham, eds., *African Experiences of Cinema* (London: British Film Institute, 1995).

8. *The Silences of the Palace (Ṣamt al-Quṣūr)*, dir. Moufida Tlatli (Tunisia: Cinétéléfilm and Magfilm; France: MT Films, 1994).

9. To date, Tlatli's second film is still undistributed in the United States: *La saison des hommes*, dir. Moufida Tlatli (Films du Losange, 2000).

10. Ella Shohat, response to Ferid Boughedir's "African Cinema and Ideology: Tendencies and Evolution," in *Symbolic Narratives/African Cinema: Audiences, Theory and the Moving Image*, ed. June Givanni (London: British Film Institute, 2000), 124. Portions of Shohat's response were originally published as "Framing Post-Third-Worldist Culture: Gender and Nation in Middle Eastern/North African Film and Video," *Jouvert: Journal of Postcolonial Studies* 1, no. 1 (1997), http://social.chass.ncsu.edu/jouvert/v1i1/shohat.htm.

11. Moufida Tlatli, "Moving Bodies: An Interview with Moufida Tlatli," by Laura Mulvey, *Sight and Sound* 5, no. 3 (1995): 18–20.

12. Viola Shafik, *Arab Cinema: History and Cultural Identity* (Cairo: American University in Cairo Press, 1998).

13. For analyses of *Silences* as a complication of national allegories and national identity, see Gil Hochberg, "National Allegories and the Emergence of Female Voice in Moufida Tlatli's *Les silences du palais*," *Third Text* 50 (2000): 33–44; and Catherine Slawy-Sutton, "*Outremer* and *the Silences of the Palace*: Feminist Allegories of Two Countries in Transition," *Pacific Coast Philology* 37 (2002): 85–104. Dorit Naaman, "Woman/Nation: A Postcolonial Look at Female Subjectivity," *Quarterly Review of Film and Video* 17, no. 4 (2000): 333–42, examines Alia's emerging postcolonial subjectivity through the paradigm of feminist psychoanalytic theory.

14. Virginia Danielson has authored a beautiful and authoritative study of the singer, her music, and the Egypt that together they helped to shape. Danielson, *The Voice of Egypt: Umm Kulthūm, Arabic Song, and Egyptian Society in the Twentieth Century* (Chicago: University of Chicago Press, 1997). This book is the inspiration for the film *Umm Kulthūm: A Voice Like Egypt*, dir. Michal Goldman (Arab Film Distribution, 1996).

15. Because the credits flash on the screen during this opening sequence, it is difficult to ascertain whether the effect is intentional. The remaining songs in the film are translated in subtitles.

16. Danielson stresses the influence that Umm Kulthūm wielded over all aspects of Egyptian identity: "She helped to constitute Egyptian cultural and social life and to advance an ideology of Egyptianness." Danielson, *The Voice of Egypt*, 2. See also Shohat's reading of this scene in "Framing Post-Third-Worldist Culture."

17. Laura Mulvey, "Visual Pleasure and Narrative Cinema," *Visual and Other Pleasures* (Bloomington: Indiana University Press, 1989), 14–26.

18. Art historians frequently point out that male figures never appear in harem and Turkish bath scenes, so as not to disrupt the male viewer's sense of ownership and mastery. In melodrama, according to Laura Mulvey, the opposite occurs: "The protagonist, with whom our sympathy and understanding lie, is subjected to the curious and prurient gaze of intrusive community, neighbours, friends and family so that the spectator's own look becomes self-conscious and awkward." Mulvey, "Melodrama Inside and Outside the Home," *Visual and Other Pleasures*, 75.

19. In Tunisia, the rule of the beys was hereditary and their power thus somewhat more autonomous than that of other local rulers directly appointed by the Ottoman sultan. They still ruled at the will of this sultan, however.

20. Mulvey, "Visual Pleasure," 19.

21. Mulvey, "Melodrama Inside and Outside the Home," 70.

22. Tlatli, "Moving Bodies," 18.

23. Organizations such as Human Rights Watch, Amnesty International, and the Committee for the Protection of Journalists continue to cite the Tunisian government for its policies of silencing dissidents through strict censorship policies, confiscation, detention, and harsh treatment of prisoners.

24. The Personal Status Code was promulgated on December 28, 1956, and has been updated a number of times over the years. For more on its underpinnings and implications, see Mounira Charrad's excellent comparative analysis of the approaches to codification of women's legal rights and social roles taken by postindependence Tunisia, Algeria, and Morocco in *States and Women's Rights*.

25. Sovereign Ahmed Bey abolished slavery by official decree in 1846. As *Silences* reveals, however, economic necessity ensured that quasi-slavery persisted in varied forms into the twentieth century.

26. Charrad, *States and Women's Rights*, 228–31.

27. Mary Ann Doane, "The Voice in Cinema: The Articulation of Body and Space," *Film Theory and Criticism*, 6th ed., ed. Leo Braudy and Marshall Cohen (New York: Oxford University Press, 2004), 373.

28. Doane observes that synchronized sound usually creates this effect in feature film. "The Voice," 382.

29. Kaja Silverman, *The Acoustic Mirror: The Female Voice in Psychoanalysis and Cinema* (Bloomington, IN: Indiana University Press, 1988).

30. Ibid., 27.

31. As the elder brother's wife, Jneina would normally occupy the position of associate head of the household, after her mother-in-law. Without a child, more specifically a son, to shore up her status, however, that role has apparently devolved to her sister-in-law.

32. Thomas Elsaesser, "Tales of Sound and Fury," in *The Film Genre Reader*, ed. Barry Keith Grant (Austin: University of Texas Press, 1986), 291; originally published in *Monogram* no. 4 (1973): 2–15.

33. Sandra Naddaff, *Arabesque: Narrative Structure and the Aesthetics of Repetition in the 1001 Nights* (Evanston, IL: Northwestern University Press, 1991), 88.

34. Ibid., 95.

35. Unlike her mother, Alia is also presumably literate, for prior to her flight from the palace Lotfi had begun teaching her to read and write.

36. This film, *Sallāma* (1945), was one of several in which Umm Kulthūm played this role. See Danielson, *The Voice of Egypt*, 107.

37. I have given, with a few modifications, the lyrics as they appear in the subtitles. While the gist of the song is obvious, even native speakers of Arabic would have a difficult time making out the exact wording over the layers of sound, dialogue, and the scene cuts that accompany Alia's performance. The song, titled "Élégie" (Elegy) on the sound track, was written especially for the film by the poet Ali Louati and arranged by Anouar Brahem. "Élégie," *The Silences of the Palace* (Caroline, 1995).

38. Abdelfatah Kilito, *The Author and His Doubles: Essays on Classical Arabic Culture* (Syracuse, NY: Syracuse University Press, 2001).

39. Doane, "The Voice," 379.

2. Speaking in Between

1. Robert Irwin dates the two tales that the vizier relates to Shahrazad at least back to a fifth-century manuscript of the Indian *Jataka*, a vast compilation of fables, stories, maxims, and legends. Irwin, *The Arabian Nights: A Companion*, 65.

2. Husain Haddawy, *The Arabian Nights* (New York: W. W. Norton, 1990), 15.

3. Galland, sometimes maligned for so expurgating the stories of the *Nights* that they came to resemble children's stories, worked with the salons of eighteenth-century France in mind, dedicating his translation to his benefactress the Marquise d'O. Lane, famous for his prolific footnotes, wrote for scholars and civil servants. Burton, notorious for his arcane vocabulary, surfeit of notes, and fascination with the erotic and bawdy, eluded prosecution for obscenity by publishing through a subscription society composed of likeminded men. Irwin furnishes an entertaining overview of the "improvements" these and other translators made to the *Nights* in his *The Arabian Nights: A Companion*.

4. The many Hollywood film versions of Ali Baba and the Forty Thieves and Aladdin, including the recent animated Disney version, fail to make any

mention of Shahrazad. In these instances, the suppression of the framing story obviates the need for the figures of powerful rulers to serve as positive role models.

5. Mernissi cites this statistic in *Scheherazade Goes West*, her sequel of sorts to *Dreams*.

6. Mernissi's books remain highly popular in Morocco, and the works she publishes there often serve further to illuminate the messages of her international publications. She directs her bilingual (Arabic and French) retelling of a popular Moroccan tale, for example, to young Moroccans whose Western-style educations have instilled in them too strong a sense of the impossible, prefiguring her message in *Dreams* by calling for a return to the wisdom of stories. Fatima Mernissi, *Qui l'emporte, la femme ou l'homme?* (Casablanca: Mu'assasat Bansharah, 1983).

7. Alan Riding cites the anonymous author of *The Almond* in his article on the runaway success of her book: "She said that even though she never expected the book to be published, she wrote it in French because it seemed less shocking to write about sex in a language that is not her mother tongue. 'In any event, if I'd written in Arabic, it would never have been published,' she said. 'Nor will it. It's a thousand years since Muslims have written openly about sex. If you find an Arab publisher, I'll buy you a bottle of Champagne.'" Alan Riding, "A Muslim Woman, a Story of Sex," *New York Times*, June 20, 2005.

8. Margot Badran and Miriam Cooke, eds., *Opening the Gates: A Century of Arab Feminist Writing* (Bloomington: Indiana University Press, 1990).

9. Fatima Mernissi, *Beyond the Veil: Male-Female Dynamics in Modern Muslim Society*, rev. ed. (Bloomington: University of Indiana Press, 1987).

10. For a detailed account of American representations of Morooco from 1942 forward, see Brian T. Edwards, *Morocco Bound: Disorienting America's Maghreb from Casablanca to the Marrakech Express* (Durham, NC: Duke University Press, 2005).

11. *The Sheik*, dir. George Melford (Paramount Pictures, 1921); *The Son of the Sheik*, dir. George Fitzmaurice (United Artists, 1926).

12. Ruth A. Ward, the photographer, also created the similar photograph that adorns the cover of *Beyond the Veil*.

13. Mernissi, *Dreams of Trespass*, 85. All subsequent page citations pertaining to this source will be presented parenthetically in the text of this chapter.

14. Fadia Faqir, introduction, *In the House of Silence: Autobiographical Essays by Arab Women Writers*, ed. Fadia Faqir (Reading, UK: Garnet Publishing, 1998), 6.

15. Sidonie Smith, *A Poetics of Women's Autobiography: Marginality and the Fictions of Self-Representation* (Bloomington: University of Indiana Press, 1987), 47.

16. Kristen E. Brustad, Michael Cooperson, Jamal J. Elias, Nuha N. N. Khoury, Joseph E. Lowry, Nasser Rabbat, Dwight F. Reynolds, Devin J. Stewart,

and Shawkat M. Toorawa, *Interpreting the Self: Autobiography in the Arabic Literary Tradition*, ed. Dwight F. Reynolds (Berkeley and Los Angeles: University of California Press, 2001), chapters 1 and 20.

17. Philippe Lejeune, *On Autobiography*, ed. Paul John Eakin, trans. Katherine Leary (Minneapolis: University of Minnesota Press, 1989), 22–23

18. Almost all of Mernissi's work touches on this topic in one way or another. See in particular Fatima Mernissi, *Le harem politique: Le prophète et les femmes* (Paris: Albin Michel, 1987), Arabic version (Damascus: Dār al-Ḥiṣād, 1990); Mernissi, *Chahrazad n'est pas marocaine: Autrement, elle serait salariée* (Casablanca: Le Fennec, 1988); and Mernissi, *Êtes-vous vacciné contre le "harem"? Texte-test pour les messieurs qui adorent les dames* (Casablanca: Le Fennec, 1998).

19. See, for example, Marie-Aimée Hélie-Lucas, "Women's Struggles and the Rise of Fundamentalism in the Muslim World: From Entryism to Internationalism," in *Women in the Middle East: Perceptions, Realities, and Struggles for Liberation*, ed. Haleh Afshar (New York: St. Martin's Press, 1993), 206–41; and Valentine Moghadam, "Introduction: Women and Identity Politics in Theoretical and Comparative Perspective," in *Identity Politics and Women: Cultural Reassertions and Feminisms in International Perspective*, ed. Valentine Moghadam (Boulder, CO: Westview Press, 1994), 3–26.

20. Malti-Douglas, *Woman's Body, Woman's Word*, 23.

21. Mernissi, *Beyond the Veil*, 8.

22. Ibid., 8–9.

23. Fatima Mernissi, *The Forgotten Queens of Islam*, trans. Mary Jo Lakeland (Minneapolis: University of Minnesota Press, 1993).

24. Because child labor is illegal in Morocco and arrangements for domestic labor are informal, statistics on the number of girls employed as domestic servants in Moroccan households are difficult to come by. Domestic service is, however, a widespread and socially accepted practice, and many urban families from the lower middle class and upward think nothing of employing an illiterate young girl from the country to do their cooking and housekeeping. These girls often receive little more compensation than room and board and naturally become easy objects of abuse. Moroccan filmmaker Farida Benlyazid targets this practice, among others, in her film *A Door to the Sky* (France Média, SATPEC, CCM, 1983). Jamila Bargach identifies the social problem of what she terms "small maids" as both a source of illegitimate children and a destiny for the girls among them in *Orphans of Islam: Family, Abandonment, and Secret Adoption in Morocco* (Lanham, MD: Rowman and Littlefield Publishers, 2002), 98, 253–54n.

25. Ironically, Mernissi has never married.

26. Mernissi, *Beyond the Veil*, 19.

27. Deniz Kandiyoti, "Identity and Its Discontents: Women and the Nation," *Millennium: Journal of International Studies* 20, no. 3 (1991): 433.

28. Shariʿa consists of the rules and regulations the Qurʾan and Mohammed set out and put into practice.

29. The Moroccan Personal Status Code, or Mudawwana (Moudaouwana), became law on November 28, 1957. Marie-Aimée Hélie-Lucas analyzes the forms that resistance to such laws has taken throughout the Islamic world in "The Preferential Symbol for Islamic Identity: Women in Muslim Personal Laws," in *Identity Politics and Women*, ed. Moghadam, 391–407.

30. As in Tunisia, the French permitted the reigning sultan to retain his position but took over the external and many internal affairs of the country. Because of Morocco's large population of Berbers, or Amazighen, however, the French developed different divide-and-rule policies from those in Tunisia. They promoted the revolt of rural tribes, for example, and also politicized divisions between Arabs and Amazighen in an effort to promote the allegiance of the Amazighen to colonial rule.

31. Morocco is today a constitutional monarchy with an elected parliament.

32. Charrad, *States and Women's Rights*, 5; 139-42 (on the *dahir*). The 1930 *dahir*, or Berber Decree, offered the Amazighen recognition of their customary law in an effort to encourage them to submit to the French colonizer. This effort continued the French practice of dividing Morocco in order to undermine the already unstable authority of the sultan by breaking Amazight ties to Islam. The decree backfired when Islamic and Amazight groups came together to protest it as an attack on Islam.

33. Although the text remains largely the same as the U.S. version, the French version of *Dreams* was never marketed as a memoir. It also contains none of the pictures that the U.S. edition does. Fatima Mernissi, *Rêves de femmes*, trans. Claudine Richetin with Fatima Mernissi (Paris: Albin Michel, 1996), 234–35.

34. Anne Donadey, "Portrait of a Maghrebian Feminist as a Young Girl: Fatima Mernissi's *Dreams of Trespass*," *Edebiyat* 11 (2000): 87; Assia Djebar, *L'amour, la fantasia* (Paris: Albin Michel, 1995); Assia Djebar, *Fantasia: An Algerian Cavalcade*, trans. Dorothy S. Blair (Portsmouth, NH: Heinemann, 1993). I analyze Djebar's novel at length in chapter 4.

35. Smith, *A Poetics of Women's Autobiography*, 49.

36. Donadey, for example, traces the portraits of women in *Dreams* back to figures in Mernissi's personal history, as well as in Moroccan and Middle Eastern history, concluding: "The many role models whose contributions [Mernissi] highlights in *Dreams of Trespass* form a chain of transmission of North-African, Middle-Eastern, Arabo-Berber, and Islamic feminism within which she finds her legitimation as the most well-known Moroccan feminist" ("Portrait of a Maghrebian Feminist," 101). Her census of these figures is both useful and compelling, yet her conclusion unfortunately minimizes the scope of Mernissi's project.

37. This message emerges very clearly from Mernissi's collection of interviews with Moroccan women in *Le Maroc raconté par ses femmes* (Rabat: SMER, 1986).

38. Spivak, "Can the Subaltern Speak?"

3. A Story without a Face

1. One of the more elaborate and best known of the tales in the *Nights*, "The Porter and the Three Ladies" is itself an intricate frame story that provides the pretext for the telling of many other stories before gathering them all together again in its resolution. It commences when a porter enters into the service of a beautiful and mysterious woman. Once he has carried her fabulous purchases to her home, he refuses to leave, insisting he be included in the party that she and her sisters must be planning. Swayed by his salacious wit, they permit him to remain on the condition that he ask no questions about anything he sees. As the party commences, three one-eyed dervishes knock on the door, as do the caliph and his vizier; all are granted entry on the condition of silence. Of course, the men all break their promises when they see the strange events that later transpire. They succeed in saving themselves from execution only by recounting their own stories, eventually persuading the three sisters to relate theirs in turn. In the end, the caliph reveals his true identity and sets everything aright.

2. Tahar Ben Jelloun, *L'enfant de sable* (Paris: Éditions du Seuil, 1985); *The Sand Child*, trans. Alan Sheridan (Baltimore, MD: Johns Hopkins University Press, 2000).

3. Tahar Ben Jelloun, *La nuit sacrée* (Paris: Éditions du Seuil, 1987); *The Sacred Night*, trans. Alan Sheridan (San Diego: Harcourt, Brace, Jovanovich, 1989).

4. In an interview with Thomas Spear, Ben Jelloun affirms, "I often say that the fact of writing in French is a way for us to be somewhat bold and also to be relevant, because, when one writes in Arabic, one is slightly intimidated by the language of the Koran." Spear, "Politics and Literature: An Interview with Tahar Ben Jelloun," *Yale French Studies* 82, no. 2 (1993): 34.

5. For a range of analyses along these various lines, see, for example, Jacqueline Kay and Abdelhamid Zoubir, *The Ambiguous Compromise: Language, Literature, and Identity in Algeria and Morocco* (New York: Routledge, 1990); Evelyn Accad, *Sexuality and War: Literary Masks of the Middle East* (New York: New York University Press, 1990); and John Erickson, "Veiled Woman and Veiled Narrative in Tahar Ben Jelloun's *The Sandchild*," *boundary 2* 20, no. 1 (1993): 47–64. Ben Jelloun's decision to reside in France is a persistent theme in interviews. He identifies himself as Mediterranean, concerned by events in France and Italy as well as in Morocco. For his thoughts on these issues, see Denise

Brahimi, "Conversations avec Tahar Ben Jelloun," *Notre Librairie* 103 (1990): 41–44.

6. Ben Jelloun discusses with Thomas Spear his belief that the writer should take a backseat to his work: "I believe it profoundly: I have said that I write so as no longer to have a face. I write not to display myself or to exploit literature for my own benefit, but rather to disappear and leave the work in the foreground. It's a bit pretentious. At the same time, it's more modest than the opposite attitude, when people hold the stage and the book has to follow." Spear, "Politics and Literature," 39.

7. Erickson praises the complex, oppositional style of *The Sand Child*, contrasting it with that of *The Sacred Night*. Erickson, "Veiled Woman and Veiled Narrative," 48 n. 2.

8. Frantz Fanon, *The Wretched of the Earth*, trans. Constance Farrington (New York: Grove Press, 1963), 240–41.

9. Ibid., 241.

10. Page numbers are from the French edition. Because many critical nuances of the tale have been lost in the English translation, I have chosen to retranslate from the French. The French for the longer passages follows in a note. "Bienvenue, ô être du lointain, visage de l'erreur, innocence du mensonge, double de l'ombre, ô toi tant attendu, tant désiré, on t'a convoqué pour démentir le destin, tu apportes la joie mais pas le bonheur, tu lèves une tente dans le désert mais c'est la demeure du vent, tu es un capital de cendres, ta vie sera longue, une épreuve pour le feu et la patience. Bienvenue!"

11. "En fait le conteur, comme les acrobates et autres vendeurs d'objets insolites, avait dû quitter la grande place que la municipalité, sous l'instigation de jeunes urbanistes technocrates, a 'nettoyée' pour y construire une fontaine musicale où, tous les dimanches, les jets d'eau jaillissent sous l'impulsion des Bo-Bo-Pa-Pa de la *Cinquième Symphonie* de Beethoven."

12. See Lisa Lowe, "Literary Nomadics in Francophone Allegories of Postcolonialism: Pham Van Ky and Tahar Ben Jelloun," *Yale French Studies* 82, no. 1 (1993): 43–61; Hanita Brand, "'Fragmentary, but Not without Meaning'—Androgynous Constructs and Their Enhanced Signification," *Edebiyat* 11 (2000): 57–83; and Jarrod Hayes, *Queer Nations: Marginal Sexualities in the Maghreb* (Chicago: University of Chicago Press, 2000). My own earlier reading follows similar lines of interpretation. Suzanne Gauch, "Telling the Tale of a Body Devoured by Narrative," *differences* 11, no. 1 (1999): 179–202.

13. "L'enfant que tu mettras au monde sera un mâle, ce sera un homme, il s'appellera Ahmed même si c'est une fille! J'ai tout arrangé, j'ai tout prévu."

14. "Un garçon—que Dieu le protège et lui donne longue vie—est né jeudi à 10 h. Nous l'avons nommé Mohamed Ahmed. Cette naissance annonce fertilité pour la terre, paix et prospérité pour le pays. Vive Ahmed! Vive le Maroc."

15. "Je suis l'architecte et la demeure; l'arbre et la sève; moi et un autre;

moi et une autre. Aucun détail ne devrait venir, ni de l'extérieur ni du fond de la fosse, perturber cette rigueur. Pas même le sang. Et le sang un matin a taché mes draps. Empreintes d'un état de fait de mon corps enroulé dans un linge blanc, pour ébranler la petite certitude, ou pour démentir l'architecture de l'apparence. . . . C'était bien du sang, résistance du corps au nom; éclaboussure d'une circoncision tardive. C'était un rappel, une grimace d'un souvenir enfoui, le souvenir d'une vie que je n'avais pas connue et qui aurait pu être la mienne. Étrange d'être ainsi porteur d'une mémoire non accumulée dans un temps vécu, mais donnée à l'insu des uns et des autres."

16. Lowe proposes a compelling reading of this passage in which Ahmed "register[s] two contrary beliefs," as a reworking of the Freudian concept of disavowal. She concludes rather abruptly, however, that his/her sense of a doubled sexuality "refers allegorically to the splitting of the subject under colonialism." Lowe, "Literary Nomadics in Francophone Allegories of Postcolonialism," 55–56.

17. Judith Butler, *Bodies That Matter: On the Discursive Limits of "Sex"* (New York: Routledge, 1993), 93.

18. "Ma condition, non seulement je l'accepte et je la vis, mais je l'aime. Elle m'intéresse. Elle me permet d'avoir les privilèges que je n'aurais jamais pu connaître. Elle m'ouvre des portes et j'aime cela, même si elle m'enferme ensuite dans une cage de vitres."

19. Butler, *Bodies That Matter*, 95.

20. Fatima Mernissi explores the obligation to marry as well as modern-day obstacles to marriage in *Beyond the Veil*.

21. "Petit à petit je fus gagné par les scrupules et l'insomnie. Je voulais me débarrasser de Fatima sans lui faire de mal. Je l'installai dans une chambre éloignée de la mienne et je me mis lentement à la haïr. Je venais d'échouer dans le processus que j'avais préparé et déclenché. Cette femme, parce que handicapée, s'était révélée plus forte, plus dure, et plus rigoureuse que tout ce que j'avais prévu. Voulant l'utiliser pour parfaire mon apparence sociale, ce fut elle qui sut le mieux m'utiliser et faillit m'entraîner dans son profond désespoir."

22. Ben Jelloun has cited "Sufi poets" as a primary influence on his work, in his interview with Brahimi, "Conversations," 43.

23. "J'ai toujours su qui tu es, c'est pour cela, ma sœur, ma cousine, que je suis venue mourir ici, près de toi. Nous sommes toutes les deux nées penchées sur la pierre au fond du puits sec, sur une terre stérile, entourées de regards sans amour. Nous sommes femmes avant d'être infirmes, ou peut-être nous sommes infirmes parce que femmes . . . , je sais notre blessure. . . . Elle est commune."

24. "Depuis qu'entre lui et son corps il y avait eu rupture, une espèce de fracture, son visage avait vieilli et sa démarche était devenue celle d'un handicapé. Il ne lui restait plus que le refuge dans une totale solitude. Ce qui lui

avait permis de faire le point sur tout ce qui avait précédé et de préparer son départ définitif vers le territoire du silence suprême."

25. "J'ai perdu la langue de mon corps; d'ailleurs je ne l'ai jamais possédée. Je devrais l'apprendre et commencer d'abord par parler comme une femme. Comme un femme? Pourquoi? Suis-je un homme? Il va falloir faire un long chemin, retourner sur mes pas, patiemment, retrouver les premières sensations du corps que ni la tête ni la raison ne contrôlent. Comment parler? Et à qui parlerai-je?"

26. "Sachez, ami, que la famille, telle qu'elle existe dans nos pays, avec le père tout-puissant et les femmes reléguées à la domesticité avec une parcelle d'autorité que leur laisse le mâle, la famille, je la répudie, je l'enveloppe de brume et ne la reconnais plus."

27. His background in psychology also makes it particularly tempting to subject his novels to psychoanalytic critiques.

28. Cynthia Running-Johnson, "Ben Jelloun, Jean Genet, and Cultural Identity in *The Street for Just One: Alberto Giacometti*," *College Literature* 30, no. 2 (2003): 162–73.

29. *La septième porte*, dir. Andre Zwobada (1946).

30. "Ce livre, mes amis, ne peut circuler ni se donner. Il ne peut être lu par des esprits innocents. La lumière qui en émane éblouit et aveugle les yeux qui s'y posent par mégarde, sans être préparés. Ce livre, je l'ai lu, je l'ai déchiffré pour de tels esprits. Vous ne pouvez y accéder sans traverser mes nuits et mon corps. Je suis ce livre. Je suis devenu le livre du secret; j'ai payé de ma vie pour le lire. Arrivé au bout, après des mois d'insomnie, j'ai senti le livre s'incarner en moi, car tel est mon destin."

31. "Fragmentaire mais non dépourvu de sens, l'événement s'impose à ma conscience de tous les côtés. Le manuscrit que je voulais vous lire tombe en morceaux à chaque fois que je tente de l'ouvrir et de le délivrer des mots, lesquels empoisonnent tant et tant d'oiseaux, d'insectes et d'images. Fragmentaire, il me possède, m'obsède et me ramène à vous qui avez la patience d'attendre. Le livre est ainsi: une maison où chaque fenêtre est un quartier, chaque porte une ville, chaque page est une rue; c'est une maison d'apparence, un décor de théâtre où on fait la lune avec un drap bleu tendu entre deux fenêtres et une ampoule allumée."

32. Of course, *maktūb* can also refer to the more prosaic note or message.

33. "Hommes! Il est une piété que j'aime et je recherche, c'est la piété de la mémoire. Je l'apprécie parce qu'elle ne pose pas de questions. Je sais que cette qualité est en vous. Ainsi, je devancerai vos interrogations et apaiserai votre curiosité."

34. "J'ai appris ainsi à être dans le rêve et à faire de ma vie une histoire entièrement inventée, un conte qui se souvient de ce qui s'est réellement passé."

35. "Et puis tout s'est arrêté, tout s'est figé: l'instant est devenu une chambre, la chambre est devenue une journée ensoleillée, le temps une vieille carcasse oubliée dans cette caisse en carton, dans cette caisse il y a de vieilles chaussures dépareillées; une poignée de clous neufs, une machine à coudre Singer qui tourne toute seule, un gant d'aviateur pris sur un mort, une araignée fixée dans le fond de la caisse, une lame de rasoir Minora, un œil en verre, et puis l'inévitable miroir en mauvais état et qui s'est débarrassé de toutes ses images, d'ailleurs tous ces objets dans la caisse sont de sa propre et seule imagination, depuis qu'il s'est éteint, depuis qu'il est devenu un simple morceau de verre, il ne donne plus d'objets, il s'est vidé durant une longue absence. . . . Je sais à présent que la clé de notre histoire est parmi ces vieilles choses. . . . Je n'ose pas fouiller de peur de me faire arracher la main par des mâchoires mécaniques qui, malgré la rouille, fonctionnent encore . . . , elles ne proviennent pas du miroir mais de son double . . . , j'ai oublié de vous en parler, en fait je n'ai pas oublié mais c'est par superstition . . . , tant pis. . . . Nous ne sortirons pas de cette chambre sans trouver la clé, et pour cela il va falloir évoquer ne serait-ce que par allusion le double du miroir."

36. Haddawy, *The Arabian Nights*, 278.

37. Antar is the hero of an Arabic-language epic set in pre-Islamic times; recorded in verse sometime between the eighth and twelfth centuries, it treats the great love and exploits of this warrior who was born the son of an Abyssinian slave, and is said to incorporate poems actually composed by this historical figure. For more information, see Peter Heath, *The Thirsty Sword: Sirat ʿAntar and the Arabic Popular Epic* (Salt Lake City: University of Utah Press, 1996).

38. "Le Secret est sacré, mais, quand il devient ridicule, il vaut mieux s'en débarrasser. . . . Et . . . vous allez sans doute me demander qui je suis, qui m'a envoyé et pourquoi je débarque ainsi dans votre histoire. . . . Vous avez raison. Je vais vous expliquer. . . . Non. . . . Sachez simplement que j'ai passé ma vie à falsifier ou altérer les histoires des autres. . . . Qu'importe d'où je viens et je ne saurais vous dire si mes premiers pas se sont imprimés sur la boue de la rive orientale ou de la rive occidentale du fleuve."

39. In addition to this explicit reference to the story "The Zahir," Ben Jelloun quotes a passage from "The Circular Ruins" and sprinkles references to many other Borges stories throughout this section. Many of these have been translated in Jorge Luis Borges, *Labyrinths* (New York: Modern Library, 1983).

40. The tale of "Abu al-Husn and His Slave-Girl Tawaddud" appears as Night 436 in volume 5 of the Burton Club edition. Richard Burton, *A Plain and Literal Translation of the Arabian Nights Entertainment, Now Entitled the Book of a Thousand Nights and a Night*, 10 vols. (Benares [Stoke Newington, London]: The Burton Club, 1886).

41. This note immediately follows the story's title.

42. Tawaddud's discourse is neither a reflection of the state of the law in

Burton's time nor quite so straightforward and has likely been much manipulated. The *Encyclopedia of Islam* places Burton's claims in perspective: "In reference to the religious disciplines, discernable here is an ideological hard core which clearly belongs in the context of the Sunnī restoration of the 5th–6th/11th–12th centuries: the defeat of al-Naẓẓām, a famous Muʿtazilī—and a poor loser to boot—in confrontation with Tawaddud, who explicitly invokes Sunnism and the Shāfiʿī law school, is eloquent in this respect. It would, however, be a mistake to exaggerate the homogeneity of the whole, which bears the marks of successive additions, and which combines, with questions of deep doctrinal importance, others which relate to a more 'popular' vision, favoring spectacular erudition and spicy or sensational subjects, and sometimes taking the form of riddles." *Encyclopedia of Islam*, CD-ROM ed., s.v. "Tawaddud."

43. "Vous seul êtes capable de comprendre pourquoi je suis ici en ce moment. Je ne suis pas un de vos personnages, j'aurais pu l'être; mais ce n'est pas en tant que silhouette remplie de sable et de mots que je me présente à vous. . . . Ce que je cherche, ce n'est pas la vérité. Je suis incapable de la reconnaître. Ce n'est pas la justice non plus. Elle est impossible. Il y a dans ce Livre des versets qui ont fonction de loi; ils ne donnent pas raison à la femme. Ce que je cherche, ce n'est pas le pardon, car ceux qui auraient pu me le donner ne sont plus là. Et pourtant j'ai besoin de justice, de vérité, et de pardon."

4. *La fantasia réclamée,* or Voice Incorporated

1. Assia Djebar, *Ombre sultane: Roman* (Paris: J.-C. Lattès, 1987); *A Sister to Scheherazade*, trans. Dorothy S. Blair (Portsmouth, NH: Heinemann, 1993).

2. The translation is from the English edition. Djebar, *Sister*, 143.

3. Assia Djebar, *Femmes d'Alger dans leur appartement* (Paris: des femmes, 1980); *Women of Algiers in Their Apartments*, trans. Marjolijn de Jager (Charlottesville: University of Viriginia Press, 1992). See chapter 2's notes for publication information for *Fantasia, an Algerian Cavalcade* and its French counterpart, *L'amour, la fantasia*.

4. Assia Djebar, *La soif* (Paris: Julliard, 1957); *The Mischief*, trans. Frances Frenaye (New York: Simon and Schuster, 1958).

5. Assia Djebar, interview by Clarisse Zimra, afterword, *Women of Algiers in Their Apartments*, 169; Assia Djebar, *Les alouettes naïves* (Paris: Julliard, 1967). Djebar's remaining early novels were *Les impatients* (Paris: Julliard, 1958) and *Les enfants du nouveau monde* (Paris: Julliard, 1962).

6. Charrad explains that Algeria supported the principle of equality between the sexes in its postindependence constitution (1963) and in its National Charter (1976) but that 1984 saw a turn to Islamicization when the government promulgated the Family Code, based on Shariʿa. Charrad, *States and Women's Rights*, 169–200.

7. Eugène Delacroix, *Femmes d'Alger dans leur appartement* (1834), Musée du Louvre, Paris.

8. Donadey briefly analyzes how Djebar encodes race in her reading of the painting, in *Recasting Postcolonialism: Women Writing between Worlds* (Portsmouth, NH: Heinemann, 2001), 108–9.

9. Quotations from *Women of Algiers in Their Apartments* and *Fantasia: An Algerian Cavalcade* are largely drawn from the very good published translations. However, Djebar's vocabulary is rich and her turns of phrase studied, and in an effort to convey the nuances and tone of her writing, I have been obliged to retranslate certain passages. Where I have reworked the translations, I supply the reference to the French edition and include the French text in the notes.

10. Winifred Woodhull, "Exile," *Transfigurations of the Maghreb: Feminism, Decolonization, and Literatures* (Minneapolis: University of Minnesota Press, 1993), 116.

11. Picasso made this series of paintings between approximately 1954 and 1957. Djebar does not specify to which of these paintings she refers. Frantz Fanon, "Algeria Unveiled," *A Dying Colonialism*, trans. Haakon Chevalier (New York: Grove Press, 1965).

12. Eugène Delacroix, *Femmes d'Alger dans leur intérieur* (1848), Musée Fabre, Montpellier.

13. Fanon, "Algeria Unveiled."

14. "variante certes de l'héroïsme et de la solidarité tribale, mais surtout ici mise en correspondance d'un corps en danger (dans le mouvement totalement improvisé) avec une voix qui appelle, défie et écorche. Pour finir, elle guérit du risque de lâcheté et permet de trouver l'issue victorieuse."

15. The year 2001 saw the breaking of the silence surrounding the systematic rape of Algerian women by French soldiers when the French courts awarded a disability pension to an Algerian man, Mohamed Garne, for psychic damages. Garne was conceived when his mother was repeatedly gang raped by French soldiers at an internment camp; the same soldiers later tortured the sixteen-year-old woman in an effort to induce her to abort. Suddenly revelations regarding the prevalence of rape by French soldiers during the war of independence filled French media, as did talk of the taboos that had prevented its exposure in the past. Florence Beauge, "Le tabou du viol des femmes pendant la guerre d'Algérie commence à être levé," *Le Monde*, October 12, 2001.

16. Gayatri Spivak, "French Feminism in an International Frame," *In Other Worlds: Essays in Cultural Politics* (New York: Routledge, 1988), 135.

17. "Ta voix s'est prise au piège; mon parler français la déguise sans l'habiller. A peine si je frôle l'ombre de ton pas! . . . Mots torches qui éclairent mes compagnes, mes complices; d'elles, définitivement, ils me séparent. Et sous leur poids, je m'expatrie."

18. *Fantasia: An Algerian Cavalcade* is the first volume of a projected quartet. The second is *A Sister to Scheherazade;* and the third, *Vaste est la prison* (Paris: Albin Michel, 1995); *So Vast the Prison,* trans. Betsy Wing (New York: Seven Stories Press, 2001).

19. Donadey, *Recasting Postcolonialism,* xxxii.

20. Woodhull, *Transfigurations of the Maghreb,* 86–87.

21. Clarisse Zimra, "Writing Women: The Novels of Assia Djebar," *Sub-Stance* 69 (1992): 77.

22. John Erickson, "Women's Space and Enabling Dialogue in Assia Dje-bar's *L'amour, la fantasia,*" in *Postcolonial Subjects: Francophone Women Writers,* ed. Mary Jean Green et al. (Minneapolis: University of Minnesota Press, 1996), 318; Jarrod Hayes, *Queer Nations: Marginal Sexualities in the Maghreb* (Chicago: University of Chicago Press, 2000), 194. See also the special issue of *World Literature Today* 74, no. 4 (1996), devoted to Djebar's work on the occasion of her receipt of the Neustadt Prize in Literature.

23. Donadey, *Recasting Postcolonialism,* 72. *Isnād* refers to the chain of authorities that validate knowledge, establishing legitimacy by grounding a position in the testimony of an eyewitness.

24. Eugène Delacroix, *Fantasia, ou exercices militaires des marocains* (1832), Musée Fabre, Montpellier. The *Robert* dictionary credits to Delacroix's paint-ing the first appearance of this particular meaning of *fantasia* in French. The full definition of the term is as follows: "divertissement équestre de cavaliers arabes qui exécutent au galop des évolutions en déchargeant leurs armes et en poussant de grands cris." *Le petit Robert,* 1996 ed., s.v. "fantasia."

25. Eugène Fromentin, *Une année dans le Sahel* (Paris: Michel Lévy, 1859) ; *Between Sea and Sahara: An Algerian Journal,* trans. Blake Robinson (Athens: Ohio University Press, 1999).

26. "—O mon ami, je suis tuée!"

27. "Et c'est le vrai tragique de cette fantasia que Fromentin ressuscite: gesticulation de la victoire envolée, assomption des corps au soleil dans la vitesse des cavales."

28. H. Adlai Murdoch, "Rewriting Writing: Identity, Exile, and Renewal in Assia Djebar's *L'amour, la fantasia,*" *Yale French Studies* 83, no. 2 (1993): 75.

29. Ewa Ziarek, "Rethinking Dispossession: On Being in One's Skin," *Parallax* 7, no. 2 (April 2001): 5.

30. "Écrire *devant* l'amour. Éclairer le corps, pour aider à lever l'interdit, pour dévoiler. . . . Dévoiler et simultanément tenir secret ce qui doit le rester, tant que n'intervient pas la fulgurance de la révélation. Le mot est torche; le brandir devant le mur de la séparation ou du retrait. . . . Décrire le visage de l'autre, pour maintenir son image; persister à croire en sa présence, en son miracle. Refuser la photographie, ou toute autre trace visuelle. Le mot seul, une fois écrit, nous arme d'une attention grave."

31. For a short introduction to the complexities of the veil in Sufi thought, see William C. Chittick, "The Paradox of the Veil," *Sufism: A Short Introduction* (Oxford: Oneworld Publications, 2000), 137–53.

32. In her study of encoding in women's recent Arabic-language novels, Nadja Odeh reminds us of the following: "The classical Arabic literary tradition allowed women only to exist under very carefully circumscribed conditions. Women were only allowed to move within one genre, the genre of *rithā'* poetry (elegy)." Odeh, "Coded Emotions: The Description of Nature in Arab Women's Autobiographies," in *Writing the Self: Autobiographical Writing in Modern Arabic Literature*, ed. Robin Ostle, Ed de Moor, and Stefan Wild (London: Saqi Books, 1998), 264.

33. Gayatri Spivak, "In a Word: *Interview*," *Outside in the Teaching Machine* (New York: Routledge, 1993), 6.

34. Gayatri Spivak, "Acting Bits/Identity Talk," *Critical Inquiry* 18, no. 4 (1992): 770–803.

35. Donadey, *Recasting Postcolonialism*, 59.

36. Benjamin Stora dissects the negative ramifications that arose from the postindependence mythification of the war in *La gangrène et l'oubli*.

37. Spivak, "Acting Bits/Identity Talk," 770–71.

38. The revolution of 1848 began with a civil war between the bourgeoisie and the working class in which the workers were violently repressed. The monarchy fell and the Second Republic took its place, proclaiming a bourgeois constitution. It lasted until 1851, when it was overthrown in its turn.

5. Shahrazad at the Vanishing Point

1. All but the most recent translators of the *Nights* silence Shahrazad in elaborate ways. In my introduction, I discussed an account of how this conclusion came to be. The passage quoted in the epigraph occurs at the conclusion of Galland's *Mille et une nuits*, and the translation is my own; the French reads as follows: "Mille et une nuits s'étaient écoulées dans ces innocents amusements; ils avaient même beaucoup aidé à diminuer les préventions fâcheuses du sultan contre la fidélité des femmes; son esprit était adouci; il était convaincu du mérite et de la grande sagesse de Scheherazade; il se souvenait du courage avec lequel elle s'était exposée volontairement à devenir son épouse, sans appréhender la mort à laquelle elle savait qu'elle était destinée le lendemain, comme les autres qui l'avait précédée. Ces considérations et les autres qualités qu'il connaissait en elle le portèrent enfin à lui faire grâce. 'Je vois bien, lui dit-il, aimable Scheherazade, que vous êtes inépuisable dans vos petits contes: il y a assez longtemps que vous m'en divertissez; vous avez apaisé ma colère, et je renonce volontiers, en votre faveur, à la loi cruelle que je m'étais imposée; je vous remets entièrement dans mes bonnes grâces, et je veux que vous soyez

regardée comme la libératrice de toutes les filles qui devaient être immolées à mon juste ressentiment.' La princesse se jeta à ses pieds, les embrassa tendrement, en lui donnant toutes les marques de la reconnaissance la plus vive et la plus parfaite." *Les mille et une nuits*, vol. 3, trans. Antoine Galland (Paris: Garnier-Flammarion: 1965), 433.

2. Burton's conclusion is elaborate and quite lengthy, but the following excerpt indicates the fate to which he consigns Shahrazad after she falls silent: "Presently they brought forward Shahrazad and displayed her, for the first dress, in a red suit; whereupon King Shahriyar rose to look upon her and the wits of all present, men and women, were bewitched for that she was even as saith of her one of her describers: A sun on wand in knoll of sand she showed, / Clad in her cramoisy-hued chemisette. / Of her lips' honey-dew she gave me drink / And with her rosy cheeks quencht fire she set." Burton, *The Book of the Thousand Nights and a Night: A Plain and Literal Translation of the Arabian Nights Entertainment*, vol. 10 (Benares: Kamashastra Society, 1885–86), 58.

3. For Rey Chow, today's discourses of ethnicity reinscribe the old Orientalist opposition between a progressive, morally superior, modern West and a despotic East that once supported the colonial endeavor. Her account of the commodification of human rights in contemporary commercial relations between the United States and China also summarizes the position of women in confrontations between the West and the Islamic world: "The commodified relations of ethnicity, in other words, are underwritten by the conviction that the other is being held captive within his or her own culture whether dead or alive and that such captivity necessitates protest and liberation [on the part of Westerners]." Chow, *The Protestant Ethnic and the Spirit of Capitalism* (New York: Columbia University Press, 2002), 23.

4. Malek Alloula's work on the colonial postcard, though problematic in its reobjectification of the very women it seeks to rescue from the colonizing gaze, remains exemplary for its exposition of the pervasiveness and mundaneness of such exoticizing images of "Oriental" women. Alloula, *The Colonial Harem*, trans. Myrna Godzich and Wlad Godzich (Minneapolis: University of Minnesota Press, 1986). David A. Bailey, Suzanne Cotter, and Gilane Tawadros have collected written texts and visual images that resist and contest colonial and postcolonial representations of Muslim women as alternately exotic and oppressed in their *Veil: Veiling, Representation, and Contemporary Art* (Cambridge, MA: MIT Press, 2004).

5. A number of informative essays on the emergence of postcolonial subject positions in contemporary France can be found in Alec G. Hargreaves and Mark McKinney, *Post-colonial Cultures in France* (New York: Routledge, 1997).

6. The best known of these pathbreaking *beur* authors are undoubtedly Azouz Begag, Farida Belghoul, and Mehdi Charef. Although they situate their novels in a variety of locations, none presents a protagonist as autonomous

and unscathed by conflict as Shahrazad. From the 1990s onward, filmmakers of North African descent, including Rachid Bouchareb, Malik Chibane, and Krim Dridi, have increasingly featured the adventures of *beur* protagonists in a French society that is frequently suspicious or even hostile.

7. Leïla Sebbar, *Shérazade, 17 ans, brune, frisée, les yeux verts* (Paris: Stock, 1982); *Sherazade: Missing: Aged 17, Dark Curly Hair, Green Eyes*, trans. Dorothy S. Blair (London: Quartet Books, 1991); *Les carnets de Shérazade* (Paris: Stock, 1985); *Le fou de Shérazade* (Paris: Stock, 1991).

8. The covers of the second and third novels of Sebbar's trilogy each reproduce a painting; *Les carnets de Shérazade* sports Matisse's *Odalisque à la culotte rouge* (1921), a painting referenced in all three novels, and the jacket of *Le fou de Shérazade* features Soutine's *Arbre couché* (c. 1923–24), not mentioned in any of the novels.

9. In his study of the evolution of urban social movements in Britain, Paul Gilroy argues that a new identity politics displaces older notions of class warfare. Sebbar's novels reflect a parallel movement in France, a shift from a politics of utopian change to one of resistance. Paul Gilroy, *There Ain't No Black in the Union Jack: The Cultural Politics of Race and Nation* (London: Hutchinson, 1987; Chicago: University of Chicago Press, 1991). Interestingly, Winifred Woodhull laments the demise of materialist feminism but takes Sebbar to task for her identity politics when the author, underscoring her commitment to social justice, promotes her particular difference as integrally French. Woodhull, *Transfigurations of the Maghreb*, 102–10.

10. The publication of Sebbar's novels predates French concern with the rising tide of Islamic extremism and the debates stirred by the Islamic head scarf.

11. All translations into English from *Sherazade* are taken from Dorothy S. Blair's able translation of the novel. Any words in brackets are my own modifications.

12. See, for example, Homi K. Bhabha, *The Location of Culture* (New York: Routledge, 1994).

13. Pheng Cheah, "Given Culture: Rethinking Cosmopolitical Freedom in Transnationalism," in *Cosmopolitics: Thinking and Feeling Beyond the Nation*, ed. Pheng Cheah and Bruce Robbins (Minneapolis: University of Minnesota Press, 1998), 292.

14. Ibid., 298.

15. See, for example, Woodhull, *Transfigurations of the Maghreb*; Anne Donadey, "Cultural Metissage and the Play of Identity in Leila Sebbar's *Sherazade* Trilogy," *Borders, Exiles, Diasporas*, ed. Elazar Barkan and Marie-Denise Shelton (Stanford, CA: Stanford University Press, 1998), 257–73; and Francoise Lionnet, *Postcolonial Representations: Women, Literature, Identity* (Ithaca, NY: Cornell University Press, 1995).

16. Pierre Loti, *Aziyadé* (1879; Paris: Gallimard, 1991).

17. Established in 1973 by a group of five founders, including Jean-Paul Sartre, who were committed to the spirit of May '68, the French daily *Libération* proclaimed itself an outlet for the opinions of the people. It differentiated itself from the established dailies by focusing on social movements and the counterculture. Somewhat ironically, the want ads that Julien reads were discontinued by *Libération* in 1982, the year in which *Sherazade* was published, when the paper began to depend on revenue from mainstream advertisers.

18. The first Intifada began in 1987, five years after *Sherazade* appeared. Already throughout the 1970s, however, recognition of the Palestinian state was a popular leftist and avant-garde cause in France, attracting such notable supporters as Jean Genet. In 1982, Israel invaded Lebanon, further fueling leftist criticisms of the Israeli government.

19. Tracing autobiographical details in Sebbar's novel, Anne Donadey cites an interview in which Sebbar denies any autobiographical connection with Sherazade and affirms, rather, her affinity with a character like Julien. Donadey concludes that Sebbar and Julien share a cultural métis identity that obliges them to seek access to their heritage through Orientalist representations, yet rather perfunctorily brands Julien a colonizer and Orientalist. Donadey, *Recasting Postcolonialism*, 112–13.

20. Elizabeth Cowie, *Representing the Woman: Cinema and Psychoanalysis* (Minneapolis: University of Minnesota Press, 1997), 133.

21. Jacques Lacan, *The Four Fundamental Concepts of Psycho-analysis*, trans. Alan Sheridan (Harmondsworth: Penguin Books, 1977), 185, cited in Cowie, *Representing the Woman*, 132.

22. Because the second and third novels of Sebbar's trilogy remain untranslated, all translations from the French are my own. The French for each selection follows in the notes. "Si [Shérazade] est vivante, s'il la retrouve . . . Et maintenant Yaël . . . A croire qu'il ne peut pas s'empêcher de vivre ses fictions. . . . Ou le contraire."

23. Donadey, *Recasting Postcolonialism*, 130.

24. Woodhull, *Transfigurations of the Maghreb*, 118.

25. Ella Shohat discusses the difficulties faced by Sephardic Jews who immigrate to Israel in "Sephardim in Israel: Zionism from the Standpoint of Its Jewish Victims," in *Dangerous Liaisons*, ed. McClintock, Mufti, and Shohat, 39–68.

26. Slavoj Žižek, *The Plague of Fantasies* (New York: Verso, 1997), 14.

27. Proponents of Amazight autonomy point out that this declaration also excludes Algeria's large Tamazight-speaking population.

28. For more on the legacy of the *pieds-noirs* and other largely forgotten immigrant groups from Algeria, see Stora, *La gangrène et l'oubli*.

29. Lacan holds that what appears in the patient's symptom is not the truth of desire but "the truth of what this desire has been in his history." Jacques

Lacan, *Écrits: A Selection*, trans. Alan Sheridan (New York: W. W. Norton, 1977), 167.

30. While the election of a socialist government in 1981, after twenty-three years of conservative rule, had the effect of granting new rights to noncitizens and so-called minority populations in France, the rise of an extreme, nationalist right during roughly the same period resulted in a more restrictive immigration policy over the period 1983–86. The extreme right, long exemplified by the ultranationalist Front National Party and its leader Jean-Marie Le Pen, appealed to the economically disadvantaged but also to those fearful of being left behind by a globalizing economy. Alec G. Hargreaves and Mark McKinney propose an informative overview of France's political climate in light of its increasingly diverse artistic production in their introduction to *Post-colonial Cultures in France*.

31. For a firsthand account of the march, see Bouzid, *La marche: Traversée de la France profonde* (Paris: Sindbad, 1984).

32. "La colère raidit Shérazade qui serre les poings. Gilles dit que la femme des *Mille et Une Nuits*, il a lu des extraits, ça lui revient, celle qui raconte des histoires au despote, est une femme douce et souple, pas comme elle . . . agressive. . . . S'il ne peut plus rire . . . Il ne l'oblige pas à parler, lui . . . à raconter des histoires, il ne va pas la violer ni la tuer au petit matin après une nuit d'amour."

33. Edward Said has underscored the complicity of the media in provoking the events it "covers," pointing out how the mere presence of television crews incites Palestinian youth to throw rocks at Israeli soldiers. Said, *Covering Islam: How the Media and the Experts Determine How We See the Rest of the World*, rev. ed. (New York: Vintage Books, 1997).

34. In an early article on postcolonial approaches to cinema, for example, Robert Stam and Louise Spence urge viewers of films to look beyond apparently positive or negative portrayals of racially or ethnically marked characters to the particularly "cinematic dimensions of film": spectator positioning, narrative structure, and cinematic style. Stam and Spence, "Colonialism, Racism, and Representation: An Introduction," in *Film Theory and Criticism*, ed. Leo Braudy and Marshall Cohen, 6th ed. (New York: Oxford University Press, 2004).

35. Žižek, *The Plague of Fantasies*, 75.

36. Donadey, *Recasting Postcolonialism*, 110–11.

37. "'Ma fille! Shérazade! Vous l'avez tuée! Ma fille est morte . . . Shérazade, ma fille! Réponds-moi . . . Ils t'ont tuée.' Mériem secoue sa mère qui sanglote: 'Imma! Imma! tu deviens folle! Shérazade n'est pas morte. C'est le film . . . Ta fille est vivante . . . Imma, ne pleure pas, ta fille vit . . . Regarde-la, elle n'est pas morte. Imma, Shérazade est vivante, vivante . . . vivante.'"

Epilogue

1. Abdelkebir Khatibi, "Nuits blanches," *Ombres japonaises* (1979; Paris: Fata Morgana, 1988).

2. "Raconte une belle histoire ou je te tue."

3. "Et si mourir était justement de dire non à ce principe suprême, de dire non—nous les Arabes décadents de maintenant, si mourir pour nous (dans l'au delà de la morale et de la métaphysique) était cette négation inouïe, encore indicible: jamais plus de Shéhérazade?"

4. "Jamais plus de ce récit et de cette mort, de cet hymen déchiré, de cette nuit blanche."

5. "Prenons le temps d'aimer Shéhérazade dans la scène théorique, hautement théorique, qu'elle a d'emblée mise en jeu."

6. In *Le livre du sang* (The Book of Blood), Khatibi develops this theory to its extreme ends, producing a hallucinatory narrative that loosely recounts the implosion of a mystical brotherhood when the androgynous youth who embodies the ideal beloved metamorphoses into a perverse and depraved seductress. Khatibi, *Le livre du sang* (Paris: Gallimard, 1979).

7. Grammatically, the *futur antérieur* expresses what will happen before another event or at a certain time in the future. It also expresses probability.

8. Edward Said, *Orientalism* (New York: Pantheon Books, 1978).

9. Réda Bensmaïa clarifies Khatibi's concern as follows: "He takes issue with the fact that Arab people were unable to distinguish between theological narratives that always situate real life in an inaccessible or transcendent future and narratives that can no longer distinguish themselves from their own ends." Bensmaïa, *Experimental Nations: Or, the Invention of the Maghreb* (Princeton, NJ: Princeton University Press, 2003), 140.

10. Khatibi's treatment of mysticism is somewhat in contradiction to his own purposes, for he seems to overlook entirely the complex history of these works, often accused of promoting erotic love and decadent behavior, not to mention of fomenting political unrest.

11. Assia Djebar, "La femme en morceaux," *Oran, langue morte* (Paris: Actes Sud, 1997).

12. "La nuit, c'est chacun de nos jours, mille et un jours, ici, chez nous, à . . ."

Index

African filmmaking, 23–24, 144n.7
agency: Maghreb artists' forging of,
  11–12, 143n.33; in Mernissi's
  women, 39–50; Sebbar's fiction,
  106, 161n.9; of Shahrazad, 5, 14
Ahmed Bey, 146n.25
*Alf Layla wa layla. See Thousand and
  One Nights, A*
Algeria: Amazighen/Amazight culture in, 117–18, 162n.27; artists'
  depictions of, 84–89; civil war
  of 1990s in, 96; colonial regime
  in, 87–89; Family Code in, 12,
  156n.6; in fictional narratives,
  58; identity with, in Sebbar's
  trilogy, 114–19; massacres of
  1996 in, 132; National Charter
  of, 156n.6; oral culture of women
  in, 87–89, 98–102; postcolonial
  transformation of, 10–12, 90–94,
  143n.30; Shahrazad's images in,
  6–12; women's status in, 82–89

"Algeria Unveiled," 85
Alloula, Malek, 160n.4
Almond, The, 148n.7
"Amal Hayaati" (song), 17
Amazighen/Amazight culture, 6–7,
  9–10, 50, 91, 117, 142n.25,
  150n.30, 150n.32, 162n.27
Amrouche, Fadhma Aïth Mansour,
  6–10
Amrouche, Jean, 9–10, 142n.25
Amrouche, Marguerite Taos, 9,
  142n.25
Antar (Arab hero), 76, 155n.37
Apter, Emily, 8
Arabian Nights: A Play, The, 144n.4
Arabian Nights, The: origins of title,
  ix, 139n.1. *See also Thousand and
  One Nights, A*
Arabian Nights, The (film), 144n.4
Arabian Nights and Days, 144n.6
Arabic literature: autobiography in,
  41–44; Europeanization of,

Suzanne Gauch is assistant professor of English and women's studies at Temple University. She has published on postcolonial literature, film, and postcolonial theory.